I0050289

MARKET ANALYSIS FOR THE NEW MILLENNIUM

Edited by

Robert R. Prechter

Published by
New Classics Library

Market Analysis for the New Millennium
Copyright © 2002/2003/2017 Robert R. Prechter
Third Edition 2017
Second Printing 2018

The material in this volume up to 500 words may be reprinted without written permission of the author provided that the source is acknowledged. The publisher would appreciate being informed by email to customercare@elliottwave.com of the use of any such quotation or reference. Otherwise all rights are reserved.

Printed in the United States of America

ISBN: 978-1-61604-109-0
Library of Congress Control Number 2003102119

Publisher: New Classics Library
Gainesville, Georgia USA

Elliott Wave International
www.elliottwave.com
Address for comments: customercare@elliottwave.com

*This book is dedicated to Robert J. Farrell,
who set the standard for professionalism
among market analysts.*

Table of Contents

Foreword

Conventional analysis is a wasteland of irrelevance. Financial analysts, economists and media commentators spend countless hours and pages discussing what effect the latest social events, political trends, central bank machinations, corporate earnings reports, etc. will have on stock prices, and yet there are no studies to back up adequately any of their working assumptions. Once you observe that financial market prices form a fractal with a set of mathematical properties, you understand that they must be independent of outside forces. Indeed, experience reveals that even the most dramatic current events have no more than an apparent fleeting effect on financial prices and rarely a predictable one.

Then what is *really* going on in the markets? The answer is that impulsive herding behavior is responsible for aggregate market pricing. Such behavior is the product of an unconscious mental process inherited through evolution. This process evolved with a purpose: to protect individuals and species, though it is not effective in every application. Since this impulse is purposeful, it must be patterned. *How* it is patterned may be open to debate, but one description — greatly the subject of this book — has survived tests of time and prediction.

People who investigate the characteristics of the human herding pattern as revealed in financial prices are working in the right direction, though with the most primitive of tools and understanding. Sometimes this leads to embarrassing errors of both thought and conclusion. Other times, it leads to brilliant insights. Those who espouse the extramarket causality of market trends enjoy a far larger community of support as well as the general presumption of authenticity. On the other hand, they never have useful insights, and they continually fail to predict trend changes. They are simply wasting their time.

"Technical" analysis accepts the primacy of shared mental states with respect to financial market pricing. That's why I pay attention to studies that attempt to investigate some aspect of those shared mental states. What are their aspects? How are they patterned? How can we benefit from the knowledge?

The financial press typically ignores the people who try to answer these questions. The reason is that one actually has to *think*, deeply, in order to understand what is really going on in the market place. It is so easy to sound learned tossing off comments about politics, economics and central bank policies that few bother expending the energy to undertake serious studies of market behavior. This book is for those of you who are willing to follow up on that latter effort.

Some of the essays herein are of seminal importance; others are so speculative as to be little more than a tentative toe in the lake of conjecture. None of them, though, uses the conventional view of market causality thus *assuring* its irrelevance at its outset. By beginning with the proper foundational understanding, each of these essays at least holds the *potential* of revealing something important. A change to the proper view of social event/mood causality, I hope, is one of the promises of the new millennium.

I would like to thank all the contributors to this book for their pioneering efforts. In some chapters, I did no editing (White, Casti, Graham & Dodd), in others minor editing (Green, Goerner, Kotick, Crittenden) and in others heavy editing or contributing (Beuttner, Montgomery, Hale, Kendall). Montgomery is an interesting case. Paul has published brilliant reports for thirty years but has never compiled his various observations into a single presentation. It took an effort to gather all his material together and string it out in narrative fashion, but the end result is well worth it. I would also like to thank Sally Webb for formatting the entire book and Darrell King for designing the jacket. I hope you enjoy reading these challenging essays.

— Robert R. Prechter, Editor

Note: All citations "originally published on [date]" refer to *The Elliott Wave Theorist* unless otherwise noted.

PART I

New Studies in
the Wave Principle

The Wave Principle is unique in that it not only demonstrates that there is a patterned social dynamic involving impulses of creation and destruction, expansion and contraction and hope and fear, it not only *describes* that pattern comprehensively and in great detail, but it is also the only approach that includes a hypothesis of *why* such patterns exist and backs it up with available scientific evidence. Indeed, the discovery that fractal geometry permeates nature demonstrates that the Wave Principle reflects the most fundamental laws of growth and order, exactly as R.N. Elliott concluded sixty years ago.

At a practical level, the Wave Principle's detailed explanation of how market dynamics operate provides a solid basis for decision making. By providing a meticulous list of rules and guidelines for interpreting that behavior, it provides the investor the opportunity to exercise reason and objectivity when approaching the task of market analysis.

The Appendix to this book provides a capsule summary of the Wave Principle. For more of the Wave Principle's essentials, please see *Elliott Wave Principle — Key to Market Behavior* (Frost and Prechter, 1978). For the science behind the Wave Principle and its wider applicability, please see *The Wave Principle of Human Social Behavior* (Prechter, 1999).

Chapter 1

R.N. ELLIOTT'S FUNDAMENTAL CHALLENGE TO MECHANISTIC SOCIAL MODELS

by Dr. Michael K. Green
originally published June 2001

Abstract: Nineteenth century physicists called into question the mechanistic approach of Newtonian physics, which was based on atomism, reductionism, the unity of the sciences and the primacy of external causality, by developing various field theories. Developments in thermodynamics also called into question the reductive approach of mechanism. R.N. Elliott, an American social thinker who lived from 1871 to 1948, applied the principles of the new physics, i.e., holism, waves, pluralism and internal self-organization, to society and developed an alternative to social mechanism. He thought that mass psychology, impelled by emotion and not reason, was the driving force of human society and that these emotional waves swept through society in a five-wave sequence. According to Elliott, aggregate stock market prices provide the most direct and detailed measure of these moods. Elliott's ideas differ fundamentally from all mechanistic macroeconomic models, including Marxism, Keynesianism, monetarism and the Efficient Market Hypothesis.

Elliott: A New Approach To Social Theory

Some thinkers receive their intellectual calling from within an intellectual tradition, which they undertake to elaborate, amend, extend or refute. Others receive their intellectual calling from some external event. The latter was the case with R.N. Elliott, an American social thinker who lived from 1871 to 1948. In his case, it was the stock market crash of 1929 and the subsequent Great Depression that led him to reflect upon the importance of social mood, i.e., the predominant emotional orientation of society at a particular time, for an understanding of human social organization and change. He had lived through the Roaring 'Twenties and seen the social euphoria of that era replaced with the social pessimism of the 'Thirties. Whereas others thought that this mood swing was the result of economic conditions, Elliott, after studying the issue, concluded that these economic conditions were a consequence of social mood swings, which unfold according to a single pattern that is variant in some aspects and, more important, invariant in others. To appreciate Elliott's contributions to social philosophy, one needs to understand fully his theoretical innovations, which carry forth the predominant movement in nineteenth century physics into social theory. Just as nineteenth century physics called into question the mechanistic views of Newtonian physics, so Elliott called into question the application of such mechanistic models to society. Once his theoretical framework is understood, then its application to society in general and American society in particular can be examined. Elliott's work is significant because it calls into question many, if not most, of the assumptions upon which current approaches to society, politics and economics are based.

PARTICLES AND FIELDS

To appreciate Elliott's innovations, one must contrast them with the mechanistic view, which was current at the time and still underlies much of social theory. According to mechanism, an entity consists of fundamental particles or atoms. Any whole within a given discipline is merely the sum of its parts. Thus, the proper procedure is to analyze a whole into its fundamental parts and then sum those parts to constitute the whole. Further, all disciplines can ultimately be resolved into a single discipline, physics, so that the doctrine of the unity of the sciences is also fundamental to mechanism. Finally, according to mechanism, the universe is basically inert so that atoms change only as a result of outside forces acting upon them. Newton formulated these laws of external causality in his three laws of motion: a body at rest remains at rest unless acted upon by an external force, a body in motion remains in motion in a straight line unless acted upon by an external force, and for every action there is an equal and opposite reaction. Thus, atomism, reductionism, the unity of the sciences, and the primacy of external causality are the four pillars of mechanism.

Elliott developed his views as an alternative to these mechanistic conceptions of the world. A key to Elliott's intellectual orientation can be found in his praise of the work of Marconi, the inventor of the radio. Marconi's work was the result of a series of century-long challenges to the mechanistic conception of the universe and seemed to vindicate a field theory over an atomistic one. As Einstein (1938, p.125) states, "During the second half of the nineteenth century new and revolutionary ideas were introduced into physics; they opened the way to a new philosophical view, differing from the mechanical one." Elliott extended this revolution to social theory. Thus, in order to understand Elliott, one must have an understanding of these new developments.

The first challenge to mechanism came when Young proposed the wave theory of light, which, by the middle of the nineteenth century, was widely accepted. The work of Fizeau and Foucault had provided significant verification of this theory. The second challenge came from developments in electromagnetic theory. The voltaic cell was invented in 1799 and made experimentation with electric charges easier. The work of Ohm, Faraday, and Maxwell further developed a field theory as an alternative to mechanism. Faraday rejected the atomic theory of matter in favor of a field theory. Maxwell developed the electromagnetic theory of light, and Hertz provided experimental verification of Maxwell's theories as well as the fundamental discoveries upon which the development of radio broadcasting and radar were based. Hertz had produced and detected waves over short distances. Marconi's achievement was to produce and detect such waves over long distances. This laid the foundations for radio. His work seemed to vindicate the concept of a field over that of particles. Elliott's work extended the field concepts of this revolutionary new philosophy to society.

The rise of thermodynamics in the nineteenth century also called into question some of the tenets of mechanism. As a result of the work of Carnot, Clausius, and Kelvin, the first and second laws of thermodynamics were formulated. These describe the behavior of complex systems in more holistic terms. As a result of this work, it was shown that macrostates could be used to describe a complex system and that these could be accounted for in terms of macrovariables that did not make reference to the atomistic constituents of the complex system. Indeed, any given macrostate is compatible with many different microstates and thus is not uniquely determined by a single microstate. Thus, the properties of wholes could be studied in and of themselves since they have properties of their own that were not merely the sum of their constituents. This left it open to study the properties of fields and systems independently of their parts.

Applying the above innovations from physics to social theory, Elliott developed a conception of society based upon systems as wholes and upon field concepts. His significant innovation at this point was to develop a method for identifying and studying the properties of a whole that cannot be reduced to the properties of its constituents. Philosophically, Elliott's conception of market behavior is similar to the approach Spinoza developed for understanding organic systems. Like Elliott, Spinoza thought that a whole should be viewed as a whole and not as a mechanical interplay of constituting parts. Spinoza thought that a whole was a self-organizing system that had a certain form and that maintained its distinctness in a causal history despite the fact that it continually gained and lost parts. As Jonas (1973, p.269) states in his explication of Spinoza's theory, a whole is "the sustained sequence of states of a unified plurality, with only the form of its union enduring while the parts come and go." Thus, a whole maintains its identity by maintaining a certain form or pattern. As was the case with electromagnetic phenomena, this form or pattern was, for Elliott, given by a wave structure. By developing a procedure for identifying the properties of wholes in terms of wave structure, Elliott rejected the reductionism of mechanism.

He also rejected both the doctrine of the unity of the sciences and the doctrine of external causality. He states: "the motion of one activity is seldom, if ever, a reliable guide for another" (Elliott, Oct 6, 1943, p.194) and "the cycle of each pattern must be analyzed by itself as to position, by its own waves, and not by extraneous elements." (Elliott, Feb-Jun 1940, p.160) Each whole must be understood in terms of its own form "irrespective of external conditions." (Elliott, Jan 16, 1940, p.156) Further, he states that external causes "tend to become relatively unimportant in the long term progress of the cycle." (Elliott, Oct 1, 1940, p.162)

Elliott spent considerable time identifying the structure of waves of progress and regress in social trends. As a result of his work, he identified a five-wave sequence that he thought was a fundamental pattern of nature. In a growth wave, wave 1 consists of an initial expansion. Wave 2 is a partial retracement of wave 1. This is followed by wave 3, which is often a strong growth spurt. Wave 4 consists of a partial retracement of wave 3. Finally, wave 5 constitutes the last and final growth spurt of the system. At this point, the growth has reached its maximum point. Then a decline begins, which retraces partially the whole progress of the previous five-wave expansion. The first wave, wave A, of the retracement is a downward thrust. This is followed by wave B, which is an upward thrust that corrects the first wave down. Finally, there is the third wave down, wave C, which completes the correction of the five-wave sequence. The process is then ready to begin another five-wave expansion period. (Elliott, Jan 16, 1940, pp.156-158)

THE WAVE STRUCTURE OF SOCIAL PROGRESS

Elliott applied the principles of holism, waves, pluralism and internal self-organization independently of external causes to develop an understanding of human society. According to Elliott (Oct 1, 1940, p.162):

> Civilization rests on change. This change is cyclical in origin and characteristic. A rhythmic series of extreme changes constitutes a cycle. When a cycle has been completed, another cycle is started. The rhythm of the new cycle will be the same as that of the previous cycle, although the extent or duration may vary.

If society is thought of as a field or medium, then what are the waves that pass through it in the five-wave pattern that is common to growing and developing systems? Elliott thought that mass psychology, impelled by emotion and not reason, was the driving force of human society. Thus, the waves that passed through society were emotional moods. As he (Elliott, Apr 20, 1943, p.182; See, also Dec 15, 1939, p.146; Oct 1, 1940, p.162; Dec 15, 1942, p.109; and 1942, p.171) states:

> In most human beings, there is a tendency to reach the crest of an emotional wave and then recede. A strong resemblance of the individual and the mass, during periods of boom and depression, is confirmed by psychiatry. There is in both a similar period of

normality. During such periods, the manic-depressive acts in a sedate and prosaic manner. During the exaltation period, his mental activity is very great indeed. He rushes about creating, planning and writing. After reaching the crisis in his exaltation, he starts on a downward wave of the depressive phase. The downward trend begins with a slight loss of confidence, develops into a condition of anxiety and ends with utter despair concerning the future. This completes the cycle, and from this point on, confidence and poise are gradually regained.

Such waves of emotion express themselves in all sorts of social phenomena. However, according to Elliott, the most direct and detailed measure of these moods is provided by aggregate stock market prices. Elliott (Apr 20, 1943, p.182) states that stocks are "an emotional human activity," and the New York Stock Exchange, because of "its marvelous machinery and organization, reflect psychology immediately and to perfection." (Aug 6, 1945, p.137) Investment decisions are not made typically by a rational assessment of risks and rewards but by relying upon others and what they are doing. As Prechter (1999, p.153) states, investors "are driven to follow the herd because they do not have firsthand knowledge adequate to form an independent conviction, which makes them seek wisdom in numbers." Because such movements are emotionally based, they can give rise to what people perceive (usually after the fact) as "abnormal markets" in which there is extreme irrational exuberance. (Apr 20, 1943, p.182) Under such conditions, individuals are overly optimistic and take on excessive risks, which leads to an economic crisis of over-investment. This is what happened in the late 1920s. After being financially burned in the economic collapse following a period of over-optimism, the crowd then goes to the opposite extreme and becomes extremely pessimistic and risk-averse. As a result, economic conditions stagnate. By charting stock prices, Elliott observed that one could trace the ebb and flow of human emotions in society through its repeated pattern of five waves up and three waves down.

Elliott's work is consistent with the work in cultural theory done by Mary Douglas and her students, Michael Thompson, Richard Ellis, and Aaron Wildavsky. As Thompson *et al.* (1990, p.2) state, "A change in the way an individual perceives physical or human nature, for instance, changes the range of behavior an individual can justify engaging in and hence the type of social relations an individual can justify living in." Human beings, they assert, are social animals who find meaning through identification with others. Identification with others requires acceptance by others, and this in turn requires that an individual adopt the preferences of his/her target group and that he/she behave accordingly. Social acceptance and identification with a group brings with it a set of preferences and a set of social relations consistent with those preferences. Preferences and social relations act in a self-reinforcing manner so as to form a consistent whole among groups of self-organizing individuals. This is true of people's perception and assumption of risk, which is also socially constructed. Wildavsky *et al.* (1990, pp.25ff) identify four attitudes toward risk around which people organize themselves. There are two ways of life that construct a tolerant attitude toward risk. At the extreme is the way of life of the risk-taking individualist in which it is felt that risk equals opportunity and that it is, in the long run, impossible to lose. The world is benign and forgiving of all risks. The second risk-tolerate view holds that the world is, for the most part, tolerant, as long as one takes adequate precautions. Risks can be managed. On the other hand, there are two attitudes toward life in which a risk-averse attitude is socially constructed. One holds that the world is a terrible, unforgiving place. The least change may trigger its complete collapse. Thus, the world is fraught with risks and dangers enough so any additional risks should be avoided. The last view holds that the world is risky because it is capricious, random and uncontrollable. According to cultural theory, social changes are due to the movement of people from one of these orientations to another. What the work of Elliott suggests is that there is a pattern to such movement and that the movement toward these ways of life can reach socially destructive extremes.

Waves in American History

Elliott attempted to show the fruitfulness of his approach by applying it to develop an understanding of American society in the past, the present and the future. His first goal was to understand the current social mood in America, and, to do this, he had to identify which phase of society's wave pattern was in force. His resources to accomplish this goal were somewhat limited. Elliott had stock market data only from 1854 to the 1940s. Nevertheless, upon the basis of the data available to him, he identified the expansionary period from 1859-1929 as a third wave, which is typically a strong expansive wave. This was followed by a wave four correction from 1929-1942. (Elliott, Aug 25, 1942, pp.81-86 and Apr 20, 1943, p.173) This was the period of the Great Depression. Reasoning backward to reconstruct the past, Elliott deduced that the period from 1776 to 1859 contained a first and second wave. Subsequent work by Frost and Prechter (2000, pp.152-159) supported Elliott's reconstruction. They conclude that from 1784 to 1837, the United States experienced its first wave expansion, and from 1837 to 1859, a second wave correction of this initial advance.

In the 1720s, extreme over-optimism developed in what came to be known as the South Sea Bubble, which Mackay (1980) described in his work, *Extraordinary Delusions and the Madness of Crowds*. The social mood retrenchment from the South Sea Bubble ended in 1784, a 64-year period of retrenchment that should give pause to those with a buy-and-hold strategy.

Elliott was not content with merely analyzing the past and the present. Once the wave structure of a system is known, then it is possible to predict in broad strokes its future course of development. In 1942, in the middle of the Depression when extreme pessimism was rampant, Elliott called for a multi-decade economic advance. This was, he reasoned, the beginning of a fifth wave expansionary period that would eventually end and then require a correction of the whole development since 1784. He saw this part of the cycle lasting through the rest of the 20th century and ending early in the 21st. Prechter's (Aug 18, 1983) subsequent studies indicated that large waves end in periods of substantial exuberance and therefore predicted in 1983 that this fifth wave would end in a speculative mania as large as that shown in the South Sea Bubble of 1720 and the stock speculation of the late 1920s.

Conclusion

In the post-Depression era, a mechanistic framework was still being used as the basis of economics. The classical view of economics, represented best in the post-Depression era by Milton Friedman, argued that the economy was naturally in a state of motion, i.e., growth, and it would remain in that state unless acted upon by an external force. Thus, the Great Depression was due to external interference by the government in the form of an ill-conceived monetary policy that prevented the economy from moving forward. For the Marxists, in the form of the theory of monopoly capitalism, the natural state of a capitalist economy was stagnation and depression, i.e., rest. Only outside stimulation in the form of governmental policies, such as the social welfare programs and the waging of war, could cause the economy to grow and could prevent the collapse of capitalism. Thus, capitalism had an inherent tendency toward aggression and warfare. Keynesianism, another post-Depression development, was a compromise between these two views. It argued that the economy might naturally be in motion and thus growing; however, it periodically encountered friction, i.e., resistance, that slowed it down. Thus, the government may need to intervene in the economy in order to maintain both growth and full employment. For Elliott, all these approaches are misguided because using external factors to explain social and economic change is mistaken. Social mood ebbs and flows according to its own inherent rhythm. External events affect an economy only insofar as they are interpreted by human beings and assigned a particular meaning. However, the way that an external event is interpreted is itself dependent upon the social mood and the degree of optimism or pessimism that is prevalent in a society at a particular time.

The current explanation for stock price change is the Efficient Market Hypothesis. This view holds that the decisions of all market participants are always informed and rational so that investment values are equilibrated immediately. This theory finds it difficult to account for the irrational exuberance that leads to stock market bubbles, such as the one in 1720, the one in 1929, and the current one that is unraveling before our very eyes. During such times when assets are overpriced, investors should be selling instead of buying, but they don't. Nor can it account for times of extreme pessimism in which investors withdraw wholesale from the markets at the very time that assets are underpriced and they should be buying. Since the market is supposed to reach equilibrium efficiently, this theory has difficulties accounting for these far-from-equilibrium states. For Elliott, both of these behaviors are part of the natural ebb and flow of social mood. Perhaps Elliott's biggest challenge to modern economics, though, is that the one-dimensional conception of human beings that underlies traditional economic theory is flawed because it ignores the emotional and impulsive side of human existence.

NOTES

Einstein, Albert and Leopold Infeld, (1938), *The Evolution of Physics*, New York: Simon and Schuster, xvi+302pp.

Elliott, R.N., (Dec 15, 1939) "Selection of Trading Mediums," Ibid, p.146 in Prechter, Robert Jr., editor, (1993) *R.N. Elliott's Market Letters (1938-1946)*, Gainesville, GA: New Classics Library, 234pp.

Elliott, R.N., (Jan. 16, 1940) "Educational Bulletin B Cycles," pp.156-159 in ibid.

Elliott, R.N., (Feb.-Jun. 1940) "Educational Bulletin C The Law of Motion," pp.159-162 in ibid.

Elliott, R.N., (Oct. 1, 1940) "The Basis of the Wave Principle," Ibid, pp.162-167 in ibid.

Elliott, R.N., (Aug 25, 1941) "Interpretative Letter No. 17 Two Cycles of American History," pp.81-86, in ibid.

Elliott. R.N., (Dec 14, 1942) "Interpretative Letter No. 25 The 13-year Triangle," pp.109-112 in ibid.

Elliott. R.N., (1942) "Educational Bulletin N The Measurement of Mass Psychology," pp.171-173 in ibid.

Elliott, R.N., (Apr 7, 1943) "Interpretative Letter No. 27 Primary No. 1 1942-1943," pp.115-119 in ibid.

Elliott, R.N., (Apr 20, 1943) "Educational Bulletin Q Psychology," pp.182-185 in ibid.

Elliott, R.N., (Oct 6, 1943) "Educational Bulletin V Technical Features," pp.194-198 in ibid.

Elliott, R.N., (Aug 6 , 1945) "Interpretative Letter No. 34 Psychology," pp.137-139 in ibid.

Frost, Alfred John and Robert Prechter, Jr., (2000) *Elliott Wave Principle — Key to Market Behavior*, Gainesville, GA: New Classics Library, 244pp.

Jonas, Hans, (1973) "Spinoza and the Theory of Organism," in *Spinoza, A Collection of Critical Essays*, edited by Marjorie Grene, Garden City, N.Y.: Anchor Books, 1973, p.269ff.

Mackay, Charles, (1980) *Extraordinary Popular Delusions and the Madness of Crowds*, London: Three Rivers Press, which is a reprint of the 1841 edition.

Pigou, Arthur, (1927) *Industrial Fluctuations*, London: F. Cass.

Prechter, Robert, Jr., (August 18, 1983), "The Superbull Market of the '80s — The Last Wild Ride," *The Elliott Wave Theorist*.

Prechter, Jr., Robert, (1999) *The Wave Principle of Human Social Behavior*, Gainesville, GA: New Classics Library, 463pp.

Thompson, Michael, Richard Ellis, and Aaron Wildavsky, *Cultural Theory*, Boulder, San Francisco, and Oxford: Westview Press, 1990, xvi+296pp.

Chapter 2

A KEY FAILURE OF LINEAR STA-TISTICAL TESTS OF FINANCIAL MARKET RANDOMNESS

by Michael Buettner

originally composed in 1995 and published January 2000

Academic economists have tended to disregard predictive models of financial markets on the grounds that markets are not orderly but random. Examining the markets with a variety of statistical tools, they have found price changes "independently and identically distributed" (IID), as reflected by insignificant correlation coefficients, a more or less "normal" (i.e., Gaussian) distribution of changes and a "noisy" power spectrum. Based on these and similar findings, some statistical economists conclude that while stocks generally move higher along a linear uptrend, day-to-day, week-to-week or month-to-month fluctuations around that trend represent nothing more than random "noise" in the system. If these fluctuations are random, they are by definition unpredictable. Thus, according to these economists, accurately predicting stock market movements is impossible.

This line of reasoning is valid only if one assumes that order in the markets must be linear. However, there is no evidence that this assumption is true. On the contrary, there exists abundant evidence suggesting that if the markets do possess some underlying order, that order is likely to be *non*linear.

To illustrate the inapplicability of linear statistical analysis to the market problem, we will construct a model of orderly market behavior that substantially matches actual stock index price movements. We will then show why linear statistical techniques are inadequate even to discern, much less describe, this model. We will thereby aid in invalidating the Random Walk hypothesis and in the process further validate the Wave Principle as a market model.

An Evolutionary Model of Market Growth: The Elliott Wave Principle

Ralph Nelson Elliott (1871-1948) discovered the first known fractal mathematical model of market dynamics. Performing his research during the 1930s, Elliott derived his model through painstaking observation of both past and current-time stock market behavior. Without the aid of modern computers and with limited sources of data, Elliott described the most basic building blocks of market patterns and how they link together to form more complex patterns at larger scales.

Elliott's first book, *The Wave Principle,* was published on August 31, 1938. With its publication, Elliott brought to the public's attention for the first time the results of his research over most of a decade. From his studies of the stock market's complex twists and turns, Elliott concluded:

> Human emotions...are rhythmical. They move in waves of a definite number and direction. A completed movement consists of five waves. Three of the five waves that form any completed movement will be in the direction of the movement; two of the waves will be in a contrary direction. The first, third and fifth waves represent the forward impulse; the second and fourth waves, the contrary, or corrective. Five waves of one dimension become the first wave of the next greater dimension or degree....Waves in the direction of the main movement, or the odd-numbered waves, are made up of five lesser waves. Corrective waves, or waves against the main movement (even-numbered waves) are made up of three lesser waves.1

The bulk of *The Wave Principle* consists of a detailed description of the various forms these five- and three-wave patterns can assume and a concise statement of the laws they appear to follow in joining together to form larger patterns. Among these laws are three unbreakable rules concerning five-wave movements:

(1) The second wave cannot carry past the beginning of the preceding first wave.

(2) The fourth wave cannot enter the price range of the first wave.

(3) The third wave is never the shortest among waves one, three and five.

Elliott refined the basic structure of his model by including numerous "guidelines," which are observations of behavior that apply often but not inevitably in the market's construction of patterns. The guidelines that are closest to being rules in their nearly universal applicability to five-wave structures are:

(1) If wave two develops as one type of pattern, then wave four usually develops as a different type of pattern. Usually, second waves develop as relatively fast, steep retracements of the prior impulsive movements, while fourth waves tend to trace out complex, more sideways-shaped patterns.

(2) Typically, one wave among waves one, three and five is "extended;" that is, it is the longest of the three movements and subdivides into component waves of nearly the size of the other main waves. Wave three is usually the extended wave.

(3) When wave three is extended, waves one and five tend to exhibit equality in their price travel and similarity in the complexity of their internal structures.

(4) Certain market movements tend to be related in size by a mathematical constant, the Fibonacci ratio or Golden Mean (ϕ), 0.618, and its complement, 0.382. Impulse waves often are related in this way to other impulse waves or series of impulse waves and often to the ensuing corrections.

Constructing a Simplified Model

In constructing a simple mathematical idealization of the Wave Principle, we have limited ourselves to the rules, guidelines and relationships described above and excluded many additional guidelines and relationships identified by Elliott. Also, while Elliott identified several types of corrective-wave patterns, our idealization incorporates only two, the "zigzag" and the "flat." In addition, our model reiterates its basic forms and relationships identically at all degrees of scale and so does not display the variability among forms shown by the actual market.

An example of the basic five-wave pattern appears in Figure 1. This rudimentary form reflects the key guidelines of Elliott's model with these specific constructs: In price, wave 5 equals wave 1, and wave 3 is 1.618 times as long. Waves 2 and 4 show alternation in the depth

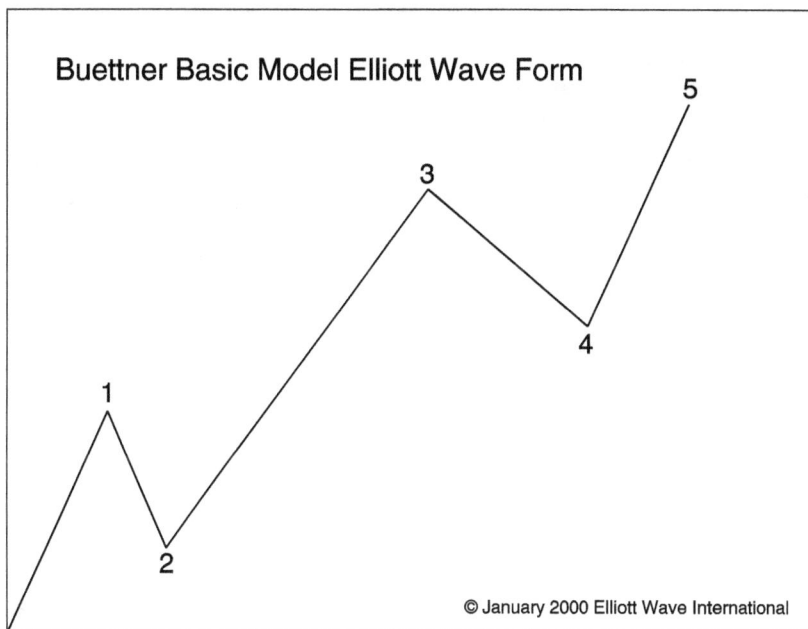

Figure 1

of their retracements, with wave 2 retracing 0.618 times wave 1 and wave 4 retracing 0.382 times wave 3, the most common relationships found between these waves. Our time units for the five waves are 5, 3, 13, 8 and 5.

When we take the rudimentary wave pattern shown in Figure 1 and show subdivisions at the next degree of scale, the result is a more complex-looking pattern (Figure 2). In this case, 34 data points are required to describe the complete pattern vs. only six data points in Figure 2. Here, we display the subdivisions of a typically extended third wave. Also, the guideline of alternation is more clearly visible in the "zigzag" form of wave (2) vs. the "flat" form of wave (4), a structure also seen in the smaller-scale waves 2 and 4 within wave (3). Within the corrections, wave c and a are equal in length. In zigzags, wave b retraces 61.8% of wave a; in flats, wave b retraces 100% of wave a. Our time units for the three waves in the zigzag and flat are 1, 1, 1 and 3, 3, 2, respectively.

Iteration of our model through five degrees of scale produces the profile shown in Figure 3, in which the number of data points has increased from 34 to more than 5000. Despite an increase in complexity

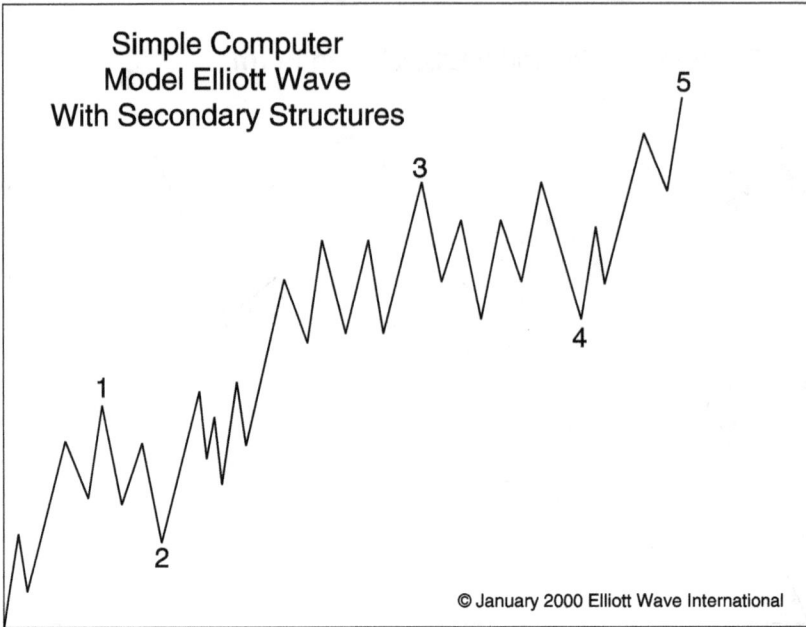

Simple Computer
Model Elliott Wave
With Secondary Structures

© January 2000 Elliott Wave International

Figure 2

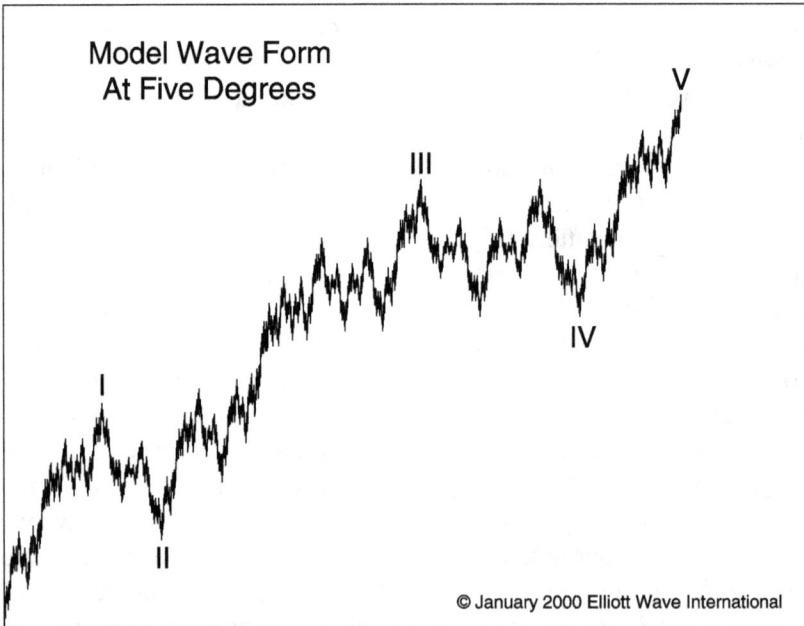

Model Wave Form
At Five Degrees

© January 2000 Elliott Wave International

Figure 3

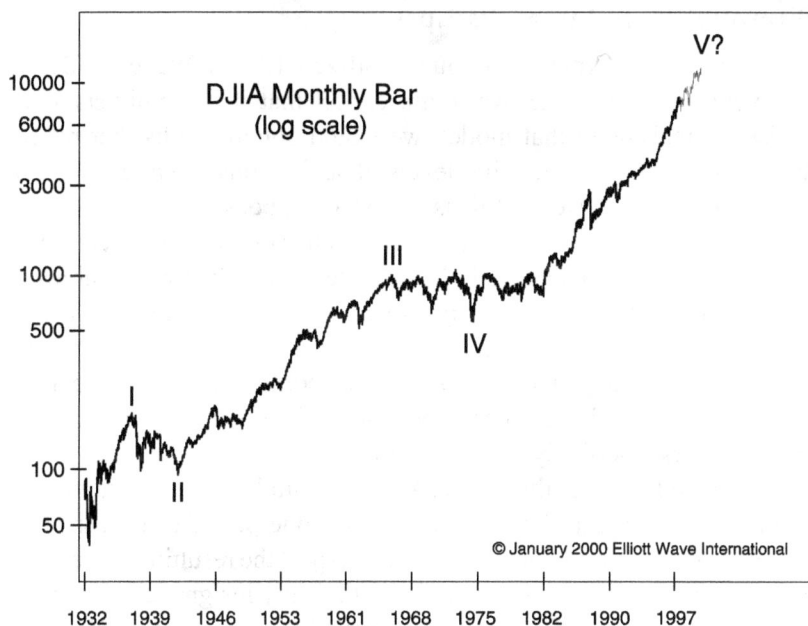

Figure 4

of more than 1000 times, the overall five-wave structure clearly still dominates the pattern.

More important, however, is the fact that at this degree of development, our mathematical idealization of Elliott's model results in a reasonably realistic-looking representation of real-world market behavior. Just how realistic-looking it is becomes evident when we compare Figure 3 with Figure 4, a chart of monthly closing prices of the Dow Jones Industrial Average from June 1932 through 1999. Knowing that June 1932 represented the bottom of the deepest bear market in United States history, we would expect the Dow to have begun a five-wave advance from that point. Indeed, that is exactly what R.N. Elliott postulated in 1938, Charles Collins reiterated in 1966 and Frost and Prechter again reiterated in 1978. At this point, one need no longer *anticipate* that development, as it has occurred. More to our present purpose, a comparison of Figures 3 and 4 demonstrates that the market model formulated by R.N. Elliott in the 1930s, even when converted into a highly simplified mathematical idealization, reproduces to a remarkable degree the overall structure of the real market during the subsequent six decades (the main difference being an exceptionally long fifth wave in the real market data).

Wave Analysis vs. Linear Statistics

Because we know that our idealized Elliott Wave model is completely deterministic, we might expect that if we apply standard statistical analysis to that model, we would obtain results that reflect this determinism, such as high levels of self-correlation and a smooth power spectrum. However, this is not what happens.

A common measure of linear dependence or independence is correlation. Positive correlation indicates a tendency for two variables to move in the same direction, negative correlation indicates a tendency to move in opposite directions, and zero correlation indicates that the variables move independently. For the more commonly cited correlation coefficient, 1.0 indicates perfect point-to-point correspondence, while -1.0 indicates a perfectly inverse relationship.

One method of analyzing market data would be to take a sample of market index prices as the x variable and the one-period change in price as y. For a random walk model, we would expect the resulting correlation coefficient to lie between zero and a statistically insignificant number. For any given sample of market data, correlation coefficients tend toward positive but very small values. Such small amounts are considered to indicate statistically insignificant relationships between the variables. In other words, price levels and price changes are considered to occur independently of one another.

Perhaps surprisingly, however, when we perform the same calculations on our idealized Elliott Wave model, we obtain very similar results. The correlation coefficients for the two data series are almost identical: 0.0231 for the Dow sample vs. 0.0229 for the idealization. Again, the small value of the correlation suggests almost complete independence between price levels and short term price changes.

As mentioned earlier, researchers have found that the stock market exhibits a "noisy" power spectrum, indicating that large and small price movements occur with essentially random frequency. Figure 5 shows Fourier transforms of the one-period differences in equal-size samples (2048 data points) of hourly readings of the Dow Jones Industrials, our Elliott Wave idealization and a computer-generated random ("brown") noise signal. All three display "noisy" profiles, evidenced by the numerous sharp peaks at irregular intervals. Both the market sample and the wave idealization appear somewhat less noisy than the random signal, especially at higher frequencies. However, both still exhibit sufficient "disorderliness" to be considered too random to predict.

Fourier Transforms

DJI Hourly

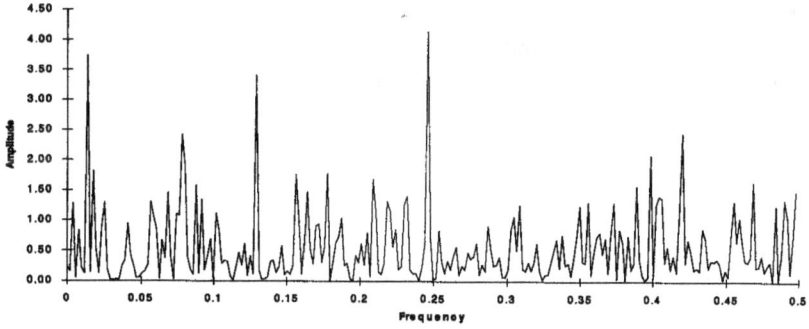

Idealized Elliott Wave

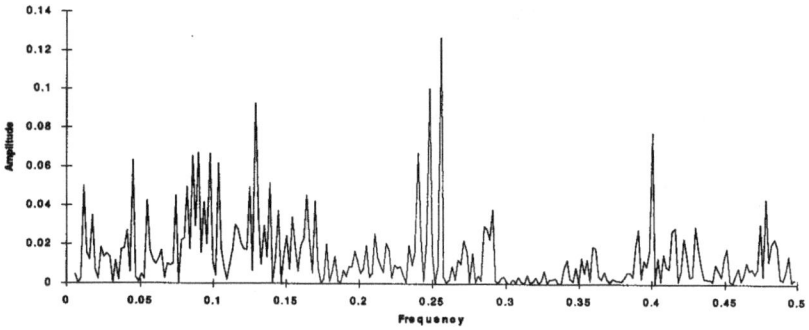

Random Noise Signal

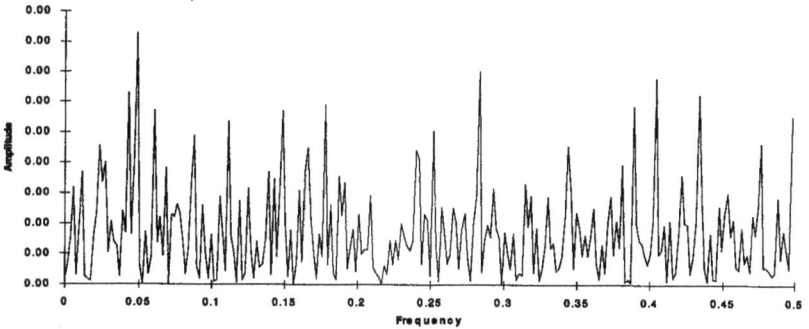

Figure 5

In the case of our wave idealization, of course, these "findings" are completely false. On the contrary, fluctuations in the model are *perfectly* predictable. With knowledge of the rules by which the model was constructed (which were, as mentioned earlier, based upon a few of the rules and guidelines under the Wave Principle), every point-to-point change in the model can be forecast *exactly*. We know, therefore, that the fluctuations in the model are not random at all. Yet *conventional linear statistical tools are incapable of recognizing this fact.*

Conclusion

Although precise rules of order dictate the movement of "prices" in our wave idealization, standard statistical analysis finds no evidence whatsoever of those rules. In other words, linear statistical methods are powerless to recognize certain types of order, specifically the type exhibited by a model of the stock market that has a six-decade history of forecasting utility: the Wave Principle, as described by R.N. Elliott in 1938. At the same time, then, that scientists are increasingly making discoveries supporting the potential validity of the Wave Principle (see *The Wave Principle of Human Social Behavior*, New Classics Library, 1999), this study destroys what has been the main basis for presuming its invalidity.

NOTES

[1] Elliott, Ralph Nelson. (1938). *The wave principle.* Republished: (1994). *R.N. Elliott's Masterworks — The Definitive Collection.* Prechter, Jr., Robert Rougelot. (Ed.). Gainesville, GA: New Classics Library.

Chapter 3

MATHEMATICAL BASIS
OF WAVE THEORY

by Walter E. White
*originally published in the 1968 and 1970 supplements
to the Bank Credit Analyst, Montreal*

"Creative mathematics begins in the more humble environment of empirics. The further removed studies are from the empirical beginnings, the greater is the danger of corruption, 'art for art's sake,' and lack of real progress."

— Von Neumann

Long-term economic patterns tie in with the Elliott concept of growth. In this paper, the writer analyzes in terms of shock and instability this concept of growth.

R.N. Elliott first introduced the idea that the stock market tends to expand in a series of waves. In previous issues of *The Elliott Wave Principle*, the editors pointed out that further work was necessary in order to understand the nature of the waves and their relation to the economy and the stock market.

In analyzing Elliott waves, the writer has discovered a general relationship between static forms in plant and animal life and dynamic waves of time. The origins of this relationship may be found in fundamental ideas of arithmetic, logic, algebra, geometry and trigonometry dating back to 500 B.C. and of differential and integral calculus. This general relationship between form and waves of time is used to describe the structure of time and the generation of dynamic waves of time in biology, physics, geophysics, electronics, economics and other sciences. It is also used to explain how the wave theory of time may be useful in studying economic time series on an hourly, daily, weekly or annual basis.

Methods of nonlinear mathematics are used to link the concept of shock, instability, static form and dynamic waves of time and to help describe the structure of time waves in the economy and the stock market as well as in a number of physical and biological sciences.

The idea of the shock seems fundamental and had an influence on Niels Bohr's discovery of the process of cognition. Bohr was a student of the philosopher Kierkegaard and his philosophic studies preceded his scientific discoveries. Kierkegaard taught that "in life only sudden decisions, leaps, or jerks can lead to progress. Something decisive occurs always only by a jerk, by a sudden turn which neither can be predicted from its antecedents nor is determined by them." These thoughts guided Bohr in developing atomic theory.*

The concept of growth initiated by a shock may be related to the logarithmic spiral of Figure 1 by the simple relationship that the ratio of the length of the arc of Figure 2 to the diameter, at any point in the evolution of the spiral, is approximately equal to the ratio of consecutive terms in the Fibonacci series (Figs. 1, 2, 3):

$$2 - 3 - 5 - 8 - 13 - 21 - 34 - 55 - 89....$$

The ratio of successive terms in the above series oscillates about the limit of 1.618, as indicated in Figure 3. The value of 1.618 is sometimes designated by the Greek letter ϕ although there is no uniformity in the literature.

The number of branches in a tree increases each year in the same ratio as the ratio of successive terms in the Fibonacci series. Logarithmic spirals occur in galaxies, flowers, shells, elephants' tusks, pinecones, leaves of trees, bumps in pineapples and in many sciences. The relationships between the logarithmic spiral, the Fibonacci series and the golden ratio known for about 2500 years has been regarded as something of a mystery by many writers. One reason for the mystery is the fact that the concepts concerning the golden ratio were evolved 2000 years before the birth of Fibonacci and many centuries before the development

---

*Though these models are useful in explicating certain characteristics of waves, the Wave Principle renders false the three presumptions of nonpredictability, non-determination by antecedents and external shock.—Ed.

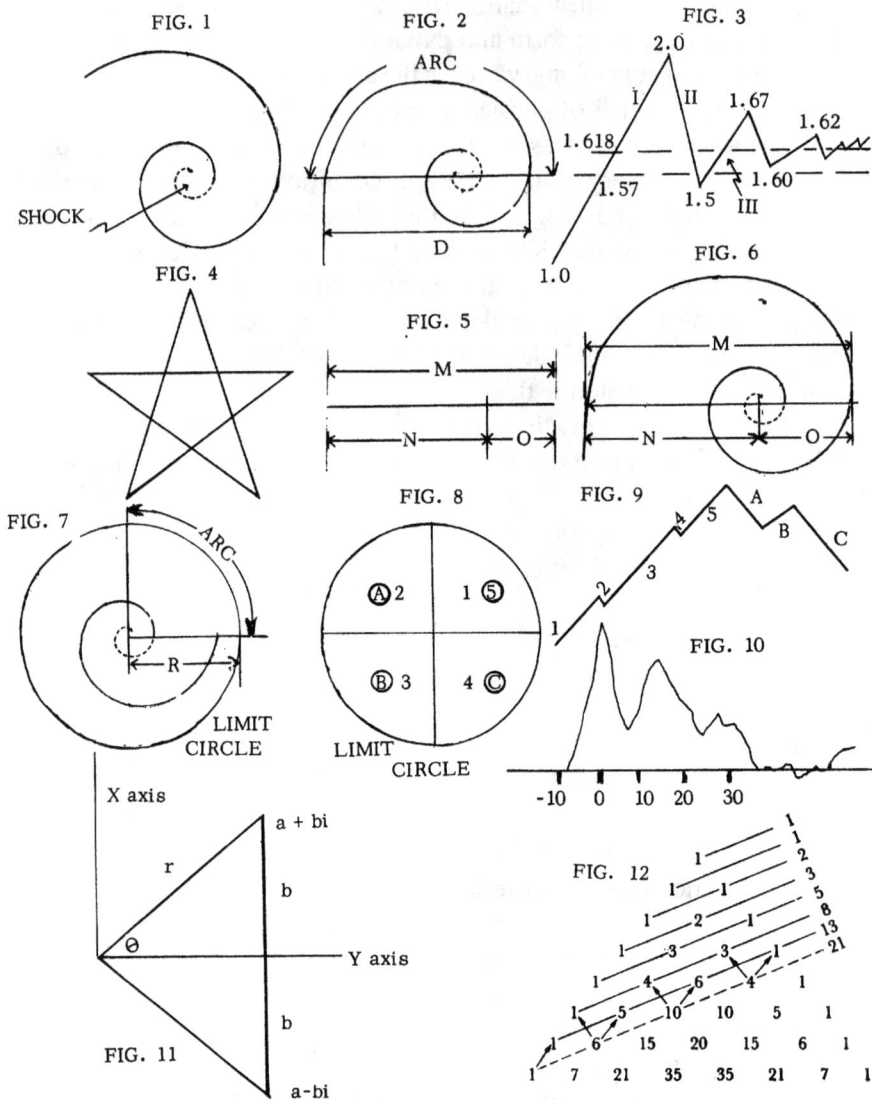

Figures 1-12

of decimal systems. These concepts were, however, important to the development of many ideas in arithmetic, logic, algebra, geometry and trigonometry, and the same concepts may be related to the development of differential and integral calculus.

Figure 4 indicates the Badge of the Order of Pythagoras. The Pythagoreans made great progress in the theory of numbers and in the geometry of areas and solids. Pythagoras played a part in the discovery of irrational numbers when he found that no common measure can be found:

> when m is the diagonal and n is the side of a square,
> *or* when a line m is divided in golden section into parts n and o.

Thus, in Figure 5, $m/n = n/o = 1.618$, and this ratio is now known as the Fibonacci ratio. In the Badge shown in Figure 4, each line is cut in the golden ratio.

An algebraic proof of irrationality may be used. Since $o = m - n$ and $m/n = n/o$, then $m(m - n) = n^2$. This equation may be solved to show that $m/n = (\sqrt{5} + 1)/2$.

Aristotle suggested an indirect proof by "reductio ad absurdum" and thus made an important step in developing the logic of mathematics.

Before decimal notations were developed, the Greeks built a ladder of whole numbers in order to approximate the irrational $\sqrt{2}$.

1	1
2	3
5	7
12	17
29	41

Each rung of the ladder contains two numbers whose ratio approaches the ratio $1/\sqrt{2}$ more closely as one moves down the ladder. The successive ratios are [respectively] less than and greater than all following ratios.

A similar ladder may be constructed for any irrational. The series known later as the Fibonacci series is related to the golden ratio:

1	1
1	2
2	3
3	5
5	8

In this ladder, the right hand member of each rung is the sum of the pairs in the preceding rung. This ratio is, alternately, a little less or a little more than $(\sqrt{5} + 1)/2$ or than the golden ratio $m/n = n/o$ of Figure 5. This ladder has not been found in ancient literature, but the Badge of Figure 4 suggests that the Pythagoreans were aware of this relationship. This series 1, 2, 3, 5, 8, 13 was known to Leonardo of Pisa, whose surname was Fibonacci, and this series is known as the Fibonacci series in current literature.

About 350 B.C., Eudoxus, a pupil of Plato, developed the Axiom of Archimedes by combining ladder arithmetic and the golden section of Figure 5. The whole theory of proportion for both algebra and geometry was developed from the three definitions of this Axiom.

In the logarithmic spiral of Figure 6, we find the golden ratio $m/n = n/o$, and the spiral provides a link to connect the static concepts in ancient literature with modern dynamic analysis. Nonlinear mathematics indicates that the spiral is one of a family of trajectories related to the stability of a system. One main characteristic of nonlinear mathematical analysis is the existence of limit cycles. An unstable spiral tends to approach a condition of stability indicated by the limit circle of Figure 7. The peak of one "wave" of Figure 3 indicates an instantaneous stability which breaks down and is followed by other attempts. The length of the "wave" in time depends upon the intensity of the shock and the relative instability indicated by the degree of convergence towards the ratio 1.618. This relative instability may be explained as follows:

For the limit circle of Figure 7, the ratio of the quarter circumference arc to the radius is $\pi/2$ or 1.57. Thus, the first three waves oscillate above and below 1.57 as well as above and below 1.618. During the third wave, however, the upper and lower limits of 1.67 and 1.50 as indicated in Figure 3 are much closer to 1.618 than the first and second waves and, therefore, the third wave will tend to be more stable. Later waves converge towards the ratio 1.618, but both upper and lower limits of these later waves will be higher than 1.57, as indicated in Figure 3.

The formation of a specific number of petals in a flower represents one form of stability in an evolving spiral. The number of petals corresponds to one of the numbers in the Fibonacci series simply because the ratio between consecutive terms in the series is the same (approximately) as the rate of growth in time indicated by the ratio of the arc to the radius of Figure 7. Since we cannot have a fractional number of petals or a fractional number of tree trunks, the Fibonacci series represents nature's way of compromising [the limit ratio] with reality.

The ratio between the arc and the diameter of Figure 2 is equal (approximately) to 1.618 at any point in the evolution of the spiral and, therefore, the Fibonacci series provides a convenient method of studying the structure of time in many phenomena. The equations for growing and decaying spirals are:

Growth, $r = e^{bx}$, and Decay, $r = e^{-bx}$, where b is the logarithm of the ratio of successive angles. For rectangular coordinates in the xy plane, the corresponding equations are: Growth, $y = e^{ax}$ and Decay, $y = e^{-ax}$, where a is the logarithm of the ratio of successive heights of ordinates.

When rectangular coordinates are used, each wave in time may be thought of as a tangent to a point moving along a spiral. Each $\pi/2$ or 90-degree rotation of the radius of the limit circle of Figure 7 generates a wave as indicated in Figure 9 and hesitates at a point of instantaneous stability. The waves 1, 2, 3 and 4 are shown in corresponding quadrants in Figure 8. Wave 5 is in the same quadrant as wave 1, and an extended 5 (5, 6, 7, 8) may result if the shock is strong enough. If the shock is not strong enough, an A-B-C type correction follows as indicated in Figure 9. The directions of the A, B and C waves are the same as the directions of the 2, 3 and 4 waves respectively. The progress after wave 5 depends upon the strength of the shock, and the conditions contributing to the strength of the shock must be assessed. Wave analysis alone will not provide a reliable answer.

The Fibonacci series provides a convenient measure function for the time waves of Figure 9. This measure function is expressed in whole numbers and can be used directly without reference to the basic equations listed above.

The following illustrates an interesting application in studying the pulse shapes of pulsars which have created considerable interest recently. Figure 10 is from page 418 of the April 26, 1968 issue of *Science* (American Association for the Advancement of Science). The author states, "Although several concepts of the object leading to two subpulses can be imagined, no schemes producing three subpulses readily present themselves."

The time structure indicates turning points at the Fibonacci numbers of 8, 13, 21 and 34 microseconds. These Fibonacci numbers, in turn, suggest that one unstable source may produce the pulse shape indicated. There are many similar applications in biology, physics, geophysics and other sciences.

An article on page 4 of the *Science Journal* (Iliffe Industrial Publications, United Kingdom) states that the annual rhythm of seed germination is passed to the embryo plant in the seed by the mother plants and that this "clock" continues to keep time for as long as the seed remains viable. This is probably another example of the relations between logarithmic growth and the structure of time.

The Fibonacci series is useful in studying economic time series, and these may be analyzed on an hourly, daily, weekly, monthly or annual basis. In economic time series, the origin of the shocks is complex. The resultant shock may be of national or international origin and may be due, in part, to extraterrestrial phenomena that affect man. Correlations between solar phenomena and economic time series have been noted for more than 100 years. Recent work indicates the possibility that extraterrestrial phenomena may contribute to the shock effect on people by one or more of the following:

(a) The effects of variations in atmospheric ions on human behavior. The effect of these ions on the electro-encephalographic rhythms of the brain has been investigated and, in most people, the alpha rhythm slows (see *Advances in Electronics and Electron Physics*, Vol. 19, pp.177-254).

(b) The effects on human behavior of variations in cosmic ray intensity changes during the 11-year solar cycle. Recent experiments in space science have explained how variations in sun spots may be "transmitted" to earth via the solar wind, resulting in variations in cosmic ray intensity (see "Magnetic Fields on the Quiet Sun," November 1966 issue of the *Scientific American*; "Plasmas in Space," November 1966 issue of *Spectrum* published by the Institution of Electrical and Electronic Engineers; and "Cosmic-Ray Studies in Interplanetary Space and on the Moon," *Spaceflight*, October 1966).

(c) The effects on human behavior of variations in the energy received from pulsars. The paper in *Science* mentioned above states that the radio energy emitted per unit area by the pulsar in each subpulse is equivalent in the radio spectrum to a value exceeding one-tenth that of the solar surface at all wavelengths.

The various relationships indicated by this analysis appear to support Elliott's claim that stock market movements are related to some law of nature. A study of the structure of time indicates that stock market price changes tend to develop in definite wave movements and that these movements cannot be described adequately by a random walk analysis.

The relationships between rectangular and polar coordinates may be generalized by using the concept of the complex plane a + bi introduced by Gauss. The two systems may be related as shown in Figure 11, where:

a	=	r cos θ
b	=	r sin θ
a + bi	=	r (cos θ + i sin θ)
a + bi	=	$re^{i\theta}$
dx/dt	=	ax - by
dy/dt	=	ax + by

where $x = e^{at} \cos bt$ and $y = e^{at} \sin bt$.

If a > 0, the spiral unwinds and moves away from the origin; if a < 0, the trajectories are spirals that wind around and move towards the origin.

From the equation a + bi = r (cos θ + i sin θ) and from Figure 11, we see that an imaginary number $bi = be^{\frac{\pi}{2}i}$ is a special case of a complex number a + bi when the cosine side of a right triangle is equal to zero.

$$bi = be^{\frac{\pi}{2}i}$$
$$= be \cos\frac{\pi}{2} + bi \sin\frac{\pi}{2}$$
$$= 0 + bi.$$

The calculus and the imaginary are both concerned with the angle of rotation (see page 1v of "Communication, Organization and Science," Jerome Rothstein, Falcon's Wing Press, 1958). Integration corresponds to a positive rotation and differentiation to a negative rotation with respect to the reference. Differentiation represents the rotations of a tangent to a point moving along a curve. Integration represents a reconstruction of the line from the rotations of the tangent.

$$\int^{-1}(\cos) = -\sin\ i^{-1} \qquad (1) = -i$$
$$\int(\sin) = -\cos\ i^{-1} \qquad (-i) = -1$$
$$\int(-\cos) = \sin\ i^{-1} \qquad (-1) = i$$
$$\int(\sin) = \cos\ i^{-1} \qquad (i) = 1$$

In the Pascal triangle of Figure 12, each term is the sum of two upper adjacent terms as indicated by the arrows. Pascal's triangle was designed to bring out the relationship between binomial coefficients and may be used in calculations of probability. Two hundred years passed before the discovery was made that the triangle contains a Fibonacci series as indicated in Figure 12. Some authorities claim that Pascal formulated the principle of mathematical induction after contemplating the triangle. Mr. D.L. Rowat of Atomic Energy of Canada, Limited, has suggested that man's thinking processes may be related to the logarithmic spiral, the Fibonacci series and the shock concept. The importance of the logarithmic spiral has been recognized for a long time. A logarithmic spiral was carved on the headboard of Isaac Newton's bed, and a reference to the spiral was made on the tombstone of James Bernoulli. Goethe mentioned a spiral tendency in nature, and the subject has been investigated by botanists for more than 200 years. Fractions representing the screw-like arrangement of leaves are often members of the Fibonacci series. Morning-glory buds form a corkscrew spiral.

Kepler tried to describe the distances between planets as a system in which bodies are alternately inscribed and circumscribed in spheres. The search today is for a dynamic rather than a static mathematical harmony.

Goedal demonstrated in his Proof that the resources of the human mind cannot be formalized completely and that new principles may always be found by discovery and by pragmatic methods. Goedal's Proof demonstrated, for arithmetic, that all possible relationships between whole numbers cannot be deduced from any one set of basic assumptions. The possible relationships are unlimited. Von Neumann and other intuitionists supported this approach.

Elliott's early work developed from observations and should be recognized as a very important step. His Wave Principle provides a measure of the structure of time and a useful guide in finding our way through the future. The rational criterion for any theory is testability, and those who have used the Wave Principle over the years know that it has a reasonable batting average. Can we afford to ignore a method that pinpoints turning points with such accuracy? The fact that the Wave

Principle works so well appears to be something of a breakthrough and also something of a connecting link between the physical and social sciences. Perhaps further work will convince more people that a simple method has been found for relating observations in economic time series to theory.

Chapter 4

WAVE FACTORS

by Robert R. Prechter, Jr.
originally published in Elliott Wave Report, *April 1976*

Elliott considered Fibonacci numbers and ratios to be the key determinants in the price and time developments of market averages. These numbers occur in a sequence derived by adding together the two previous numbers in the series, beginning with 1. Thus: 1, 1, 2, 3, 5, 8, 13, 21, 34, 55, 89, 144, etc. The ratio between adjacent numbers approaches one specific number the closer the series gets to infinity. That number, to three decimal places, is .618 when the smaller number is the numerator, and 1.618 when the larger number is the numerator. These two ratios are inverses, so that .618 x 1.618 = 1. Moreover, the ratios are related to their own squares as follows: $1 - (.618)^2 = .618$ and $(1.618)^2 - 1 = 1.618$. 2.618 and .382 express the ratio between *alternate* Fibonacci sequence numbers. With this minimal background, we can proceed to inspect the internal wave components [This paragraph was originally published in the April 1977 Update.—Ed.]

A correction ended in October 1975. Figures 1 and 2 show the wave count from that point. [Wave-degree notations originally in this report have been standardized per *Elliott Wave Principle* (1978).]

The Time Element

Let's first examine wave (3). It is made of waves, 1, 2, 3, 4, and 5. Their time lengths break down as follows:

Wave 1	52 hours
Wave 2	16 hours
Wave 3	153 or 157 hours
Wave 4	70 or 66 hours
Wave 5	155 hours

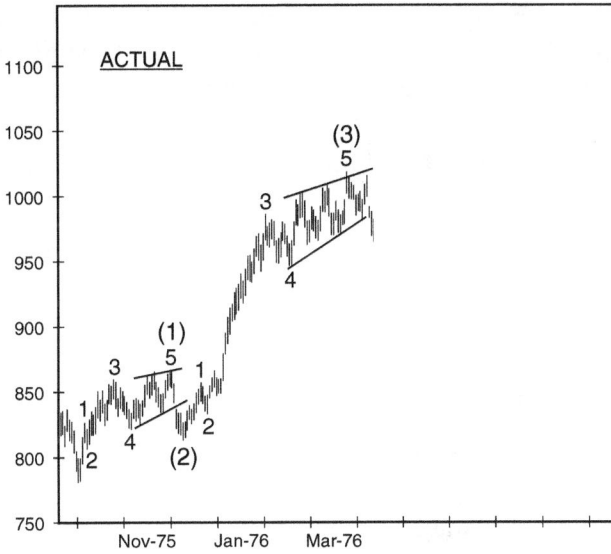

Figure 1

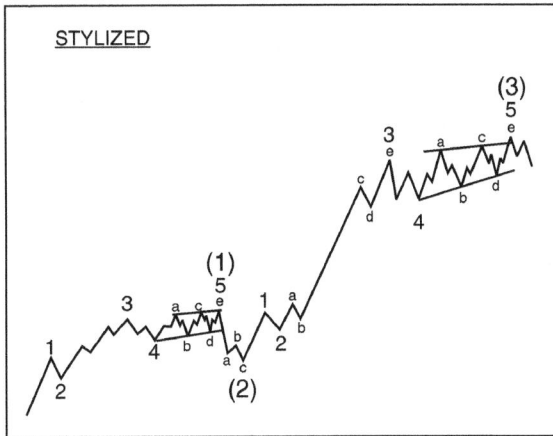

Figure 2

The choices given for waves 3 and 4 result from the question of the failure, discussed earlier.

Each number is understood to be ± 2, since the plotting for one hour masks the possibility that the bulk of that hour could have been in the opposite direction. I.e., two hourly plots of 960.18 and 958.00 could represent a slide through 960.18 climaxing at 950.01 in the first five minutes of the second hour, the remainder of which was spent advancing to 958.99. We must be aware, however, that adding an hour to adjust one interval wave necessitates subtracting one from some other wave, and vice versa.

Now, if we adjust waves 1 and 2 by one hour and average waves 3 and 4 to their centers, we get the following:

    Wave 1   51 hours
    Wave 2   17 hours
    Wave 3   155 hours
    Wave 4   68 hours
    Wave 5   155 hours

and several interrelationships become immediately apparent. First of all, wave 3 = 5 exactly. Secondly, wave 1 = 3 x wave 3 (and 3 x wave 5). Next we see that wave 1 = 3 x wave 2, and wave 4 = 4 x wave 2. Can this all be coincidence? Each time period is related to the others:

    Wave 1 : wave 2 as 3 : 1
    Wave 1 : wave 3 as 1 : 3
    Wave 1 : wave 4 as 3 : 4 ($3 : 2^2$)
    Wave 1 : wave 5 as 1 : 3
    Wave 2 : wave 3 as 1 : 9 ($1 : 3^2$)
    Wave 2 : wave 4 as 1 : 4 (2 : 8) ($2 : 2^3$)
    Wave 2 : wave 5 as 1 : 9 ($1 : 3^2$)
    Wave 3 : wave 4 as 9 : 4 ($3^2 : 2^2$)
    Wave 3 : wave 5 as 1 : 1
    Wave 4 : wave 5 as 4 : 9 ($2^2 : 3^2$)

The numbers in parentheses reduce the non-Fibonacci numbers to Fibonacci-based expressions.

What we have, then, is a *base unit* of 17 hours, of which each wave is a whole-number-multiple expression:

    Wave 1 = 17 x 3
    Wave 2 = 17 x 1
    Wave 3 = 17 x 9
    Wave 4 = 17 x 4
    Wave 5 = 17 x 9

These relationships argue that wave 3 was indeed a single entity.

The time elements of the larger wave currently developing are as follows:

Wave (1) = 248 hours
Wave (2) = 30 hours (adjusted to 31 hours; see next page.)
Wave (3) = 446 hours

A striking pattern emerges. First, wave (1) is to wave (3) precisely as 5 is to 9. The factor is 49.6. If we multiply 49.6 by the Fibonacci ratio (.618), we get 30.65, the approximate length of wave (2). All right, suppose instead of 30 hours, we adjust wave (2) to 31 hours (30.65 is closer to 31 than 30) and assume that wave (1) borrowed an hour from the preceding wave as well. 31 into 248 is *exactly* 8. Thus, wave (3) = 8 x wave (5), and of course 8 is a Fibonacci number.
Thus we have:

(1) : (2) as 8 : 1
(1) : (3) as 5 : 9, and
(2) : (3) as 1 : 9 x 1.618 (or approx. as 1 : 14.4, where 144 is
a Fibonacci number),

and, in terms of a time factor,

(1) = 49.6 x 5
(2) = 49.6 x .618
(3) = 49.6 x 9

so in units of time, our wave now looks like this:

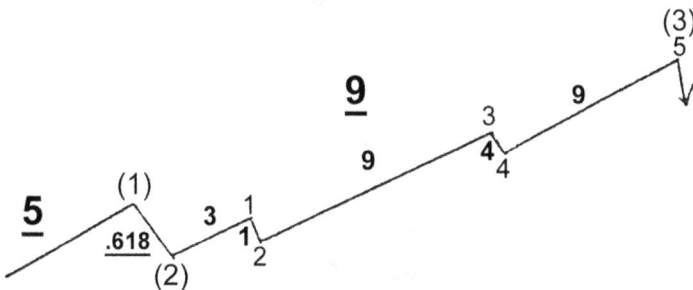

Figure 3

Now, since wave (2) is related to the base number 49.6 by the Fibonacci ratio, we know that 31 and 49.6 are to each other as two numbers in the Fibonacci series. Checking the ratio table [see Table 4-A in *Beautiful Pictures*], we find in this case 5 and 8, and the divisions into waves (1) and (2) give us a factor of 6.2 exactly. Thus,

(1) = 6.2 x 40 (5 x 8)
(2) = 6.2 x 5
(3) = 6.2 x 72 (2^3 x 3^3) or (2 x 3 x 13),

where the figures in parentheses express the multiples in Fibonacci numbers.

The Price Element

What about the number of points in our wave structure? For the large formation, we have,

(1) = 78.01 points
(2) = 45.89 points
(3) = 195.69 points

Immediately, we can deduce that wave (1) : wave (3) as 2 : 5, with a factor of 39, so that

(1) = 39 x 2 and
(3) = 39 x 5,

where 39 can be expressed as 13 x 3, two Fibonacci numbers.

Furthermore, wave (2) is very close to .618 x wave (1), suggesting a Fibonacci relationship. Now the wave can be expressed as multiples of the factor in approximately in these terms:

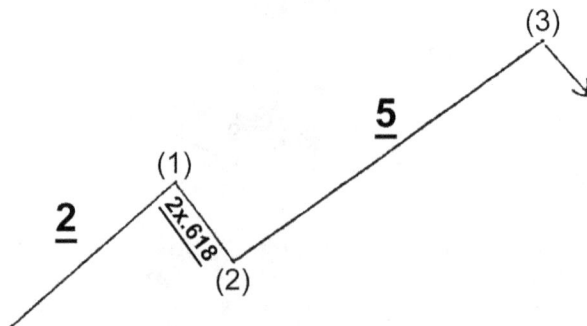

Figure 4

Upon more precise inspection, we find the following relationships, all of which utilize only Fibonacci numbers:

(1) : (2) as 5 : 3
(1) : (3) as 2 : 5
(2) : (3) as 8 : 34,

and in terms of round numbers of units, we have the following multiples of a factor of approximately 7.75:

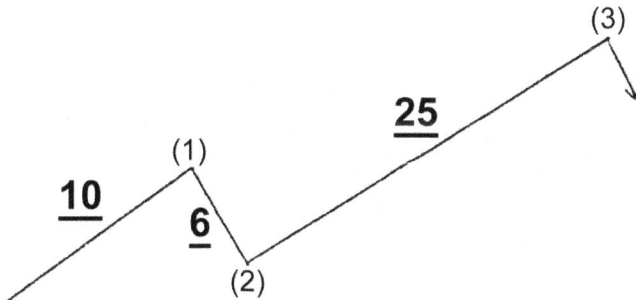

Figure 5

[*This analysis implied that waves (4) and (5) would also adhere to these time and price factors. As shown in the next report, they did.—Ed.*]

UPDATE: APRIL 1977 *ELLIOTT WAVE REPORT*

If, as the random walk proponents suggest, market moves have no form, then internal components would rarely "make sense" mathematically, and then only by statistically insignificant fluke occurrences. However, there seems to be enough evidence that mass psychology, as recorded in the Dow Jones Industrials, forms patterns that are uncannily interrelated.

Time Factors

With reference to Figures 6 and 7, the five Intermediate waves had the following time lengths:

Wave (1) : 248 trading hours
Wave (2): 31 trading hours
Wave (3): 446 trading hours
Wave (4): 961 trading hours
Wave (5): 209 trading hours

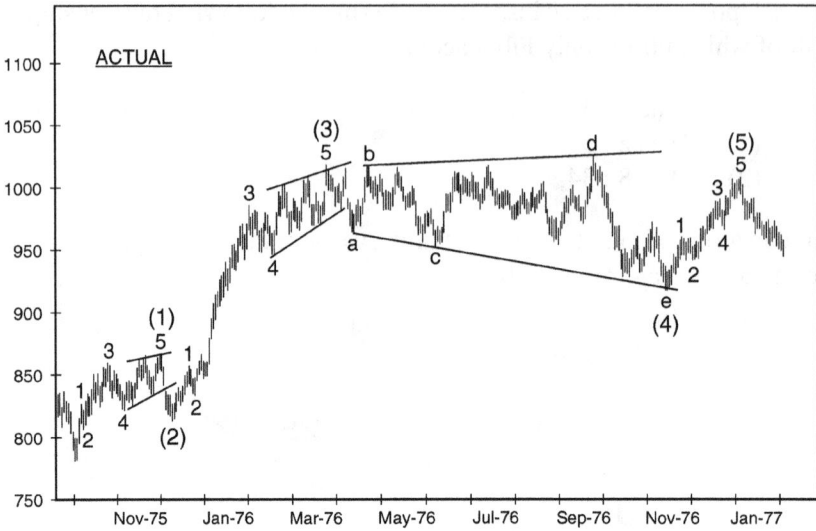

Figure 6

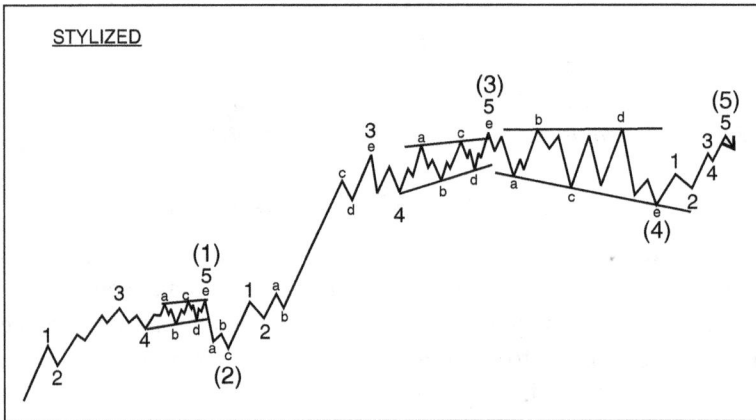

Figure 7

At first glance, the time spans seem random, but as we are about to see, they are not. To make the ratio relationships perfect, wave (5) must be reduced by 11 hours to 198 hours. Possible reasons for why this was necessary will be discussed at the end of this section.

49.6 hours happens to be the factor times which our whole number and Fibonacci ratio multiples give us the lengths of each of these waves. It is not clear whether there is a reason that approximately 50 hours has been an important subdivision within this expression of mass psychology. The breakdown is as follows for the advancing waves (see Figure 8):

TIME FACTORS OF 49.6 HOURS
(x = 49.6)

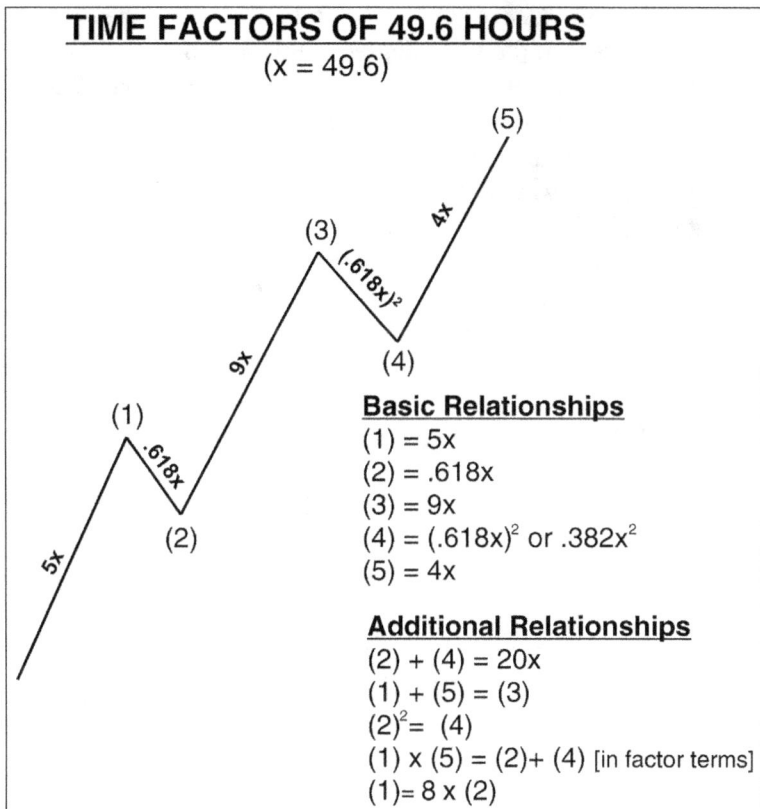

Basic Relationships
(1) = 5x
(2) = .618x
(3) = 9x
(4) = $(.618x)^2$ or $.382x^2$
(5) = 4x

Additional Relationships
(2) + (4) = 20x
(1) + (5) = (3)
$(2)^2$ = (4)
(1) x (5) = (2)+ (4) [in factor terms]
(1)= 8 x (2)

Figure 8

Wave (1) = 49.6 hours x 5
Wave (3) = 49.6 hours x 9, and
Wave (5) = 49.6 hours x 4

Can the brief December break be related to the entire "trading range" from March to November? A little figuring reveals the following durations for the corrective waves:

Wave (2) = 49.6 x .618
Wave (4) = $(49.6 \times .618)^2$

Observe that if we take the length of (2) at 31 hours and square it, we get exactly 961 hours, the length of (4)! Stated another way, using a factor of 31, wave (2) is x and wave (4) is 31x or x^2. Can these observations be coincidence? Or are they related because they are each corrective processes of the same degree within an Elliott wave?

We have seen that the advancing waves are related to the 49.6 hour factor by whole numbers, while corrective waves are related through the Fibonacci ratio. What happens if we add together the entire time span of the two corrective waves? $31 + 961 = 992$. It is unlikely to be coincidence that 992 divided by a whole number (20) gives exactly 49.6! Thus, while the two *individual* corrective periods, which are also square and square root of each other, are expressions of the Fibonacci ratio times the basic time factor, the *entire* corrective process is a *whole number* expression of the basic time factor, *as are the advancing waves*. Finally worth noting is that the sum of the two shorter advancing waves exactly equals the length of the longer advancing wave, so that $(1) + (5) = (3)$.

Without elaborating, see how uncannily this 50-hour time factor works into even the interior developments of corrective wave (4), as illustrated by Figure 9.

In the accompanying table, brackets show adjacent waves that appear to have "borrowed" hours, one from another, so that adding the two gives a closer approximation of a factor multiple. Note that these time expressions are not "cycles," first since total time for each unit varies, and secondly because some relate highs to lows and others highs to highs or lows to lows.

A) March high to April low:	50 hours	**(50 x 1)**
B) April low to May high:	147 hours ⌐	**(50 x 3)**
C) May high to June low:	105 hours ⌐	**(50 x 2)**
D) June low to June high:	50 hours	**(50 x 1)**
E) June high to July high:	101 hours	**(50 x 2)**
F) July high to August low:	195 hours ⌐	**(50 x 4)**
G) August low to September high:	105 hours ⌐	**(50 x 2)**
H) September high to October low:	99 hours	**(50 x 2)**
I) October low to November low:	108 hours	**(50 x 2)**

Similar time factor relationships are noticeable within intermediate wave (3). Its internal breakdown has a time factor of 17 hours, which is to the 50-hour factor as one is to three. The five waves within (3) are 51, 17, 155, 68, and 155 hours, or in 17-hour factor terms, 3x, 1x, 9x,

RELATING THE 50-HOUR FACTOR
TO THE INTERNAL STRUCTURE OF WAVE ④

MAJOR SUBDIVISIONS

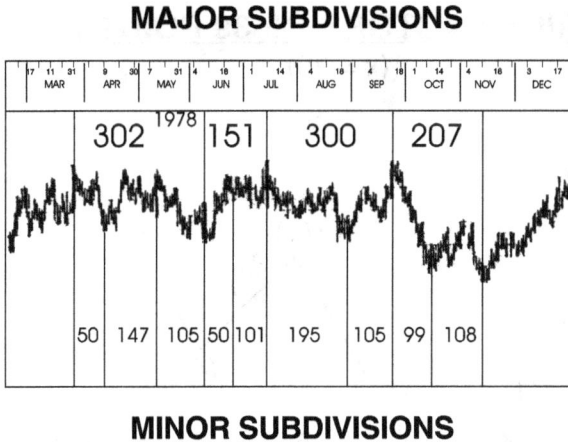

MAR	APR	MAY	JUN	JUL	AUG	SEP	OCT	NOV	DEC

302 1978 151 300 207

50 | 147 | 105 | 50 | 101 | 195 | 105 | 99 | 108

MINOR SUBDIVISIONS

Figure 9

4x, and 9x. The third and fifth waves are exactly the same duration. The same durations expressed in 50-hour factor terms give approximately the following multiples: 1x, .382x, 3x, 4(.382x) and 3x, which again places the minor corrective waves 2 and 4 in Fibonacci-ratio-based expressions, as are waves (2) and (4).

Price Factors

When wave (3) was over, the following lengths for the first 3 waves were recorded:

Wave (1): 78.01 points
Wave (2): 45.89 points
Wave (3): 195.69 points

Using only Fibonacci numbers, (1) is to (2) as 5 is to 3, (1) is to (3) as 2 is to 5, and (2) is to (3) as 8 is to 34. The price factor, which could be deduced at that time, was 39 points. To complete the picture, we find that wave (4) spanned 101.23 points and wave (5) 84.02 points. Wave (4) here is measured not from the orthodox high of wave (3) but from the nominal market high in September at 1021.86, so that the full span of the wave is included. Now we can see that in terms of the 39 point factor, the following relationships hold (see Figure 10):

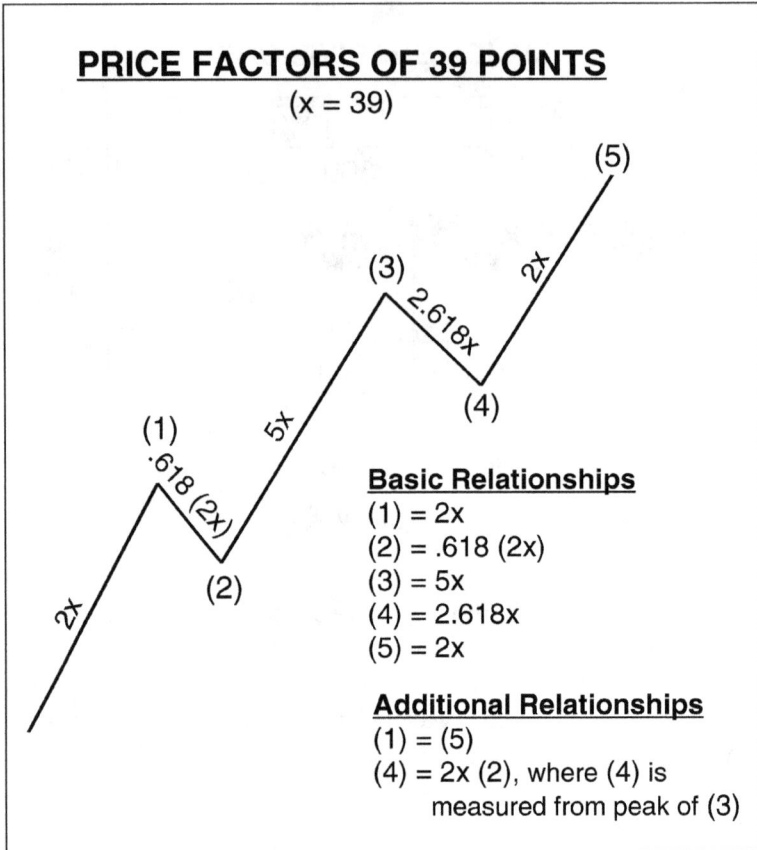

PRICE FACTORS OF 39 POINTS
(x = 39)

(5)

(3)

2.618x

2x

(1)

5x

.618 (2x)

2x

(2)

(4)

Basic Relationships
(1) = 2x
(2) = .618 (2x)
(3) = 5x
(4) = 2.618x
(5) = 2x

Additional Relationships
(1) = (5)
(4) = 2x (2), where (4) is
     measured from peak of (3)

Figure 10

Wave (1) = 39 x 2
Wave (2) = (39 x 2) x .618
Wave (3) = 39 x 5
Wave (4) = 39 x 2.618
Wave (5) = 39 x 2

Again, we see advancing waves expressing whole number multiples of a numerical factor, while correcting waves are related by an expression involving the Fibonacci ratio. Again, we have waves one and five nearly equal, and together they are close to twice the advance recorded during wave (3). Again, wave (5) is a bit longer (6 points) than it "should" be ideally, *as it was in terms of time*, showing that even the aberrations are in step.

Several other price relationships are worth mentioning. The total net decline of wave (4) (measuring from the peak of wave (3) and ignoring the intra-wave highs set in September) was 91.33 points. 91.33 is exactly twice the size of wave (2), which covered 45.89 points. Stated another way, using a factor of 45.8, wave (2) is 1x and wave (4) is 2x. In terms of price, then, wave (4) equals wave (2) x 2, and in terms of time, wave (4) equals wave $(2)^2$. Thus waves (2) and (4), representing one swift break in December 1975 and a long trading range throughout half of 1976 respectively, are surprisingly intimately related.

Of further interest is the internal breakdown of wave (3) itself, within which the five component waves are 37.15 points, 15.90 points, 139.56 points, 26.52 points, and 61.39 points. In 15.5-point factor terms, they equal 5/21x10 (where both 5 and 21 are Fibonacci numbers), 1, 9, 1.618 and 4. Note that the 15.5-point factor of the minor wave is to the 39 point factor of the major wave exactly as 2 is to 5. Remember that the two time factors are related as 1 is to 3. 1, 2, 3 and 5 are all Fibonacci numbers.

Data Precision

All we have available for this study is the price upon each hour's end. Price points can have a wide range of movement intra-hour. All time lengths should be understood as plus or minus 2 due to uncertainties at each end of the wave concerning how much of the beginning and ending hours were actually taken up by the wave in question. It would be possible for an intra-hour extreme to occur more than an hour away from the hourly extreme, but "theoretical intraday" price bars near these waves' ends indicate that for these waves, the hourly and intra-hour extremes were very close to each other. It is certainly possible that these remarkable price and time interrelationships might prove to be even more precise if we had access to intra-hour data.

Conclusions

At least this much can be fairly reliably stated as a result of this work:

    1) The idea that the market is a "random walk" is probably false.

    2) With knowledge concerning internal price and time factors, Elliott waves can be more reliably interpreted and predicted.

3) It takes at least three waves to generate enough information to propose the time and price factors operating for all five waves. Thus, ending points for fourth and fifth waves will be easier to predict or confirm using internal mathematical factors than those for the first three.

4) Last and most important, turning points in the market may be more easily recognized *at the time of occurrence* if price and time factors fall into place *together*, along with the completion of an acceptable wave form.

UPDATE: AUGUST 1977 *ELLIOTT WAVE REPORT*

The internal breakdown of the wave B triangle was perfectly described by Elliott forty years ago in his *Financial World* articles. The converging trendlines contain all rallies and declines from the February low to the apex in May. The internal breakdown consists of five waves of three steps each. The final step often gives a minor "false breakout" above the triangle trendline before resuming the trend in force prior to the formation of the triangle. May 18 did provide such a false breakout. Each rally peak was accompanied by stampede-type block figures, a surge in volume, and a disappearance of short selling. [Figure 3-12 in *Elliott Wave Principle* shows the details of this triangle.—Ed.] Wave B lasted 346 ± 2 hours, or the 49.6-hour factor times 7, fulfilling the whole-number multiple requirement for advancing waves within the preceding wave, suggesting continuity into this corrective period. The net price gain was the 39-point price factor times 1/3.

UPDATE: MARCH 1978 *ELLIOTT WAVE REPORT*

Still in its experimental stage is a study of internal wave factors. In the April 1977 report, the advance labeled (3) was discovered to contain a price factor of 39 points, by which the impulse waves were related in whole Fibonacci number terms while the corrective waves were related by the Fibonacci ratio. Now it is evident that the (A), (B), and (C) waves of the 1977-78 decline (see Figure 11) also have an internal factor, this time of 25.4 points, in which wave (A), at 75.65 points, is 3 times the factor, wave (B), at 14.16 points, is .618 times the factor, and wave (C), at 202.88 points, is 8 times the factor. Not only are the impulse waves related by whole numbers that are Fibonacci numbers, but the corrective wave is related by the Fibonacci ratio, as was the case in the preceding study.

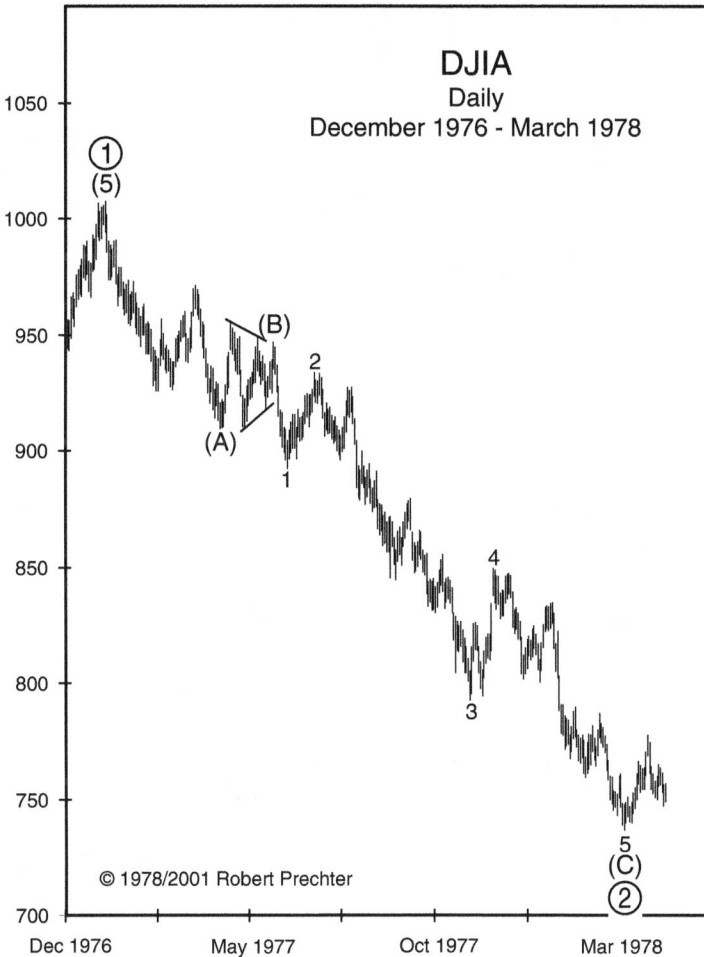

DJIA
Daily
December 1976 - March 1978

© 1978/2001 Robert Prechter

Figure 11

As a final touch, can it be coincidence that the new 25.4-point factor itself, which is the factor in a *corrective* wave, is just over .618 times the 39-point factor of wave (3), which is an *impulse* wave? This relationship fits the underlying theme of our observations.

In the (A)-(B)-(C) corrective wave under discussion, wave (A) lasts 230 hours, wave (B) 346 hours, and wave (C) 1174 hours. The factor is 115, so that wave (A) equals 2 times the factor, wave (B) equals 3 times the factor, and wave (C) equals 10.2 times the factor. Wave (C) would equal exactly 10 times the factor at the minor low four days prior to March 1st at 745.06.

Chapter 5

The Hidden Similarity of
Two Wave Forms

by Robert R. Prechter, Jr.
originally published in Elliott Wave Report, *August 1977*

The construction of the 1977 corrective formation has an uncanny resemblance to the 1975 market correction from July to October. Figure 1 shows the 1977 period up to July 29 on a continuous hourly basis plotted at four hours to the box. The corresponding 1975 period is plotted above it, with the initial waves A, B and C at one hour to the box and waves X, (A), (B) and (C) at three hours to the box, in order to display the similarities in wave form regardless of time differences.

As the chart shows, both corrections to the wave C lows show declines of 10.8% from the high. They begin with a very similar five waves down composing wave A, which dropped, about 7.3% from the highs in each case. Both "B" waves are contracting triangles, the first legs of which make new lows below A by approximately the same percentage (1.6%). Both triangles are composed of five waves of three legs each, both have "false breakouts" at the peak of the fifth triangle wave, and both show rallies and declines progressing by the Fibonacci number sequence starting with the first down wave. Finally, the three waves in each year labeled X, (A) and (B) have about the same relative lengths: 53.43, 48.65 and 36.84 in 1975, and 34.60, 30.19 and 23.60 in 1977, producing ratios across the years of 1.54, 1.61 and 1.56. (Hourly readings omit intrahour data; the tendency appears to be very close to 1.618.)

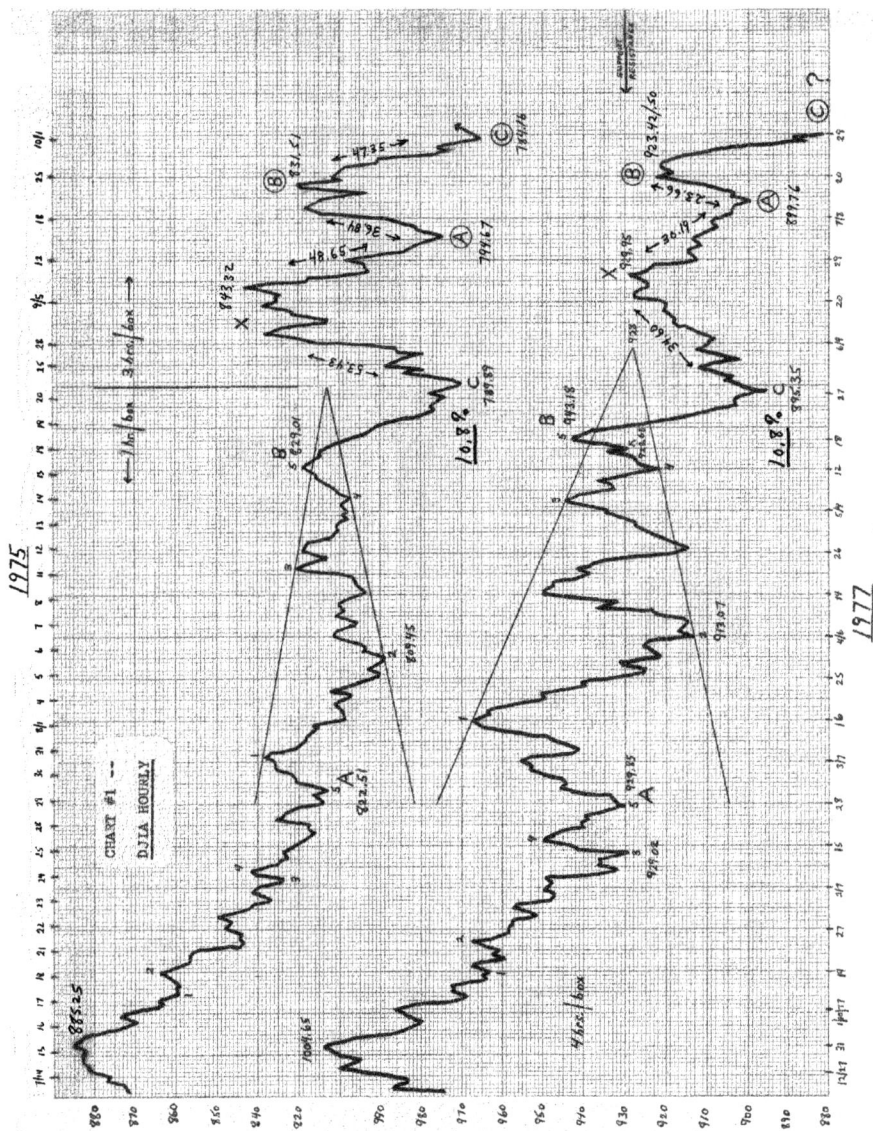

Figure 1

FORECASTING WORKSHEET

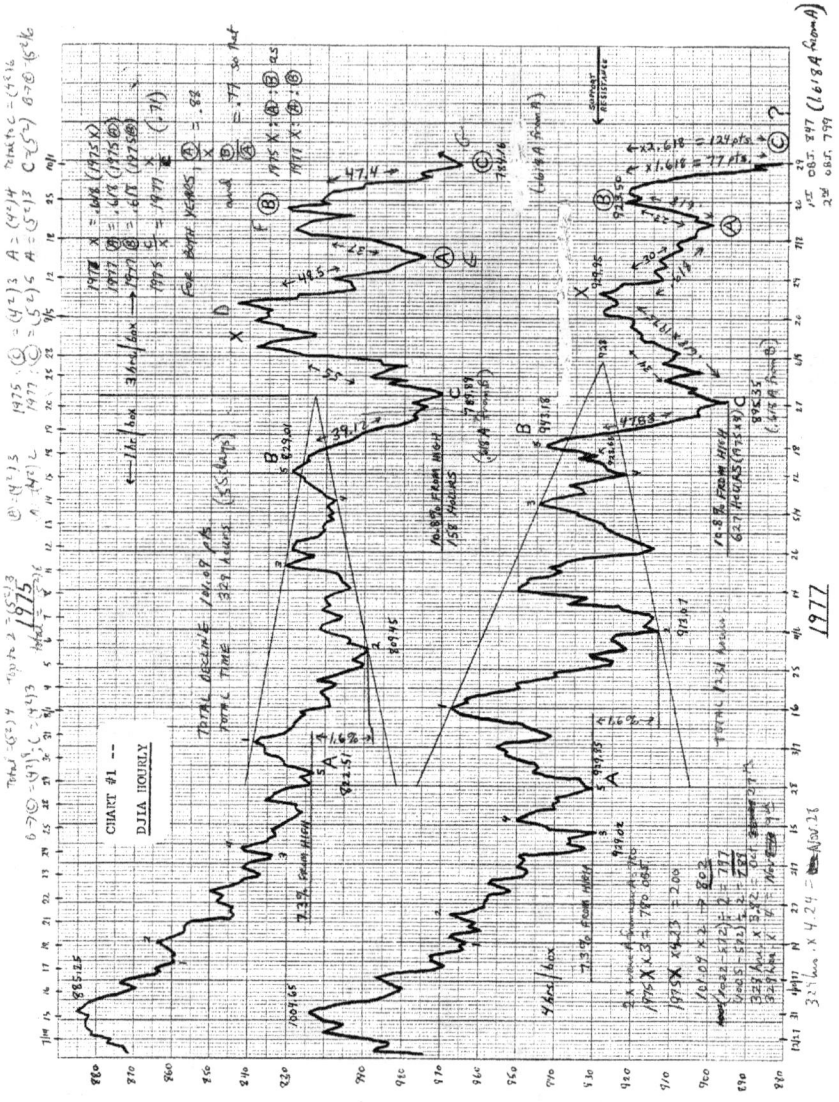

Figure 2

UPDATE: DECEMBER 1977 *ELLIOTT WAVE REPORT*

1975 vs. 1977

The key to the 799 target projection for the October low was the phenomenally close relationship of the action in 1977 to that in 1975, as first illustrated in the August report. The "look" of each of these periods is quite different when viewed on the average daily or weekly bar chart (see Figure 3). However, when the time parameter is compressed by four for the 1977 period on an hourly chart, amazing correlations in form are immediately apparent (see Figure 4). Quite possibly, the assumption that each of these corrections is a second wave in a five-wave sequence is strengthened by these findings.

With the help of some simple calculations, the parallels between the two periods are listed below, most to within an error factor of one percent. This error factor may be even more surprisingly small, since hourly quotes ignore intra-hour extremes, where the true "top tick" and "bottom tick" actually occur.

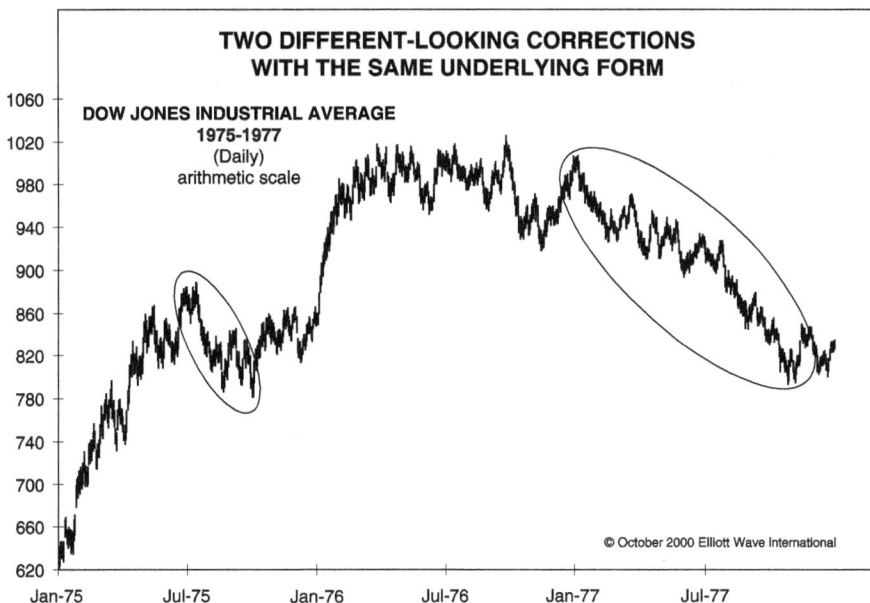

Figure 3

Price Relationships

Since the correct Elliott labeling of the 1975 and 1977 corrections appear in other reports, the letters A through G will be used here for easier cross-reference in revealing the following phenomena relating to price movement (see Figure 4):

1. Wave A in each case ends 7.2% from the highs.
2. Wave 2 of the wave B triangle ends 1.6% below wave A in each case.
3. Wave C ends 10.8% from the highs for each period.
4. Wave B in each case is a "symmetrical" or "contracting" triangle (descending tops, rising bottoms), composed of five waves of three legs each, with precise internal and external mathematical relationships as outlined in the August report. [See pp.115-116 and Figure 3-12 in *Elliott Wave Principle*.—Ed.] The net gain of wave B in 1975 is one-half that of 1977.
5. Wave C is .618 times the length of wave A in each period.
6. Wave G in 1975 ends below A by exactly .618 times the length of wave A, while wave G in 1977 ends below A by approximately 1.618 times the length of wave A (to within 10 points).
7. The length of wave D is to wave C in 1977 as the length of wave C is to wave D in 1975. In other words, they are exactly inversely related. The ratio is .71.
8. The length of wave E divided by wave D is the same for both years, .88, and
9. the length of wave F divided by wave E is the same for both years, .77. Thus,
10. D: E: F in 1975 exactly as D: E: F in 1977.
11. The length of wave D in 1977 = .618 times wave D in 1975.
12. The length of wave E in 1977 = .618 times wave E in 1975.
13. The length of wave F in 1977 = .618 times wave F in 1975.
14. The length of wave G to the August low in 1977 = 1.618 times wave G in 1975.
15. The length of wave G to the October low in 1977 = 2.618 times wave G in 1975.
16. The length of the 1977 correction at point G equals twice the length of the entire 1975 correction.

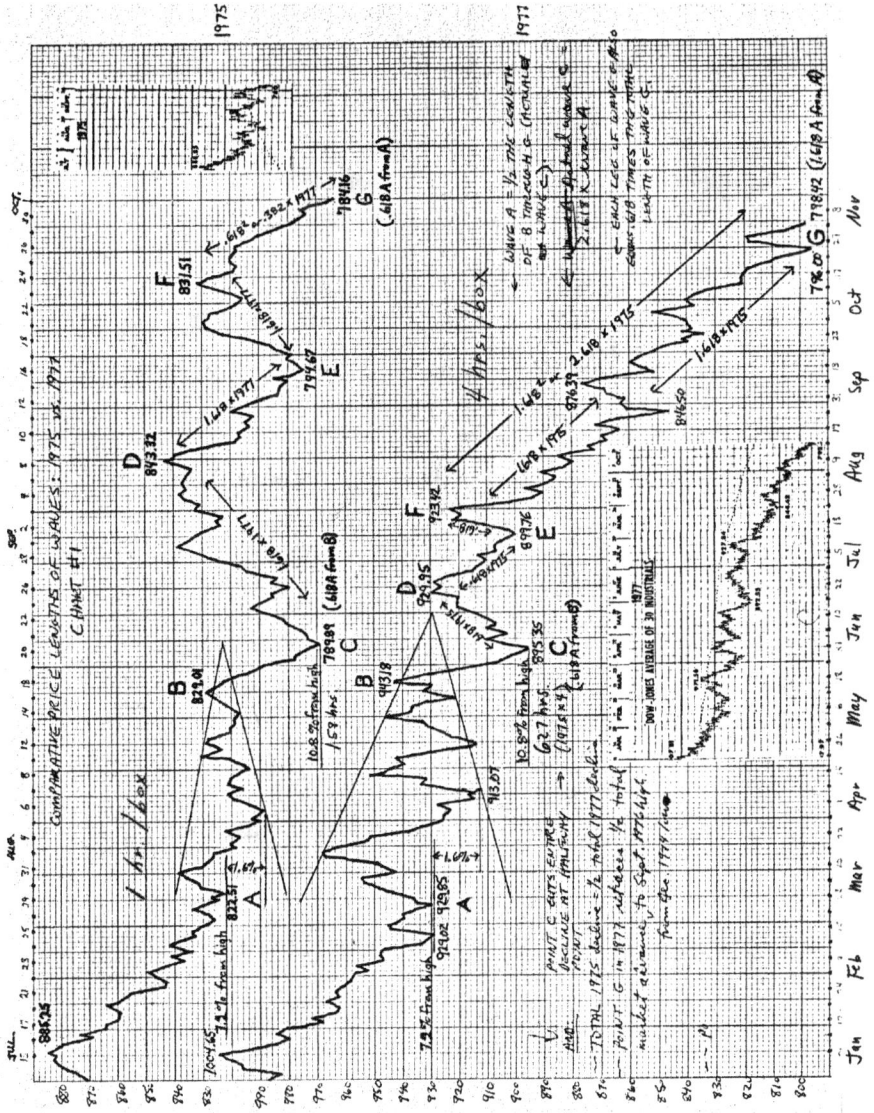

Figure 4

17. Wave G is neatly cut by the August-September rally so that each resulting leg is not only the same price length but equal to .618 times the length of the *entire* G wave *and* equal to 1.618 times the G wave of 1975.

The parallels are even more impressive when one realizes that between the two corresponding periods, one stock was substituted for another in the DJIA (MMM for A), actually making the 1977 average a different one from the 1975 average. The resulting implications regarding mass psychological perception of the levels of market averages are beyond the scope of this report. [See *The Wave Principle of Human Social Behavior*, p.167.—Ed.]

Time Relationships

Time relationships are somewhat less striking but nonetheless nearly perfect. Bold typeface designates Fibonacci sequence numbers.

1. Waves A through C in 1977 last 4 times as long, at 627 ±2 trading hours, as the same waves in 1975 at 158 ±2 trading hours.
2. The point labeled "C" in each period cuts the time length of each period up to "G" approximately at the halfway mark price-wise as well as time-wise. This is not only the point after which the 1977 wave begins to look and act differently from the 1975 wave in terms of price, but in terms of time as well. From that point,
3. Wave D in 1977 lasts 1.618 times as long as wave D in 1975.
4. Wave E in 1977 lasts **2** times as long as wave E in 1975.
5. Wave F in 1977 is the same duration as wave F in 1975.
6. Wave G in 1977 at the August low lasts **5** times as long as wave G in 1975.
7. Wave G in 1977 at the October low lasts **13** times as long as wave G in 1975.

Also notable is that the net travel of waves B through G in 1977, at 147 points, is not only twice the length of wave A at 74.5 points but at **21** weeks, lasts 2.618 times wave A at **8** weeks.

Conclusion

Needless to say, all these waves are countable by the Elliott method without any reference whatsoever to their price or time lengths. Indeed, it is sometimes necessary to apply Elliott's counts and labels in the first place in order to determine the points from which these measurements should be made. However, no other market approach has the framework ever to discover, or even postulate, the types of interrelationships presented here. Very few market approaches even suggest that the market has a "memory" for what it did last week, last month or last year, as it most obviously does. In fact, it seems that the band leader of a military parade shows more tendency for random walk that the Dow has done in 1977.

The Next Level of Support

DJIA support levels below the October low include the **780s** area and the **740s** area, since $572 + (1005 - 572) \times .50 = $ **788**, 1977's wave B minus (1975's wave Ⓒ)3 = **781**, $929.85 - (1005 - 930)2 = $ **780**, $1022 - (1022 - 572).618 = $ **744**, $1005 - (885 - 784)2.618 = $ **742**, and (A x 2.618) from the peak at B = **746**. [The 1978 and 1980 hourly lows occurred at 740, and the 1982 hourly low occurred at 777.—Ed.]

Given the overwhelming evidence of internal precision manifest in the recorded progress of the major market averages, one can certainly rely on the conclusion that whether or not a particular expected advance or decline develops, the market will continue to unfold in patterns discovered by R.N. Elliott over forty years ago.

UPDATE: APRIL 1978 *ELLIOTT WAVE REPORT*

The relative weakness of the 1977-8 decline after the late May low, as contrasted to the 1975 correction carried even further to produce another new low in 1978, a **740.30** hourly reading on March 1. When it was done, the length of wave C = 2.618 x wave A, where wave C is the entire decline following point B.

This drop corresponded to the December 1975 shakeout, which was wave 2 or B in the 1975-1976 advance. Despite the difference in appearance, the precision of relative wave lengths extended right into this period. The November rally in 1977 (wave 4) was .618 times as long as the October-December 1975 rally. The fifth-wave diagonal triangle from the November 1977 high to the March 1978 low broke into five subwaves, the first and fifth of which were exactly the same length as the December 1975 shakeout and the third of which was 1.618 times that length.

The big picture provides a final crowning touch. Roughly speaking, the duration of the entire bull market rise to the orthodox high on December 31, 1976, at 24 months (December 1974 to December 1976) is 1.6 times the duration of the 1977-1978 correction, at 15 months (December 1976 to March 1978). Finally, the price length of the entire 1977-1978 decline of 264.35 points equals 2.618 times the length of the entire 1975 correction of 101.09 points! Thus, the 1977-1978 decline is perfectly related to the entire initial bull market rise, to the 1975 correction, and internally to its own components. [For a full presentation, see Chapter 4 of *Elliott Wave Principle.*—Ed.] Despite all this detailed discussion, Elliott himself would have labeled this common 5-3-5, A-B-C correction a simple "zigzag."

Not only can we conclude that the market remembers every single move it has made in the past, but also that corrective processes are essentially *all of the same nature*. Waves may take on a different price shape, but the basic internal structures and the mass human action they represent are all cast from the same mold.

Chapter 6

AN EXAMPLE OF FIBONACCI RELATIONSHIPS IN THE STOCK MARKET

by Robert R. Prechter, Jr.
originally published July 1, 1982

When approaching the discovery of mathematical relationships in the markets, the Wave Principle offers a mental foothold for the practical thinker. If studied carefully, it can satisfy even the most cynical researcher. A *side element* of the Wave Principle is the recognition that the Fibonacci ratio is one of the primary governors of price movement in the stock market averages. The reason that a study of the Fibonacci ratio is so compelling is that the 1.618:1 ratio is the *only* price relationship whereby the length of the shorter wave under consideration is to the length of the longer wave as the length of the longer wave is to the length of the entire distance traveled in both waves, thus creating an interlocking wholeness to the price structure. It was this property that led early mathematicians to dub 1.618 the "Golden Ratio."

Some of the advantages of Elliott's use of Fibonacci ratios as compared to currently popular numerological "Gann" assertions are as follows:

1. Fibonacci ratios are independent of the unit of price measurement, the unit of time measurement, and chart scale.

2. Fibonacci ratios are few. The only ratio which occurs often enough in markets to be of practical importance is **1.618**. Of secondary importance are **.50**, **1.00** (equality), and **2.618**, which are all ratios found in the Fibonacci sequence. The inverses of these ratios are alternate expressions of the same relationships.

3. The Fibonacci ratio's occurrence in markets is not based upon mystical assertions. The Wave Principle is based on *empirical evidence*, which led to a *working model*, which subsequently led to a tentatively developed *theory*. In a nutshell, the portion of the theory that applies to anticipating the occurrence of Fibonacci ratios in the market can be stated this way:

a. The Wave Principle describes the movement of markets.

b. The numbers of waves in each degree of trend correspond to the Fibonacci sequence.

c. The Fibonacci ratio is the governor of the Fibonacci sequence.

d. The Fibonacci ratio has reason to be evident in the market.

As for satisfying oneself that the Wave Principle describes the movement of markets, some effort must be spent attacking the charts. The purpose of this article is merely to present evidence that the Fibonacci ratio expresses itself often enough in the averages to make it clear that it is indeed a governing force (not necessarily *the* governing force) on aggregate stock prices.

When the Ratio Occurs

Elliott discovered that a Fibonacci relationship between *adjacent* waves occurs more often within corrective patterns. A Fibonacci relationship between *unconnected* waves which are nevertheless part of a single pattern occurs more often within five-wave sequences when the third wave is the longest. Price relationships, by the way, are calculated with reference only to vertical points traveled.

Past Examples

Other publications have pointed out, sometimes in advance for forecasting purposes, the 1.618 relationships found in the following time periods: **1921-1928**, where the final wave (1926-1928) of the sequence is 1.618 times as long as the first three (1921-1925); **1932-1937**, where the final wave (1934-1937) is 1.618 times as long as the first three (1932-1933); **1930-1939**, which contains four swings, each of which is related to the ensuing swing by 1.618; **1949-1966**, where 1957-1966 is 1.618 times 1949-1956; and **1966-1974**, where the distance from 1966 to 1974 is 1.618 times the length of the 1966 decline.

The period from 1974 to the present has been less documented, but deserves mention for the frequent occurrence of the 1.618 ratio during this period. All Fibonacci relationships in all the interlocking waves during this span could not possibly be illustrated, but a few of the most striking will serve to illustrate the influence. In order to give an overview of recent Fibonacci history and bring us to the present, I have outlined both the bigger picture from 1974 to 1982, and on a closer basis, the period from August 1980 to December 1981. Let's start with the smaller wave pattern.

August 12, 1980 – December 11, 1980 (Figure 1)

This sideways pattern began from the point at which the orthodox top of five waves from April 21 to August 12, 1980 ended. (An "orthodox" turning point is one that marks the end of an Elliott Wave pattern, ensuing minor new highs or lows notwithstanding.) The height of each A-B-C pattern in this sequence is related to the preceding A-B-C pattern by 1.618 (with 1% error and 6% error respectively). The height of the final A-B-C is 2.618 times the height of the first. If the December low (899.57) had been 905.84, the second calculation would have had 0% error. If we label the first pattern "X", the second "Y" and the third "Z", then X:Y as Y:Z; X:Y as Y(X+Y); Y:Z as Z:(Y+Z). The whole pattern is an interlocking expression of the Fibonacci ratio.
Regarding Figure 2:

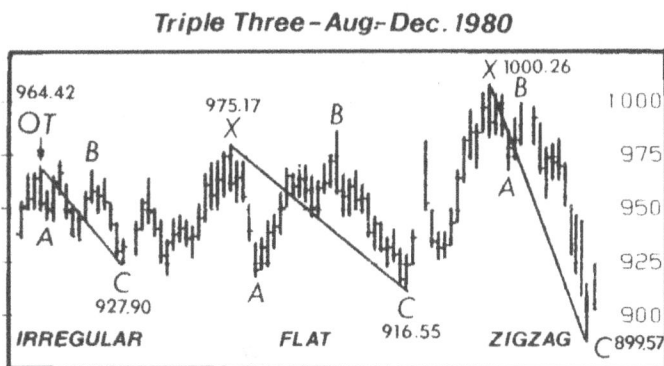

Triple Three – Aug.– Dec. 1980

```
2nd ABC = 1.618 x 1st ABC (1% error).
3rd ABC = 1.618 x 2nd ABC (6% error).
3rd ABC = 2.618 x 1st ABC (5% error).
```

Figure 1

(1) With division at 894.37, all calculations have 0% error.
(2) The December 1980 low at 899.57 is a compromise between an ideal 905.84 and for the XYZ pattern and an ideal 894.37 for the PQR pattern.

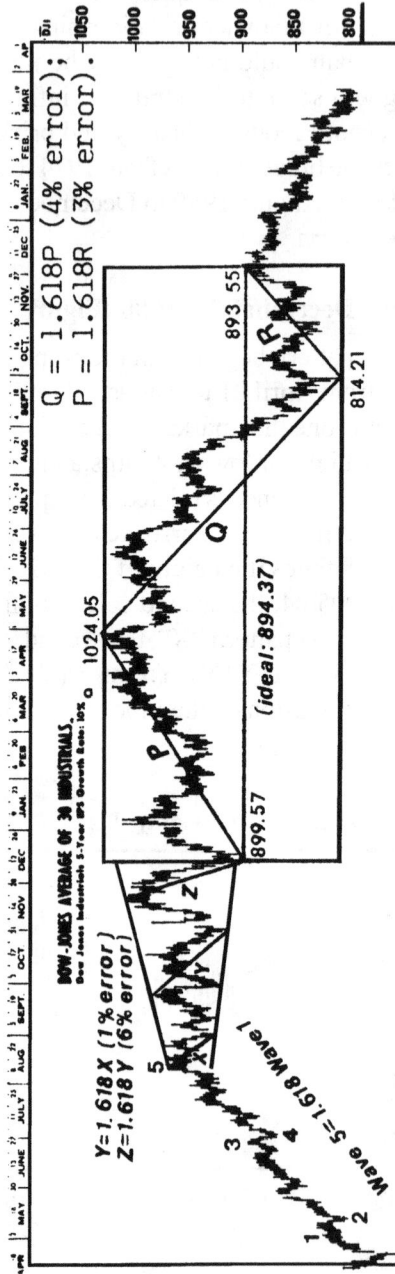

Figure 2

December 11, 1980 – December 4, 1981 (Figure 2)

The April-September decline is 1.618 times the December-April advance (4% error), and the December-April advance is 1.618 times the September-December advance (3% error). The April-September decline is 2.618 times the September-December advance (1% error). Each calculation would have had 0% error if both the December 1980 low (899.57) and the December 1981 high (893.55) had been 894.37. In other words, the entire height of the pattern is divided into a Golden Section at 894. If we label these lengths P, Q and R, note that R:P as P:Q, R:P as P:(R+P) and P:Q as Q:(P+Q). On the chart, we can draw a rectangle, encompassing all this price action, which is divided into the Golden Section proportion at its exact beginning and end.

1974-1982 (Figure 3)

Now we come to the most interesting pattern, the big picture from 1974. Each wave since 1974 is related to an adjacent wave by 1.618 (or in the center of the pattern by equality), within the percentage errors listed. The only large deviation is the "overshoot" in the 1978 October massacre. During the October-December 1978 period, the first ideal retracement level at 806 was penetrated eight times in whipsaw action. All of these penetrations were extremely volatile, so much so that *five of them left intraday gaps in the Dow*. Among the three that did *not* leave gaps were a nevertheless volatile 9-point up opening hour and a 17-point down opening hour. That kind of action may indicate that the market sensed the importance of the exact Fibonacci retracement level despite the overshoot. The next largest deviation occurred because of the mild overshoot at the November 1979 low, which was again due to a "massacre" type market.

1974-1982 (Figure 4)

A second way of looking at this period is to *average* the tops in 1976, producing 1013.08, and the tops in 1980-81, producing 1011.51. It so happens that a rounded average of the two, which gives a central peak point of *1012*, is the exact point which provides *0% error* for the Fibonacci relationships involved. Similarly, the average of the tops in 1978-1980 is *908,* and the average of the bottoms in 1978-1979 is *789*. The three average price points make all the Fibonacci ratio relationships perfect except for the average of the 1978-1979 bottoms, which is 15 points below the ideal low of 804. However, 789 has its own particular *raison d'etre*.

The Fibonacci Ratio in the Dow From 1974

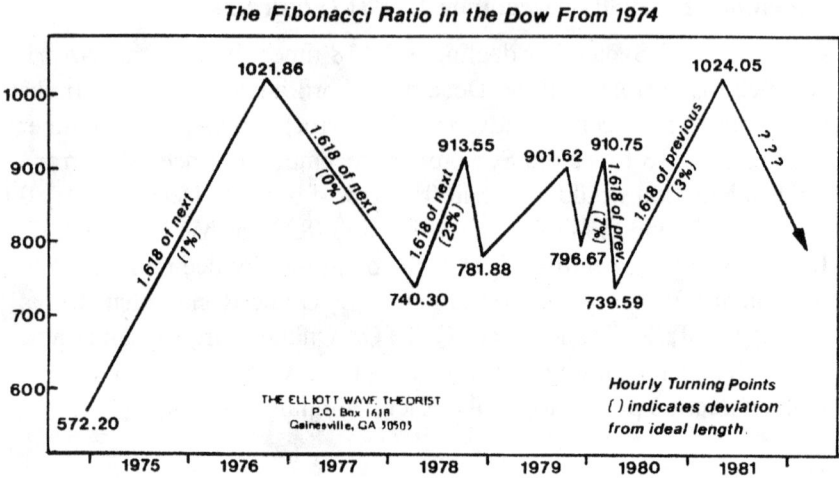

Figure 3

The Fibonacci Ratio Using Average Turning Points

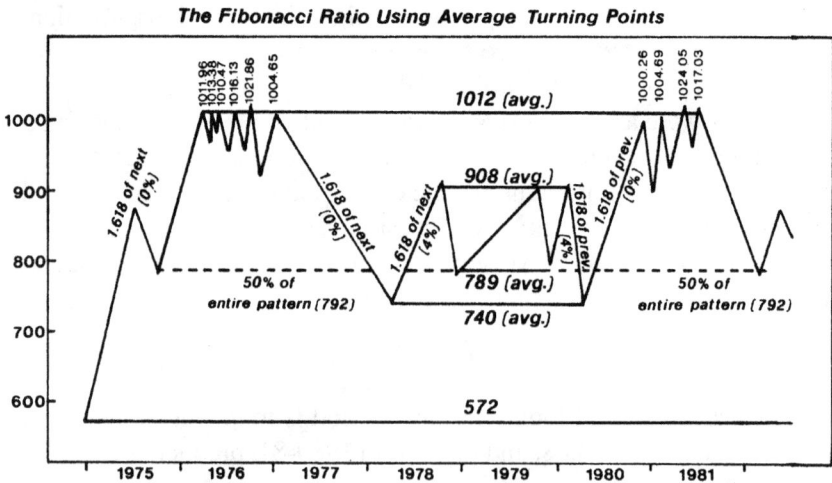

Figure 4

The 789-792 Level

So far this year, the 789 level has acted as solid support for the Dow Industrial Average. It marked the exact hourly low in March and, as of this writing, the hourly low so far in June. This same support point has stopped cold three declines since 1974. Why? The 792 level just happens to fall right at the halfway (50%) level of the entire pattern back to the 1974 low! Perhaps this fact explains why the two bottoms in 1978 and 1979 were "off" a bit from their ideal Fibonacci target at 804, and gravitated to 789.

789 also happens to be the level at which the decline from the peak in December 1981 would be 1.618 times the length of the April-May 1981 decline. These two declines *can* be labeled as fifth and first waves respectively. To see another example of this type of relationship, see the 1980 five-wave advance in Figure 2, where wave $5 = 1.618$ x wave 1.

With reference to Figure 3, I've calculated that if the down wave which began in 1981 were to fall 1.618 times the length of the preceding advance, it would bottom at 563.79, and create a symmetrical pattern from 1974. That level should not be taken as a forecast at this point, but would certainly become likely if 789 is broken on the downside any time this year. On the other hand, if 789 holds, another new bull market could well get underway. [The final low for the year was 777. —Ed.]

Fibonacci's Extent

As we have seen, perfection in these relationships is approached but not attained. The possible reasons are: (1) The DJIA is an imperfect meter for measuring the mood of the entire society, reflecting only Dow stock investors, which is a subset of all investors, which is in turn a subset of society; (2) Fibonacci expression in human mood is more complex than simple ratios and involves additive sub-sequences within each relationship.

Does the Fibonacci ratio apply to every move in every market? Definitely not. My studies show that there are many times when one should *not* expect a Fibonacci relationship. Knowing *when* to look for one is the key to successful application, and I haven't found any exceptions to Elliott's discoveries in that regard. Even if old Fibonacci doesn't rule the world, I can't help thinking that if he were a trader, he might well own the New York Stock Exchange.

Chapter 7

THE NECESSITY OF ACCOUNTING FOR IMMATERIAL MENTAL STATES WITHIN FINANCIAL ANALYSIS

by Paul Macrae Montgomery
originally published November 2000
from issues of Universal Economics, *1983 - 1995*

The Logical Primacy of Mental States in the Price Structure of Investments

> One must reject traditional beliefs a priori because there is
> a problem. Inquiry does not start unless there is a problem,
> and the presence of a problem means that traditional answers
> are inadequate.
>
> — F.S.C. Northrop

Economic and capital market prediction has been so consistently unreliable that financial forecasting is universally acknowledged as constituting "a problem."[1] The very existence of this problem is itself prima facie proof of the inadequacy of traditional economic beliefs. The thesis of this chapter is that the fundamental false principle underlying traditional economic science in general, and capital market theory in particular, involves the failure to recognize the logical primacy of mental states in the price structure of investments. One practical consequence of this theoretic flaw is the persistent failure of conventional economic science accurately to predict capital market behavior — or virtually any other economic data series. If mental states, which are immaterial, are indeed as relevant as will be suggested herein, then the investment problem is to a very significant extent a subcategory of the human behavioral problem. This being the case, there can be no adequate *investment* theory that does not integrate adequate concepts of *behavioral* theory. Furthermore, recent discoveries have shown that there can be no adequate *behavioral* theory that does not integrate the concepts of modern field theory, neurophysiology, and other disciplines far removed from the purview of traditional economics. It follows therefore that economic science and investment theory are both in need of extensive supplementation by radically different first principles.

> The market's pricing mechanism remains based in such a degree upon faulty and frequently irrational analytic processes that the price of a security only occasionally coincides with the intrinsic value around which it tends to fluctuate.
> — David Dodd

The mistaken assumption implicit in conventional economic theory is the notion that economics is somewhat analogous to classical mechanics, wherein a certain action in one part of a system invariably produces a given reaction in another part of that system. Such forecasting implicitly assumes, by way of illustration, that if the budget deficit goes down by A, and if the inflation rate decreases by B, then interest rates supposedly should go down to C. Or if interest rates fall by X, and corporate earnings rise by Y, then stock prices supposedly should go up to Z.[2]

While the necessary interconnection of events implicitly assumed in this type of prediction does of course obtain within *physical* systems, it cannot occur within *economic* systems, which are fundamentally quite different. Whereas physical systems concern material objects, the central nexus of economics is *"value,"* which is not inherent in any physical object, but rather derives exclusively from the human *desire* for certain particular objects at certain particular times. Therefore, the ultimate subject of economics is neither gold bullion nor savings accounts nor money supply nor bond coupons nor cash flows nor any physical goods whatsoever, but *human desires* — i.e., *immaterial mental states*. The fundamental difference between "values," or immaterial mental states, which are the subject of *economic* science, and material objects, which are the subject of *physical* science, is that mental states do not obey the same Law of Conservation of Momentum that physical states obey. This law states that an isolated object in motion will continue in motion with the same momentum throughout time. It is this conservation principle that provides order and permits precise prediction in physics. If an isolated object's momentum did *not* remain constant but rather fluctuated through time, then consistently accurate prediction would be logically impossible within the physical sciences. Mental states, and hence economic values, unlike physical momenta, do *not* remain constant with time. Mental states, rather, are in constant flux through time. Since they do not obey the conservation principle, it is not logically possible using principles similar to those that govern physics to deduce what the status of mental states, and therefore people's values, and therefore the level or direction of any economic series, will be at any particular future time. Therefore, a scientific economic dynamic, and hence consistently accurate economic and capital market prediction, is logically impossible within the framework of classical economic theory and methodology.

If economics were similar to the physical sciences, then the effect that a tax refund, or a large budget deficit, or a change in inflation, or a discount rate cut would have on the prevailing level of interest rates would be predictable. However, since the central nexus of economics — i.e., value — is constantly changing, the effect that various events will have on interest rates is not consistent. For example, sometimes the extra cash resulting from a tax refund will be spent immediately for current consumption, sometimes it will be saved, sometimes it will be invested in bonds, sometimes it will be used for speculation, and sometimes it will simply sit in a demand deposit account. All of these alternatives, not to mention countless others, are dependent upon the contemporaneous net state of mind of the populace. As for the capital markets, while we all have experienced cases where bonds go up immediately after a cut in the Federal Reserve re-discount rate, we have also seen bonds come crashing down after a such a cut. While we all have experienced cases in which stock prices go up immediately after an increase in corporate earnings and/or a decrease in interest rates, we have also seen cases in which they come crashing down after identical changes. The reactions of debt and equity prices to such economic developments seem to depend upon the contemporaneous state of mind of the market's participants. The fact that mental states do not obey the conservation principle means that the effect that any given quantum of economic data has on the capital markets is not *constant*.[3] The effect is rather *variable,* depending upon the significance that the contemporaneous net state of mind of the populace happens to place upon that particular quantum of data at the particular time it is received. Since this popular state of mind is not predictable within the assumptions of, nor by the methods of, contemporary economic theory, neither is the future level of interest rates or stock prices predictable thereby. This being the case, the problem of accurately forecasting stock and bond prices can *never* be solved by collecting infinitely more "fundamental" data or by manipulating myriad other variables within the framework of conventional economic theory. *If the problem of forecasting the price structure of the capital markets is to be solved at all, the answer must lie within some radically different first principles of economic science — principles that are not subject to the logical problems inherent in classical economic theory.* It is true, of course, that conventionally derived economic forecasts sometimes have hit the mark. However, since there is no *necessary* connection between any current state of the economic system and any future configuration of interest rates or stock prices, those few forecasts that have proved correct are not the deductive consequence of economic theory. They are rather the result primarily of *random chance*. In addition, since such data series have a propensity to *trend*, and since most economists simply extrapolate trends, they can sometimes look "right" for a time for the wrong reason.

The fact that adequate capital market prediction is logically impossible under the assumptions of classical economics does not mean that interest rates and stock prices are therefore theoretically unpredictable under *any* assumptions. Mental states may not obey the laws of classical mechanics, but they might obey laws of *some* sort. If it were possible to ascertain the laws that mental states actually *do* obey, then it would be possible to determine the precise significance that a brain — or a collection of brains — would place upon given economic quanta at given times.[4] Consequently, interest rates and stock prices would become both explainable and predictable — at least in theory. We will now briefly examine some recent capital market behavior, firstly in order to illustrate the fundamental inadequacy of traditional theory, and secondly to suggest how this observed problem might be amenable to some radically different first principles.

> The investment value of a stock is the present worth of all the dividends to be paid upon it.
>
> — John Burr Williams

Amending the Dividend Discount Model of Stock Valuation

Stock prices (S) typically are viewed as the dependent product of two independent variables, viz., the income stream that they produce (I) and the multiple, or discount factor, that is applied to that income stream (D). There are, however, some problems with this approach, most notable of which is the observed failure of conventional theory adequately to predict, or even fully to describe after the fact, the actual behavior of equity prices. For example, according to theory, the proper rate at which stock market income should be discounted is the rate of return that could be earned on alternate investments. Therefore, conventional analytic practice is to discount stock market cash flows by a rate equivalent to the yield available from long-term bonds.[5] It obviously follows, other things being equal, that any change in long-term interest rates should produce a proportionate (though not necessarily equivalent) change in the current market value of both the bond market and the stock market.

In actual practice, however, stock market prices and yields have *not* moved proportionately with bond market prices and yields. Neither have they moved proportionately with earnings. As a result, actual stock prices have frequently been far different from what theory would calculate them to be by applying the prevailing discount rate to the income stream of the underlying business enterprise. It must be emphasized that we are not at this point addressing the *predictive* failures of conventional theory. Since future earnings and interest rates are themselves necessarily unknown, forecasting future stock prices on the basis of such variables is tenuous at best. What we are addressing here, rather, is the observed failure of conventional investment theory to explain the actual behavior of stock prices *even in retrospect*. For example, Figure 1 depicts the actual behavior of the S&P Industrials from July 1982 through December 1999. The S&P Industrial Index, as opposed to the 500 Index, is well suited for this purpose because it does not include utility issues, which in investors' minds are somewhat similar to bonds. It therefore well represents stocks *qua* stocks. Plotted below the S&P Industrials is a depiction of how this index should have behaved, based exclusively on the changes in interest rates and dividend streams that occurred during this period of time. Note that at the end of the period, the S&P Industrials stood at an actual price of 1841 as opposed to its theoretically calculated price of 562, a discrepancy of approximately 227%. This huge discrepancy means that if in July 1982, a divinely

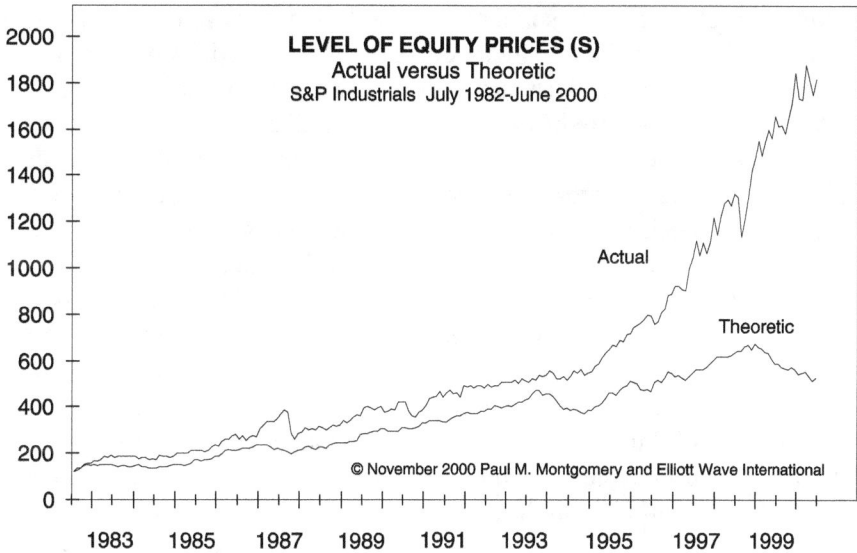

Figure 1

favored investor had been blessed with perfect foreknowledge of exactly where both interest rates and stock dividends would be eighteen years later, he *still* would have miscalculated the actual level of stock prices by more than 200%. (This particular example implicitly assumes that stocks were priced at their "proper value" at the beginning of the period, but the magnitude of the discrepancies through time would be essentially identical, irrespective of the propriety or impropriety of the initial market value.)

It should be pointed out here that intolerable discrepancies between the actual and theoretic price structure are not specific to one particular valuation model. Except for the *extent* of the discrepancy between theoretic and actual market prices during certain periods, there is little material difference, whether one employs models based upon dividends, as we do in Figure 1, or trailing earnings, expected earnings, "real" earnings, cash flows, EBIT or normalized returns on current cost book. Similarly, there is little theoretic difference whether these models use a discount factor based on nominal bond yields as we do, or "real" interest rates, historic returns or LIBOR. One could employ numerous elaborate and sophisticated models, but the significant point remains that *any* valuation methodology that is limited to conventional economic variables consistently fails to describe the actual behavior of stock prices—both predictively *and* retrospectively.

Since the behavior of the traditional independent variables — cash flows and discount rates — cannot adequately describe the real world behavior of stock prices, it necessarily follows that there must be at least one additional variable in a proper capital market equation. We suggest that the missing variable within the price structure of the equity market relates to the fluctuating mental states of investors mentioned earlier. The two conventionally recognized variables — income streams and discount rates — may indeed determine the theoretic *"net present value"* of the equity market, but only by adjusting this calculated *present value* by an additional variable related to the stock market's contemporaneous *"psychologic value"* can the *actual* level of equity prices be derived.

We suggest that stock prices might better be considered as the dependent product of *three* independent variables. In this revised view, the conventional income stream (I) remains the first factor. However, the second conventional factor, the income multiple, will be separated into two distinct variables. One part is the discount rate (D) derived from the prevailing level of long-term interest rates. The *other* part can be described as the contemporaneous premium or discount that equity ownership happens to command with respect to debt ownership. Simply put, people sometimes are willing and desirous to pay significantly more for stocks than their fundamentally calculable value, and sometimes people are willing and desirous to pay significantly less. This latter function — the relative *desire* to own equities — apparently fluctuates independently of the two fundamental factors. While the precise nature of this factor so far remains largely unexplained, since it is hypothesized to be the product of immaterial mental states, it shall herein be denominated as the *psi* factor, or Ψ. Therefore, according to this alternate way of looking at stock prices (S), reality can be described by the following equation:

$$S = I \div D \times \Psi$$

While the first two terms of this equation are quite familiar to most stock valuers, the last term, Ψ, requires some further amplification. Mathematically, this term describes the result that is obtained when contemporaneous bond yields are divided by contemporaneous stock yields. This result, the Bond Yield/Stock Yield Ratio, will be termed the *psi* factor (Ψ) in the present context. This third variable is of critical significance because without it, the income/discount rate equation does not properly describe actual stock prices. It must be emphasized that — at this point anyway — *psi* is merely a descriptive tautology, not yet predictive.

Besides making the equity market equation a more accurate reflection of reality, an additional benefit derived from dividing bond yields by stock yields in this fashion is that it has the effect of filtering out — to a large extent anyway — such powerful fundamental factors as book values, corporate earnings, inflation, taxes, payout ratios and the prevailing level of interest rates. Once these fundamental variables are essentially neutralized, the remaining components of the price structure — whatever they may be — are isolated and thereby rendered more accessible to study.

As a practical example of the additional insight this tripartite way of viewing stock prices provides, we proffer the charts in Figures 2a through 2d, which depict each of the four factors in the equation $I \div D \times \Psi = S$ as they actually obtained between July 1982 and June 2000. The first three variables, taken together, necessarily calculate the fourth term — which is the actual contemporaneous level of stock prices. More specifically, in July 1982, the S&P Industrials were paying cash dividends of $7.18 (I), the yield on Moody's AAAs was 14.6% (D), and bond yields were 2.44 times the level of dividend yields (Ψ). Hence by the preceding equation, the contemporaneous level of the S&P Industrials (S) could be described as follows: $I \div D \times \Psi = S$ or

$$\$7.18 \div 14.61\% \times 2.44 = 119.9.$$

In December 1999, by comparison, dividends had risen to $17.38, bond yields had dropped to 7.55%, and the Ψ factor had soared to 8.00. By this same suggested equation, the S&P Industrials at that time could be described as follows: $I \div D \times \Psi = S$, or

$$\$17.38 \div 7.55 \times 8.00 = 1841.$$

At this point, of course, the Ψ variable, i.e., the ratio of bond yields to stock yields, is determinable only from knowledge of the S variable,

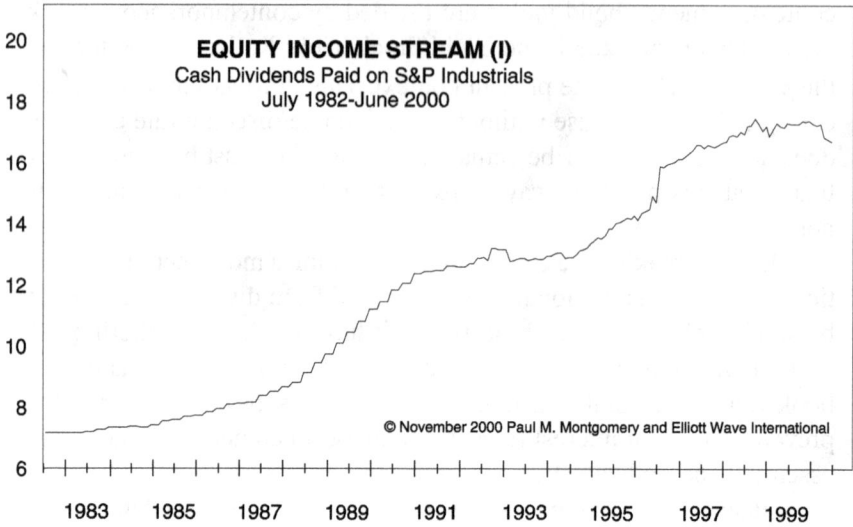

Figure 2a

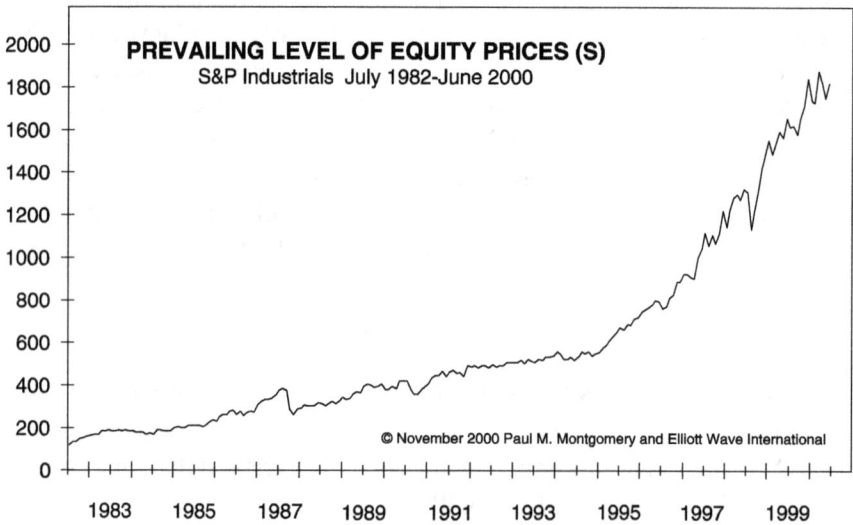

Figure 2b

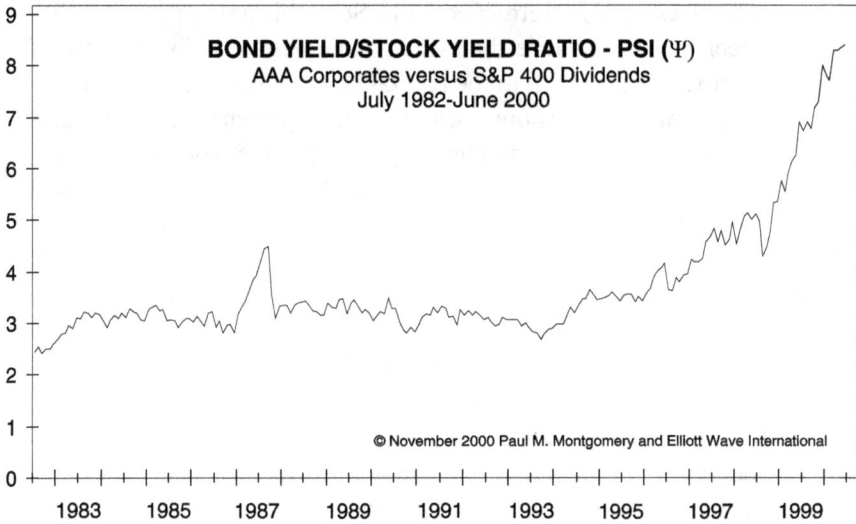

BOND YIELD/STOCK YIELD RATIO - PSI (Ψ)
AAA Corporates versus S&P 400 Dividends
July 1982-June 2000

© November 2000 Paul M. Montgomery and Elliott Wave International

Figure 2c

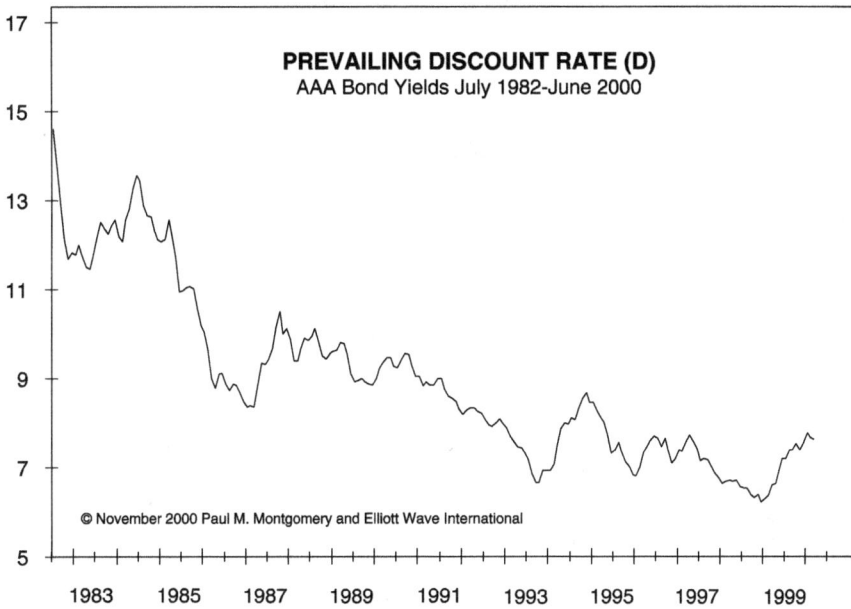

PREVAILING DISCOUNT RATE (D)
AAA Bond Yields July 1982-June 2000

© November 2000 Paul M. Montgomery and Elliott Wave International

Figure 2d

i.e., stock prices, applied retrospectively. So to this point, predictability has not been enhanced. Nevertheless, an immediately obvious benefit of this new tripartite approach to the capital markets is that it makes more readily apparent precisely *how* stock prices have gotten to and from their respective levels between any chosen points in time. By this formula, for example, from July 1982 to December 1999, dividends increased by an amount sufficient to lift stock prices roughly 142% ($17.38 ÷ $7.18 = 2.421). Falling interest rates were sufficient to lift the market an additional 94% (14.61% ÷ 7.55% = 1.935). A shift in investor preference from debt-generated income towards equity-generated income was sufficient to lift prices an additional 227% (8.00 ÷ 2.44 = 3.2788). The product of these terms equals the 1535% that the S&P Industrials actually gained during their historic bull market run from July 1982 to December 1999. Considering Ψ, then, causes us to isolate and focus on the variable that actually had the greatest effect on the movement of stock prices during this period.

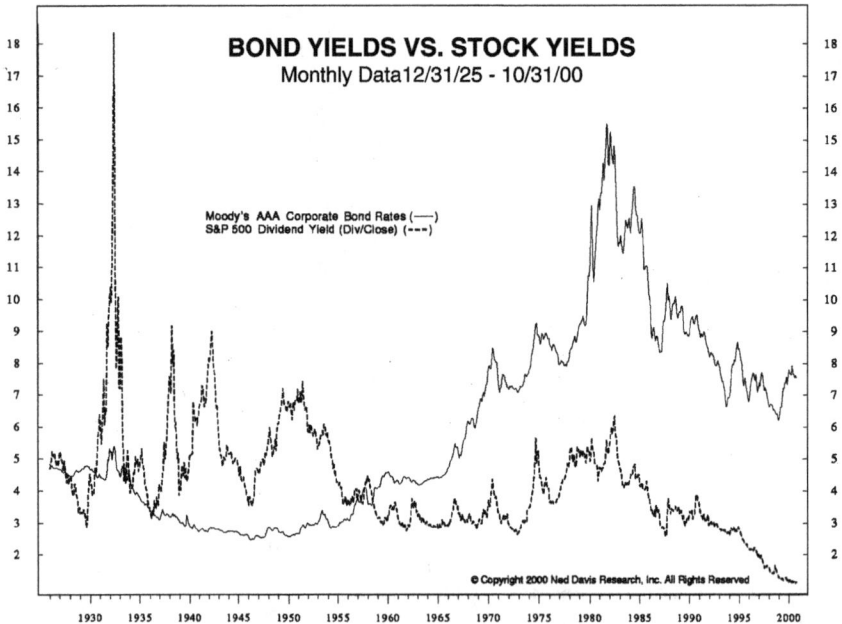

BOND YIELDS VS. STOCK YIELDS
Monthly Data12/31/25 - 10/31/00

Moody's AAA Corporate Bond Rates (——)
S&P 500 Dividend Yield (Div/Close) (- - -)

© Copyright 2000 Ned Davis Research, Inc. All Rights Reserved

Figure 3

Figure 3 depicts Aaa bond yields and common stock dividend yields between 1926 and 2000. It is immediately obvious that stock market yields have not simply moved proportionately with the coupon rate on long term bonds as theory might suggest. In fact, there does not immediately appear to be any consistent differential relationship whatsoever between interest rates and dividend yields. *Sometimes stocks yield several times as much as bonds, sometimes bonds yield several times as much as stocks,* and sometimes the relationship is somewhere in between. So in the real world, the rate of return available from equities is *not* a constant function of prevailing interest rates, as theory would have it. Stock market returns are rather some *variable* function of bond market returns *even over long periods of time.*

In order better to examine the long-term effects of this variable function, Figure 4 depicts seven decades of history for this variable. It reveals massive swings in investor preferences, from stocks to bonds and then back again to stocks. From the ratio's peak in 1929 to its low in 1942, people became so disenchanted with equities that the *psi* factor dropped from roughly 1:1 to an all-time low of roughly 1/3:1 — a nearly threefold difference in relative valuation. Apparently, the experience of the stock market crash and the Great Depression so traumatized the investing public that, at their most dispirited point, people were willing to pay nearly three times as much for one dollar's worth of *guaranteed* bond income as they were willing to pay for an identical amount of *non-guaranteed* stock income.

Now observe what happened to the relationship between stocks and bonds in the second half of this century, as a whole new generation of investors reached majority. To this generation, the stock market crash and the Great Depression were part of an irrelevant past. Their great fear was of "inflation," and their great hope was for "growth." Concurrent with this change in attitude, the Bond Yield/Stock Yield Ratio, which had suffered such a long eclipse, began to enjoy an even longer ascendancy, having reached a year-end peak of 6.5:1 in 1999. (The weekly figures reached 8.7:1 in the week ending July 14, 2000.) It is profoundly important to observe hereby that the *psi* factor is not limited to short term emotional mentation *but may be a dominant influence in valuation even over long periods of time.*

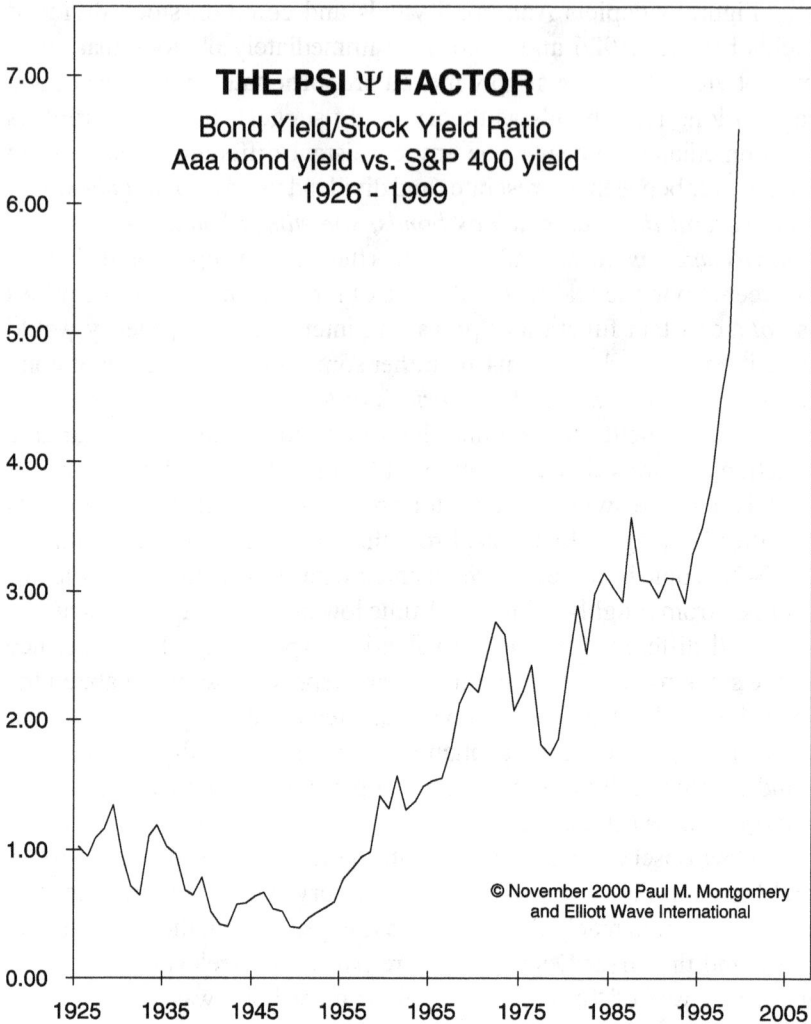

THE PSI Ψ FACTOR

Bond Yield/Stock Yield Ratio
Aaa bond yield vs. S&P 400 yield
1926 - 1999

© November 2000 Paul M. Montgomery
and Elliott Wave International

Figure 4

The importance of Ψ over the long term is hardly confined to the United States. Figure 5 displays the Bond Yield/Stock Yield Ratio for Japanese securities from January 1950 through the first half of 2000. In the late 1940s and 1950s, stock dividend yields in Japan consistently exceeded the yield on Japanese bonds — just as was the case in the U.S. Then, in 1957, bond yields in Japan began to exceed stock yields.

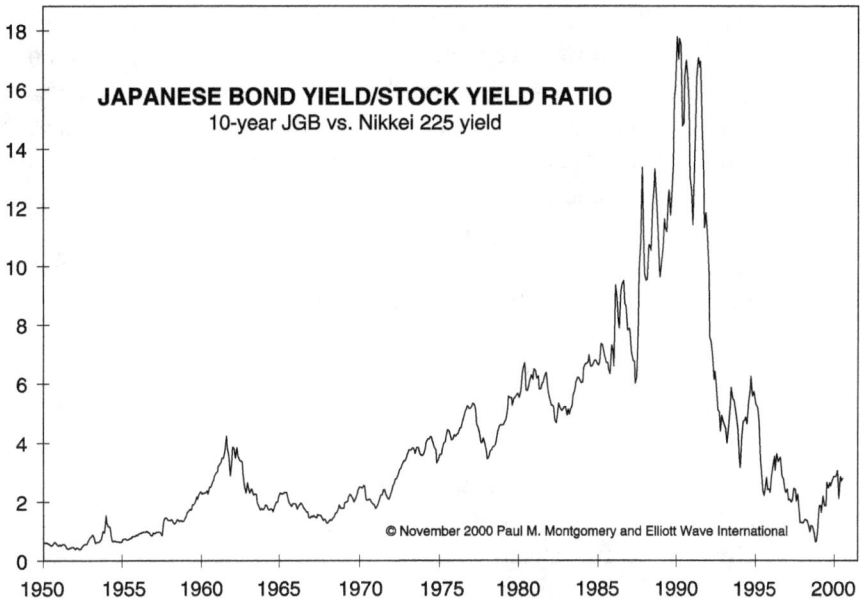

JAPANESE BOND YIELD/STOCK YIELD RATIO
10-year JGB vs. Nikkei 225 yield

© November 2000 Paul M. Montgomery and Elliott Wave International

Figure 5

(One year later, the identical development took place in the U.S.) Subsequently, this critical variable embarked upon a dramatic and sustained
rise. As mentioned above, the Bond Yield/Stock Yield Ratio in the U.S.
reached 8.7 to 1 this year. In Japan, however, this same ratio soared to
an incredible 17 to 1 in December 1989, at which point it peaked and
then headed back downward. Since that all-time peak some ten years
ago, the decline in this Japanese equivalent of *psi* has been so persistent
that in October 1998, this critical variable was once again below unity.
That is to say, stock dividend yields once again exceeded bond coupon
yields, for the first time since 1957.

In June 1949, the Nikkei stock index closed at 146.92. In October
1998, it closed at 13,564.51. This nearly one hundred-fold appreciation
in stock prices can be almost completely "explained" by the changes in
dividend and interest rates that occurred over these same five decades
— much as conventional theory would have it. *However*, while these
13,000 points may be attributable to the "fundamentals" — i.e., to
dividends and interest rates — the 26,000 points up to the 1989 all-time
peak of 38,915.82, as well as the 26,000 points from that point back

down, are *not* attributable to these "fundamentals." These enormous moves, both up and down, were instead almost totally dependant upon changing human *attitudes* regarding the relative desirability of these two asset categories. So even over periods of time measured in decades, immaterial mental states can have, and indeed have had, more than *twice* as much influence on the price structure of investments as the most tangible economic fundamentals.

The dominance of the *psi* factor is felt just as strongly on the short term. In fact, it can readily be demonstrated once again to be, at times, the single most important component of the price structure. Between September and November 1987, for example, S&P Industrial dividends remained constant at $8.52, and AAA bond yields dropped negligibly, from 10.18% to 10.01%. The Ψ factor, however, plunged from 4.49 to 3.09 during this same period of time. This 31% drop in the Ψ factor in just three months was sufficient to erase roughly one-third of the value of the Dow Jones Industrial Average, despite the fact that business cash flows and the prevailing discount rate both remained essentially unchanged.

So while tangible fundamental factors such as income streams and interest rates obviously are extremely important to the price structure of investments, precisely as traditional theory would have it, immaterial mental states, or the *psi* factor, would appear to be at least as significant.

While distilling the price structure down to its constituent parts in this fashion is clearly enlightening so far as analyzing past market behavior is concerned, there is an enormous potential theoretically inherent in such an approach because it conceivably could enable one to anticipate more accurately the future level of stock prices. Conventional methodologies incorporate cash flows and discount factors as the only independent variables responsible for stock prices. In the real world, the latter variable is itself actually a product of *two* factors; viz., interest rates times the "stock/bond premium (or discount)." *If* this third variable, this stock/bond ratio, is not random but follows an order of some sort, then it should be possible to improve upon forecasts based on cash flows and interest rates alone. This is especially the case given the fact that each of the three components of the stock market price structure appears to follow a radically different dynamic. Each of these components, therefore, ideally requires a radically different analytic approach. For example, according to common experience, the dividend component of the equity price structure (I) is fairly orderly and is probably best determined by applying conventional fundamental analysis to basic business enterprise. On the other hand, the discount factor — or the interest rate component of the price structure (D) — appears to be highly *resistant* to fundamental analysis (see Endnote 1). It is generally agreed that the part of the equity price structure determined by the *discount rate* must be investigated by methodologies quite different from the methodologies brought to bear upon forecasting the *income stream* component of the price structure. The third and final component of the equity price structure, the Ψ factor (in this case the Bond Yield/Stock Yield Ratio) might be presumed to be the most elusive of the three inasmuch as it is likely to be almost purely a psychological phenomenon and hence immediately dependent upon immaterial mental states. If the actual level of stock prices at any time is a multiplicative function of *all three* of these variables, then superior information regarding the probable future state of any *one* of these three variables — other things being equal — would constitute a marginal advantage, theoretically conducive to excess investment returns.

Before we attempt to elucidate a basis for predicting immaterial mental states, we will investigate *why* the psyche imposes itself so powerfully upon the equation.

The Triune Brain's Challenge to EMH

> Wonderful as is the development of the human brain, it originated as an enlarged ganglion, and its first response is still that of the ganglion.
>
> — G.C. Selden, *Psychology of the Stock Market*

The Efficient Market Hypothesis assumes that while the future may not always be knowable, investors will always change their perceptions about it in a perfectly rational manner as new information arises concerning their holdings. A corollary to this theory is that, inasmuch as information is generally disseminated instantly and ubiquitously, stock market prices virtually always accurately reflect economic verities. This hypothesis has a certain undeniable appeal, but as a complete model of the capital markets, it is woefully inadequate. The hypothesis is challengeable not only because it is contrary to experience, but also because it is based on a demonstrably incomplete model of human neurophysiology and behavioral dynamics. What the Efficient Market

Hypothesis does describe, and describe quite well, is that particular portion of human psychology and capital market behavior that is primarily directed by the computer-like left neocortex of the human forebrain. This particular portion of our brain *does* perform orderly and rational operations such as calculating the net present values of our holdings. But as most observers of human behavior acknowledge, there is much more to human thought and action than the coldly rational. Certain recent neurologic discoveries, in fact, seem to be especially enlightening in the attempt to understand the capital markets, particularly the discoveries that the human brain functions in a *cyclic, bicameral,* and *triune* fashion.[6]

The triune concept of the brain (see Figure 6) holds that the human forebrain actually comprises a hierarchy of three fundamentally distinct brains in one. These three formations — the reptilian complex, the limbic system, and the neocortex — are each radically different from the others in anatomical structure, in chemical composition and in function. They are so different, in fact, that we might be said to have three different minds: a primal mind, an emotional mind and a rational mind.

The reptilian complex is the most phylogenetically primitive brain system, consisting primarily of a large mass of ganglia at the base of the forebrain. This primal brain apparently is intimately involved in dozens of prototypic behavior patterns essential to the survival of the species. Activities such as establishing territory, selecting leaders, hunting, hoarding food, mating and breeding as well as migration and herding (or flocking) behavior all seem to be under the direction of the primitive reptilian complex. Many of the behavior patterns this brain organizes are very complex, but they are all, nonetheless, inflexible, stereotypic and predictable, even to the point of being obsessive-compulsive. This brain system apparently lacks the appropriate neural circuitry for learning to cope with new situations, rendering our reptilian mentality an utter slave to inherent biologic programming.

Surrounding the reptilian complex are various neural and endocranial complexes known collectively as the limbic system. This brain system processes some signals from the outside world, olfactory ones for example, but it is primarily occupied with receiving and processing signals from our internal world, i.e., those produced by cardiovascular, somatic, proprioceptive, neuroendocrinal, visceral and other activities. The limbic system derives its information and directs our behavior almost exclusively in terms of emotional feelings, especially those

Left Cortical

Bond Value $(V_o) = \sum_{i=1}^{i=n} \pi_i v^i + C v^n$

Theory of Investment Value, 1938

The investment value of a stock is the present worth of all dividends to be paid upon it.
John Burr Williams, 1938

$$P_{z,t_1+t_2} \, dz = \int_{-\infty}^{+\infty} P_{x,t_1} P_{z-x,t_2} \, dx \, dz$$

Theory of Speculation, 1900

Right Cortical

The higher a people's intelligence and moral strength, the lower will be the prevailing rates of interest
Eugen von Bohm-Bawerk, c.1910

Well, it's a Bull market you know.
Reminiscences of a Stock Operator, 1923

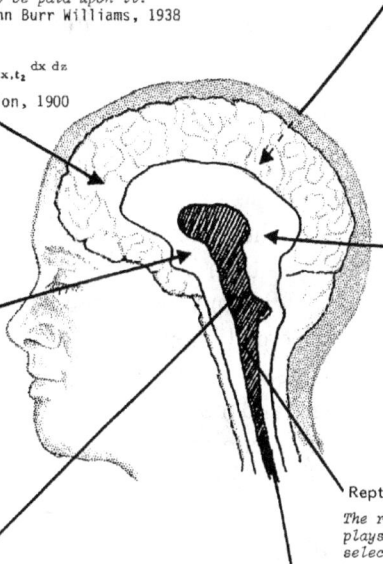

Limbic

When dealing with the Fed, [the financial markets] are dealing with wild animals.
Maxwell Newton, 1985

Limbic

The market's pricing mechanism remains based to such a degree upon faulty and frequently irrational analytic processes that the price of a security only occasionally coincides with the intrinsic value around which it tends to fluctuate.
David Dodd, 1987

Reptilian

The reptilian brain in mammals plays a crucial role in... selecting leaders.
Paul D. McLean, 1970

Reptilian

The gyroscopic action of the prices recorded on the tickertape produces an effect somewhat similar to that of watching the water as it flows over Niagara Falls. Dozens of people, without any suicidal intentions, have been drawn into this current and dashed on the rocks below. And thousands daily are influenced by the ticker to commit the most fatuous blunders.
Psychology of Speculation, 1926

Reptilian

Wonderful as is the development of the human brain, it originated as an enlarged ganglion, and its first response is still practically that of the ganglion.
Psychology of the Stock Market, 1912

Cyclic Principles

*Much shall rise that now lies buried,
And much shall fall that is held in honor today.*
ARS POETICA c.20 BC

Figure 6

emotions associated in any way with the two basic life principles of *self-preservation* and *procreation,* such as ecstasy, anxiety, panic, foreboding, the fear of being alone, threat of annihilation, etc. In limbic mentation, "the net present value of future cash flows" is totally meaningless because the only sense of "time" is the current instant, and the only sense of "value" is immediate physiologic relief. Emotional cerebration can occur independently of rational thought because the two processes are the product of two different cerebral mechanisms. Dealing primarily with internally generated signals, the ancient limbic system has the capacity to generate extremely strong feelings of conviction, which attach to our beliefs about the outside world *completely irrespective of whether they are true or false.* It is thus one of the fundamental properties of emotional mentation that — both in different people, and in the same people at different times — it can support diametrically opposite sides of the same question with equal intensity.

The neocortex is the seat of the rational mind. Surrounding the matrix of the limbic system and the upper brain stem, this layer of neural tissue is most significantly occupied with the production and processing of language and symbolic logic and with associated functions such as reading, writing, mathematics, etc. The neocortex's primary function is processing visual, auditory and tactile signals arising in the external material world. The neocortex (and to some extent the limbic system) is hemispheric in form and bicameral in function.

The primary distinction between the two cerebral hemispheres is not so much in the type of data they deal with — since the same informational content can be processed by either hemisphere — but in the methods by which the identical data are processed. The dominant, or left, forebrain is apparently specialized for sequential, verbal, numeric, logical, rational, analytic methods of processing its data in a discrete, discontinuous, unstructured, materialistic and mechanistic manner. The non-dominant, or right, brain, on the other hand, processes these same data simultaneously in terms of a nonverbal, intuitive, holistic, continuous, patterned, aesthetic and harmonious gestalt. Certain problems, such as calculating the *net present value* of a stock or the yield to maturity on a deep discount bond, are processed primarily by the dominant neocortical hemisphere so as always to produce the same result. More multi-faceted problems with open solutions, such as figuring out the best way to win a war, allow for many different solutions and require both sides of the neocortex. The first type of problem is solved *predictably* in the part of the brain that works like a computer, processing the same input data each time, in the same way, to reach the same result. The second type of problem, of which the investment problem is one, is solved far less predictably, given the multitude of possible solutions. This difference is critical to recognize in that the variability of *potential* solutions allows investors to *rationalize* their decisions in terms of external "facts" at times when those decisions in actuality are primarily based upon internal direction from the limbic system. This variability also introduces the factor of *uncertainty,* which further exposes the decision-making process to input from the emotional limbic system and from the inflexible lower brain stem.

Even over relatively long periods of time, the lower brain processes may be the predominant influence on stock or bond prices. At almost any time, for example, virtually any competent analyst can take current economic conditions and construct a neocortical case for a bull or bear market. Sufficient external conditions always exist to account for a major rise or fall in prices. However, it is only when the market becomes sufficiently emotional, i.e., when investors become sufficiently *internally* aroused about these external conditions, that a dramatic movement in prices eventuates. It is activity within the hippocampus much more than activity within the Federal Reserve Board, in the Oval Office or in other markets that determines the behavior of any particular series of financial prices.

Financial market behavior appears to provide numerous demonstrations of analysts' capacity to rationalize trends as externally caused. As one example, in 1987, market observers cited a weak dollar as the reason why bond prices collapsed. As shown in Figure 7, however, the dollar had been falling (foreign currencies rising) since February 27, 1985. In fact, from that date until late March, the U.S. Dollar Index (not shown) slipped from roughly 167 to roughly 97 — better than a 40% decline. Throughout this rout of the dollar, the bond market actually rose. Then, when the Dollar Index slipped almost imperceptibly from 97 to 95 in April, bond prices collapsed. The economic theory behind the rationalizations sounds valid; e.g., a falling dollar raises prices and decreases the real net present value of the future cash flows from a bond portfolio, and bond prices necessarily fall as a result. Practically, however, it seems passing strange that a 40%, 25-month long decline

FALLING DOLLAR HAD NO EFFECT ON BOND PRICES FOR 25 MONTHS

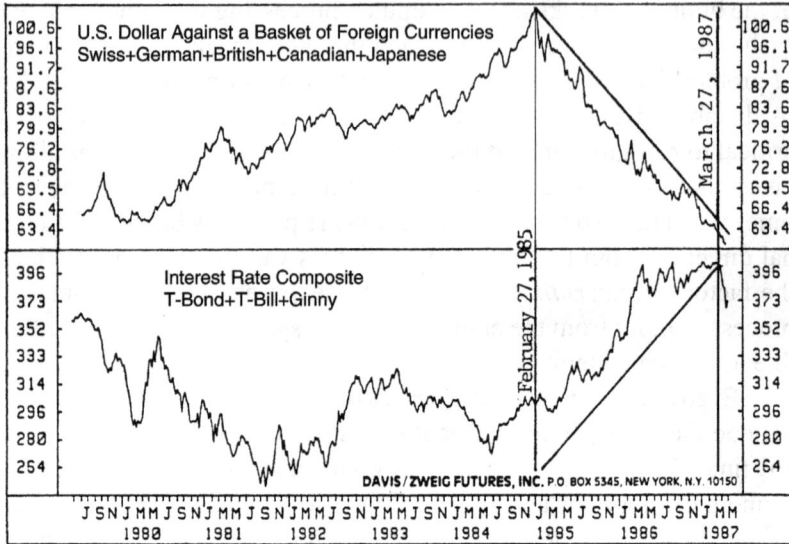

Figure 7

in the dollar would be *good* for bonds, whereas a 2% one-month long continuation of this decline would be devastating for bonds. The same logic applies to the rising CRB Commodity Index, the surge in gold, and all the other economic events that were cited as the reason for that deluge in the credit markets.

The point is that, at times, purchases and sales of securities may be driven *not* by logical conclusions from the left neocortex regarding *external* conditions, as economic theory claims, but by the limbic system's attempt to *alleviate internal perturbation*. Bonds plunged when holders could no longer tolerate the distress attendant upon ownership. Such limbic cerebration can occur entirely independently of rational thought because the two states are products of two quite distinct cerebral mechanisms. As a consequence, securities might at times be quite aggressively acquired, or aggressively jettisoned, absolutely irrespective of their calculable present values or yields-to-maturity. Whatever the *external* fundamentals may be, the most dramatic movements in security prices occur when market participants become sufficiently *internally* aroused — and only then. Conventional economic theory simply does not address itself to the problem of determining either the time or the price at which market participants — actual or potential — will become excited enough to act. Ignoring the critical problem of determining just *when* the primitive brain centers will become sufficiently aroused to excite the neocortex, unsettling investors sufficiently to force them to act, is what underlies the inevitable failure of conventional economic theory adequately to predict the capital markets.

The neocortex is also capable of being overwhelmed, at times, by the phylogenetically primitive lower brain stem, which serves to direct instinctive responses that are both stereotypic and highly inflexible. Typically in highly complex behavior, such as investment behavior, the more rostral, or "higher," brain centers such as the neocortex exercise a large degree of control over these animalistic "lower" brain centers. However, these primitive ganglia can at times effectively dominate the higher cerebral processes because they are programed to serve such powerfully motivating ends as pain avoidance, security and survival. For example, there are probably few things more unsettling to the nervous system than the gain or loss of large sums of money, which, emotionally if not practically, impinges upon our very survival. Consequently, when we are surprised by a dramatic market move, either up or down, or when we go through a protracted period of excess market volatility, the rapid succession of gains and losses is capable of generating neural impulses quite strong enough to overwhelm the neocortex. In such circumstances, the ancient lower brain stem may well assume predominance, paralyzing us into inaction, forcing us into rigid behavior patterns, propelling us into the stampeding herd, or otherwise prompting us to behave quite differently from the way the neocortex would have prompted us to behave in the absence of these unsettling neurophysiologic signals.

So apparently the human brain, the basis of all our behavior, actually consists of at least three, perhaps four, or even five (the limbic system appears to have two parts) separate biologic computers, each unique in form and function, and each with its own unique type of intelligence, its own private memory, its own unique rules of logic, and its own sense of time and space — all functioning simultaneously, all operating in parallel, and each influencing behavior to one degree or another. As a consequence, the colossally relevant fact is that virtually all human activities, *especially* highly complex ones such as trafficking in financial instruments, necessarily involve *all* of these neural centers, not just the computer-like left neocortex of the forebrain. They involve the right neocortex, wherein individual bits of data are not nearly so important as the overall *form or pattern of experience*. They also involve our relatively primitive midbrain, or limbic system, which processes data of an *internal and emotional* nature. Finally, they involve our phylo-genetically ancient lower brain stem, which directs *reflexes, instinctive responses* and other activities essential to basic survival.

A further complication to the human behavioral problem derives from the fact that the human brain, in contrast to a computer, is not a steady-state system but rather undergoes cycles in state function. If specific data are repeatedly put into a computer program, they necessarily always generate the same specific result. However, when specific data are put repeatedly into the human brain, they do *not* necessarily always generate the same result because the result is only *partially* determined by the data. *It is also partially determined by the state the system happens to be in at the time the data are received.* For example, studies show that stock market returns are significantly greater on days that New York City is very sunny than they are on days when there is heavy cloud cover.[7] The explanation for this phenomenon arguably relates to the tendency of sunlight striking the retina to alter the activity of the pineal gland, thereby changing the balance of those neurotransmitters in the brain that are associated with depression and elation. Since there is considerable evidence that the *entire* constantly fluctuating electromagnetic spectrum has a much greater effect on human brain function than just the visible band thereof,[8] it follows that the *total* electromagnetic field might play a great role in human psychology and thus in the price structure of investments.

Whatever the precise mechanism, and whatever their exact contribution, these non-rational, immaterial mental factors, fluctuating through time, demonstrably have a significant impact on the price structure of the stock market. From this discussion, it should be apparent that the most basic neural circuitry of the human being is such as to ensure that capital market prices will deviate periodically from even their *retrospectively calculated* "rational" value.

It is highly likely that some of these internal, instinctive, non-rational aspects of our nature partially explain the variable relationship that has been observed to exist between debt securities and equity securities — the factor we are calling the *psi* variable in the stock market equation. A bond, for example, generally represents security in that it guarantees by force of law that the holder will be paid specified amounts of money at specified times in the future. A stock, on the other hand, guarantees nothing, but it does provide the holder with the hope that he may receive unlimited riches at some indeterminate time. Since the clinical evidence is that *hopes* regarding one's wealth and *fears* regarding one's security are significantly determined by subcortical functions, these processes are *necessarily at work in determining the perceived value of stocks versus bonds.*

Furthermore, and of critical importance, is the fact that *these lower brain centers all operate in an exquisitely orderly fashion.* They each have, as noted, their own special intelligence, their own private memory, their own rules of logic, and their own sense of time and space. But unlike the cortex, whose operations are relatively accessible, the subcortex lacks the requisite neural circuitry to articulate verbally exactly what it is doing. Since it does not have the means to explain itself, we must study the behavioristic principles upon which it operates by their *results,* i.e., the behavior patterns that the subcortex motivates. That is exactly the approach taken by one particular unconventional line of inquiry, and as we shall see, substantial progress has been made in describing the orderly behavior patterns of the subcortical brain, at least as it relates to aggregate, or group, behavior such as that exhibited by capital markets.

A Ubiquitous Pattern of Subcortical Brain Function

> He that studies what ought to be done rather than what is done
> learns the way to his downfall rather than to his salvation.
> — Machiavelli

Now we arrive at the critical point. The process revealed by the *psi* factor, first of disaffection for equities and a swelling preference for bonds, and then of increasing desire for equities and a dampened enthusiasm for bonds, is *not disorderly, linear or random.* As market students will immediately recognize, it rather constituted, over most of the past century, a near-perfect example of the Wave Principle of aggregate human behavior as elucidated by Ralph Nelson Elliott. Figure 8 is a long term picture of the relationship shown in Figure 4, on semilog scale. As you can see, these historic metamorphoses in investor attitudes began with a textbook corrective process of three major waves (labeled a-b-c), two in the direction of the larger trend (down), and one counter

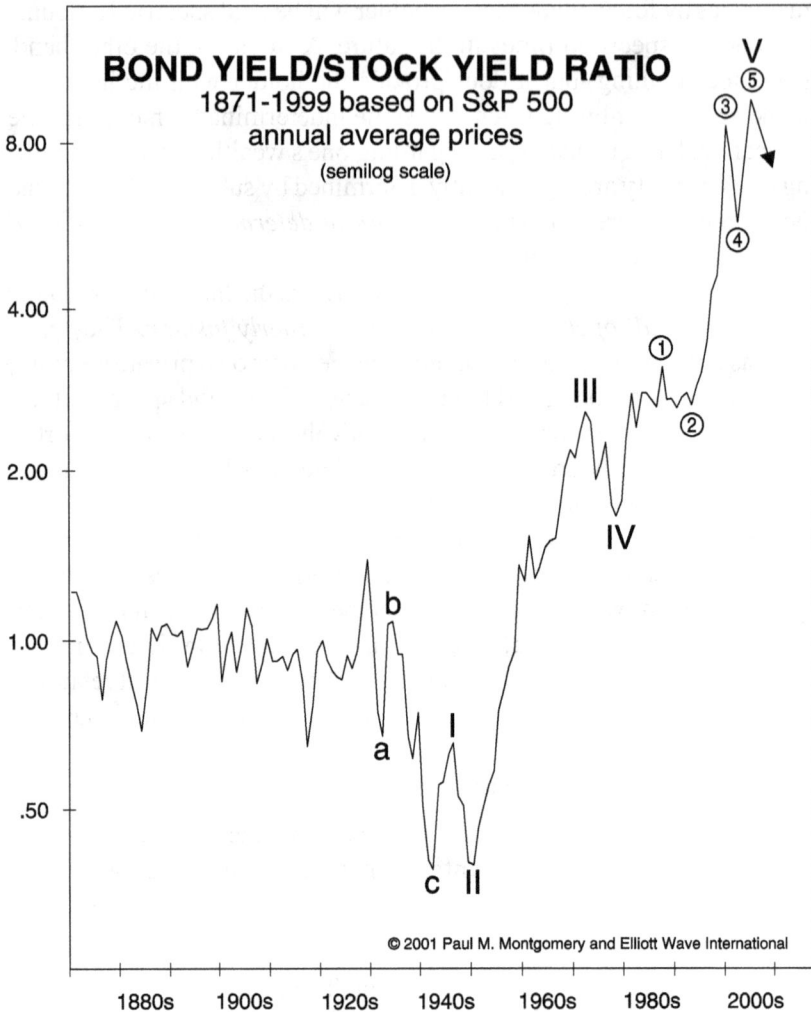

Figure 8

to the trend (up), just as Elliott theory would have it. From there began a classic five-wave advance. Wave I up carried into the mid-1940s and was followed by a corrective wave II into the early 1950s. Next was a dramatic impulse wave III up into the early 1970s, which was the strongest wave, following Elliott's guidelines. This upwave was followed, again according to form, by a three-step corrective wave IV, which ended in 1978. Then the presumed final wave V advance began. This move has been properly subdividing into five waves, which are tentatively over, as indicated by the arrow in Figure 8.[9]

First during the heady days of the 1987 stock market rally, and then ever since 1998, many observers have expressed amazement at the apparent "uncoupling" of the debt and equity markets. Our expressed view, however, is that *far from being "uncoupled,"* stocks and bonds have actually been dancing together *with exquisite precision,* a precision that had been elegantly detailed long ago. The typical observer's confusion arises from the fact that the steps to this dance cannot be found in Graham and Dodd or anywhere else within the familiar canon of conventional analytical thought. They are to be found only within the tenets discovered and elucidated by that pioneer of the study of psychologic market patterns, R.N. Elliott.

We all have seen a market grind on, in wanton disregard for any and all outside circumstances, as if it were under the control of some inexorable force or pattern. During a bear market, innumerable terrifying fundamental facts are paraded forth to account for the decline, but once the bear dies and prices reverse dramatically to the upside, all of this bad news is ignored and good news becomes the focus, thereby providing fodder for the ravenous bull. Just as our bodies assimilate all manner of ingesta yet maintain their idiomorphic form in the midst of this constant physiochemical flux, so the capital markets assimilate all manner of news and yet maintain *their* contemporaneous form, be it bull or bear, in the midst of constant social, political and economic flux.

Whence comes this persistent and idiomorphic form? While superficially, such behavior appears absurd, *it is irrational only within the limited logical framework of the left neocortex.* This pattern is apparently *perfectly valid mentation* within the logical framework of the *right neocortex,* according to which overall patterns are the basic postulate to which all the discrete facts of experience must conform themselves. It is also perfectly valid according to the logical principles of the *subcortex,* under which the conviction that attaches to an idea depends entirely upon the intensity of the associated neural arousal and not at all upon the congruence that idea may or may not have with external reality. Likewise, the Elliott Wave Principle *reflects an internal law of mentation independent of outside events, not a mechanical reflection of external forces.* In other words, the patterns and cycles characteristic of human brain function are themselves *irreducible causal factors* behind the price structure of investments, deserving equal if not greater status than the external "fundamental" factors typically adduced to explain market behavior.

Figure 8, then, demonstrates convincingly that in fact there *has* been a consistent relationship between interest rates and dividend yields for this period. *It is a dynamic consistency, however, not a static one.* Simply by taking into account the Wave Principle, the idea of a consistent relationship between stock and bond yields can suddenly and dramatically be demonstrated. Therefore, theoretically at least, all one has to do to predict financial market prices accurately is to replace the inapplicable Law of Conservation of Momentum with laws that our composite brain actually obeys. The one law yet discovered that repeatedly applies to aggregate human behavior, and therefore to market behavior, is the Wave Principle.

There is, of course, no guarantee that *psi* will always trace out clear and distinct Elliott Wave patterns of progress and regress as was the case during the decades just examined. Since our bicameral, triune, unsteady-state brain functions according to *numerous* principles — rational, non-rational, cyclic — it is only natural that *all* of these principles evidence themselves in the price structure of investments. W*hich* of these principles will predominate at *what* particular time is a question that remains to be fully answered. For example, during the years immediately preceding the seven decades examined here, dynamics other than these described by Elliott may — or may not — have held sway. We can see from Figure 8 that prior to the 1920s, the bond/stock ratio was relatively flat, apparently cycling back and forth across a central tendency. Capital markets being infinitely complex, it is always possible to identify some changing "fundamentals" that correlate with apparently changing capital market dynamics. For example, the moderate alternation between stock and bond dominance that characterized the late 19th and the early 20th century occurred when this country was on the Gold Standard — which effectively guaranteed bond holders that the interest and principal they received would maintain their purchasing power through time. The Bond Yield/Stock Yield Ratio abandoned its moderate cyclic behavior and embarked upon its impulsive Elliott behavior soon after this country abandoned the Gold Standard, thereby abrogating the implicit guarantee that our currency — and bonds denominated therein — would maintain its integrity. This new state of affairs arguably injected an entirely new long term *uncertainty* into the capital markets — especially the credit markets — and as discussed earlier, the more uncertainty in a given situation, the more the subcortical brain is called into service. The result of subcortical activity in this case apparently was to produce a sequence of Elliott wave patterns that dominated the capital markets for decades. In other words, there are times when the *psi* factor is hardly important and times when it is utterly dominant. The degree of uncertainty may regulate the degree of its participation in the valuation equation.[10]

The fact that certain psychological principles are evident in the behavior of the Bond Yield/Stock Yield Ratio is of particular theoretic significance in that it strikes straight at the heart of fundamental investment theory. It might be relatively easy to admit, for example, that intangible, non-rational mental states hold sway in some highly leveraged, zero sum futures market, where concrete, calculable values are virtually nonexistent. It is much more difficult, however, for conventional theory to rationalize the presence of such immaterial, non-rational factors deep within the venerable *Dividend Discount Model*. They are there nonetheless, and because they are there, they are likely to be everywhere else in the marketplace.

THE D AND I FACTORS: UNDER THE SAME INFLUENCE

— by Paul Montgomery and Robert Prechter

The concern of the preceding essay has been primarily to demonstrate the logical necessity of according immaterial mental states at least equal status with cash flows and interest rates within the price structure of investments. The bulk of the preceding discussion deals primarily with the *income statement*—the ratio of bond income to stock income—while the common concern of investors is with the *balance sheet*—the ratio of the relevant security to cash. Since income statement concerns and balance sheet concerns can be equally unsettling psychologically, much the same neurologic dynamic is likely at work in either case.

Ultimately, the inadequacy of conventional economics is far larger than this initial conclusion implies, inasmuch as cash flows and discount rates are *themselves* consequences of human behavior. It necessarily follows that *all* of the factors within the economic equation — not just the part we have termed Ψ — are ultimately dependent upon immaterial mental states. Thus, the role of mental states in investment markets is not just an *equally* important factor, but a factor of *primary* importance. The preceding discussion addressed I and D, which explain, *after the fact,* a portion of the valuation of investments. However, *before and during the fact,* the investment universe is a highly *uncertain* one. In a *certain* universe, investors should be relatively indifferent as to the particular source of their income, and consequently, most financial instruments should consistently price themselves so as to provide somewhat comparable rates of return. In such a universe, stock prices should react to changes in earnings and interest rates in a relatively predictable fashion. However, since we always live in a highly *uncertain* universe, it is not possible to enter actual earnings, or cash flows, or interest rates, or inflation, or taxes, or payout ratios, or *actual* anything into our dividend discount models. All we can really put into these equations are our *ideas* regarding these factors — ideas that often involve hopes and fears and linearly projected expectations. This means that to a significant extent, the conventional variables within this theoretic price structure of investments, i.e., discount rates and income streams — the supposed *concrete* factors in the valuation equation — at the time of their useful employment in the equation are *themselves* necessarily dependent upon ideation. Once we acknowledge this fact, the entire investment problem is violently wrenched out of the comfortable and calculable *external* world of property, plant, equipment and cash flows and catapulted into the *internal* world of the human psyche. The human psyche, *especially under conditions of uncertainty,* operates quite differently from a bloodless computer mechanically cranking out net present values.

As evidence of the form that those mental states produce in the "D" factor of the valuation equation, it is necessary to examine the wildly variable history of the discount rate that is typically used for stock market valuation, i.e., *bond yields,* as shown in Figure 9. The wave labeling shown here has been developed in its various stages as it was unfolding over the past dozen years by Robert Prechter in *The Elliott Wave Theorist* and Paul Macrae Montgomery in *Universal Economics.* As you can see, since the 1940s, bond yields *themselves* have fluctuated according to the Wave Principle of R.N. Elliott. The implication of Figure 9 is that D is *governed by the very same dynamic consistency,* i.e., the Wave Principle, that governs Ψ.

Now we see that fluctuating mental states govern a *substantial* portion of the valuation equation, in fact, *most of it*. This fact even more strongly indicates that a scientific economic dynamic is logically possible *if* and *only if* it is firmly based on the logical primacy of immaterial mental states. Finally, we can see by the patterns, which

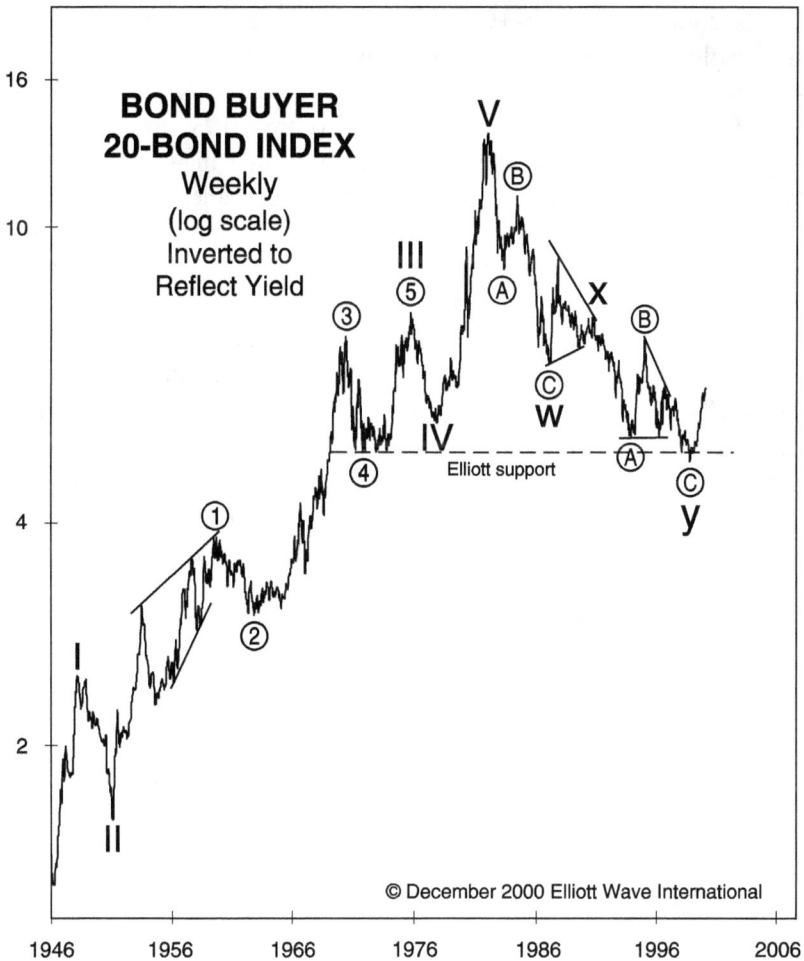

**BOND BUYER
20-BOND INDEX**
Weekly
(log scale)
Inverted to
Reflect Yield

Elliott support

© December 2000 Elliott Wave International

Figure 9

follow observations detailed by R.N. Elliott decades ago, that it is in fact possible accurately to *describe in advance* and therefore, to a great degree, to *predict* the manner in which these mental states will behave.

Of course, the I variable, the income stream from stock invest-ments, is produced by economic activity and distributed according to the (often competing) desires of company managers on one hand and investors on the other. Thus, Elliott wave practitioners contend that even I is ultimately determined by the emotional mentation of people and therefore is subject to the same laws of dynamic behavior. Sometimes it is substantial, as it was in 1932 and 1942, for example, and other times it is negligible to non-existent, such as in the present. These changes appear to have a psychological base. Figure 10 shows a textbook Elliott wave progression in economic activity from 1982 to the present, supporting the case that the very production of I may be dependent upon trends of production that fluctuate in accordance with the Wave Principle. If either contention is true, then even the most stable variable in the valuation over long periods of time will behave dynamically and in concert with fluctuating mental states.

Of course, the Wave Principle itself was discovered through meticulous observation of the patterns within the solution variable, S.[11] Thus, *all four* variables in the equation, D, I, Ψ and S, have at least some basis in the proper first principle of financial analysis, the one that addresses the immaterial mental states that presented us with our original problem. By replacing the false first principle of physical mechanics with the proper first principle of non-rational human mentation, the Wave Principle, we are finally properly positioned to make significant progress in financial and economic analysis.

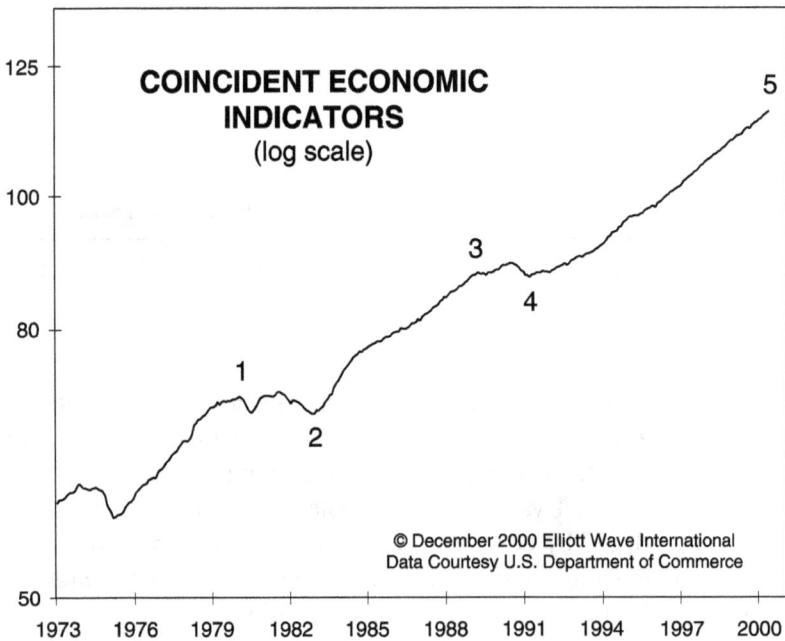

COINCIDENT ECONOMIC INDICATORS
(log scale)

© December 2000 Elliott Wave International
Data Courtesy U.S. Department of Commerce

Figure 10

Implications

The very fact that the attempt has been made to articulate the complex principles of human brain function as they relate to market behavior is of enormous philosophic and practical significance. What it means is that in the equation $I \div D \times \Psi = S$, the Ψ variable is no longer a residual, and the D, and perhaps I, variables are no longer unpredictable. To the extent that Ψ can be quantified and Ψ, D and I can be anticipated, the equation is no longer merely descriptive. It has become *predictive*, since $I \div D \times \Psi$ is at least theoretically capable of predicting stock prices, which $I \div D$ by conventional methods is demonstrably incapable of doing — either practically, as experience has shown, or theoretically, which is the thesis of this paper.

We find, therefore, that the Elliott Wave Principle addresses, apparently usefully, the problem of immaterial mental states, which is the missing first principle and thus the fatal flaw in modern investment theory. These mental states, which are by turns rigid, cyclic and patterned, are not merely the consequence of economic activity but independent, irreducible causal factors behind human behavior and hence within the price structure of investments. To the extent that the dynamics of the Wave Principle can be understood, a properly scientific approach to investment has, for the first time, become a logical possibility.

NOTES

[1] A forecasting survey of leading economists published semi-annually by the *Wall Street Journal* reveals that these experts have been able to forecast the direction of interest rates, just six months into the future, worse than a coin flip by half. [The existence of herding psychology explains consistently doing worse than chance.—Ed.] Further, the most sophisticated models of stock price behavior deviated from reality by 100% or more.

[2] See pp.362-365 in *The Wave Principle of Human Social Behavior.*

[3] Or there is fundamentally no "effect" at all, which is the essence of socionomics.—Ed.

[4] Socionomics asserts that the brain assigns value to economic quanta primarily to rationalize decisions already made by the pre-rational portion of the brain.—Ed.

[5] This relationship actually $V_O = \dfrac{D_1}{(1+i)} + \dfrac{D_2}{(1+i)^2} + \cdots \dfrac{D_N}{(1+i)^N}$, where V is the present value of the stock, D1 is the first dividend, D2 the second

dividend, etc., and I is the interest rate at which these dividends are discounted. While some methods utilize "earnings" or "cash flow" instead of dividends, considering internal reinvestment policies the various income streams are functionally equivalent (see Miller and Modigliani, "Dividend Policy, Growth, and the Valuation of Shares," *Journal of Business,* October 1961). We also employ the common shortcut method of capitalizing cash flows; viz. dividing current income by current cap rates. While not identical, this method is sufficient for the present purpose.

[6] This discussion is derived from the triune concept of Dr. Paul D. MacLean, the bicameral notion of Roger Sperry, and the cyclic state electrodynamic theory of life of Harold Saxton Burr, F.S.C. Northrop and Dr. Leonard J. Ravitz.

[7] Edward M. Saunders, Jr. "Stock Prices and Wall Street Weather," *The American Economic Review* vol. 83, no. 5, December 1993, pp.1337-1345.

[8] Leonard J. Ravitz, "History, Measurement, and Applicability of Periodic Changes in the Electromagnetic Field in Health and Disease," *Annals of the New York Academy of Science,* vol. 98, part 4, October 1962, pp.1144-1201.

[9] Elliott wave patterns in the capital markets typically display extended third waves, whereas Elliott wave patterns in commodity markets typically display extended fifth waves. Since some groups of stocks, such as the Internet group, essentially trade as commodities as their yields are nil, the current upward explosion in the Bond Yield/Stock Yield Ratio may display in some groups and averages a fifth wave acceleration characteristic of commodity market dynamics.

[10] Periods of flatness and cyclicality and periods of persistent advance are themselves part of the dynamic of the Wave Principle, the former two being predominant in "corrective" periods, the latter in "impulsive" periods. For example, the 19th century was a corrective period, which typically separates trending markets. Hence, the *apparently* differing dynamics seen in Figure 8 may each fall within Elliott wave dynamics and therefore within the purview of Elliott wave analysis. Even the so-called fundamental *cause* of the difference, the abondonment of the Gold Standard, *was a result of a change in the mental state of humans.* However one chooses to describe these dynamics, the fact remains that ultimately, they are *all* the product of immaterial mental states.—Ed.

[11] For examples of wave patterns in the stock market, see *Elliott Wave Principle* as well as pp.35-37 in *The Wave Principle of Human Social Behavior.*

PART II

Finance and Philosophy

Chapter 8

CLASSICAL PHILOSOPHY
AND THE CAPITAL MARKETS

by Paul Macrae Montgomery
originally published June 2000
from issues of Universal Economics, *1983 - 1995*

With two dice you can manufacture what looks like a business cycle...or price fluctuation.

—Paul Samuelson

God does not play dice with the universe.

—Einstein

The quarrel between technical analytic theory and random walk theory is not easily resolved merely by appeals to the evidence, because their differences are basically conceptual rather than factual. The technical school interprets capital market data from a "Greek" perspective on the world, whereas the random walk school views the identical data from a "Modern" perspective. These two philosophies are fundamentally quite different and generally have been considered irreconcilable.

Greek thought, excepting atomism, was grounded most significantly on the "Harmony of the Spheres" and related notions of ratio, proportion and form attributable to Pythagoras. Epitomized by the Ideal Forms of Plato, the mathematical astronomy of Eudoxus, and the geometry of Euclid, Greek science was based essentially on harmony and continuity of pattern. Form was held to be so fundamental that it was proper to speak of *"formal causes."* That is to say, that pattern itself has causal properties to the extent that matter is constantly striving to follow, or being driven to follow, some intangible, immaterial form or proportion. Matter was a secondary consideration inasmuch as the behavior of material particles was viewed as essentially a product of the basic order and fundamental forms of nature. Greek science reflected this philosophy throughout. Aristotle's biology with its "fixity of type" is one example, and the medicine of Hippocrates with its concern for temporal and spatial pattern is another. Such a Weltanschauung is virtually nonexistent today, but the technical analytic theory of capital market behavior constitutes a rare contemporary example of the Greek point of view. Its claim, that market prices somehow tend to follow certain predeterminable patterns, is very firmly within the tradition of the formal causes of Greek thought.

Modern science and philosophy, however, are in violent opposition to this Greek thought. The Modern view virtually ignores the forms, harmonies and patterns that the Greek view held to be fundamental and instead holds matter to be fundamental. Its philosophy is empiric and pragmatic, and its science views nature not as a single harmonious system but as an aggregation of material particles. The forms and proportions of geometry, mathematics and nature, which the Greek view held to be primary, are held to be at best secondary phenomena without any causal properties. The apparent harmonies and patterns that occur in nature are believed to be merely temporary effects produced by the behavior of discrete, discontinuous particles.

This materialistic, mechanistic, unstructured, particulate view of the universe, traceable to Leucippus, Democritus, Epicurus, Lucretius and the other atomists, now completely dominates contemporary thought. It returned to vogue in the seventeenth century concurrent with the development of the mechanical astronomy of Galileo and the physics and astronomy of Newton. This atomistic conception of nature next appeared in the chemistry of Lavoisier, with its emphasis on "Elements" as basic "building blocks" of the physical universe. It became dominant in medicine and biology after the discoveries of Harvey and Darwin. Finally, Schleiden and Schwann gave Modern thought its basic biologic "building block," the "cell." Interest since has shifted from the cell to the gene to the DNA molecule, but the philosophic significance is identical, inasmuch as the predominant reaction to these scientific discoveries has been to interpret them in the context of a materialistic, particulate, and discontinuous view of the biologic universe, identical to the prevailing view of the physical universe. The mechanistic conception of biologic systems eventually produced the psychologic dynamics of Pavlov and Skinner, and the political and economic systems of Marx,

Engels and Keynes. Finally, this materialistic, discontinuous, action/reaction philosophy extended itself even into capital market theory, as latter-day atomists have proclaimed that market prices are "random" and follow no forms beyond those of chance and "Brownian Motion."

It is easy to see, even from this very cursory review, why the essentially Greek viewpoint of technical analysis has been incompatible with the archetypically Modern viewpoint of random walk theory. The former maintains that market prices reflect a system of patterns and forms which continually perpetuate themselves in the midst of continuous economic flux. The latter maintains that any patterns or forms that may appear in the market merely reflect a temporary relationship among price data, which are themselves the mechanistic result of myriad disconnected, randomly surfacing economic events. Therefore, price "patterns" and market "forms" are merely transient epiphenomena, totally without causal or predictive significance.

The success of Modern science is beyond question, so it is entirely appropriate for the less exact and less mature sciences such as economics to attempt to incorporate its principles, as random walk theory has done. Recently, however, the entire Modern point of view, with its emphasis on discontinuity rather than on continuity, and on particles rather than on patterns, has been found to be in need of *drastic* revision.

Modern thought is valid in the proper context, but it is inadequate to explain, or even describe, all phenomena. The discoveries of wave mechanics, quantum theory, and most particularly relativity theory, require that the all but forgotten Greek concepts must be given equal status with the Modern. Einstein united these previously incompatible philosophies with his insistence that *fields both condition and are conditioned by the particles in it.* Relativity field physics retains the Modern position that constituent elements have causal properties, but it also reaffirms the neglected Greek claim that the unity and forms of nature are themselves causal factors. The implications of this discovery are so important and so universal that *all* the sciences and *every* area of human activity must be re-examined with an eye towards bringing them in line with field physics. Thus far, the most spectacular result of just such a thoroughgoing reexamination of modern thought is the verified Electrodynamic Theory of Life.[1] It now has been theoretically and empirically demonstrated that an electrodynamic field actually compels atoms and electrons to take certain pathways in living systems, directing growth, maintaining idiomorphic forms and perpetuating characteristic behavior patterns in the midst of physiochemical flux. Since capital market behavior is a subcategory of human behavior, it follows that form and pattern should be evident in market price data as well, which is precisely the primary assumption of technical analytic theory.

Failing to realize its implicit philosophic bias, modern economic science tends to confuse *data* with *evidence* and tends to exclude from consideration any system not based on its own materialistic first principles. Thus, much of what passes for "science" in the field of economics is actually pure speculative philosophy. Therefore, much of the criticism of technical analysis is ultimately nothing so much as fanatic assertion.

Again, this is *not* to say that the Modern viewpoint is invalid. Economic news events most certainly *can* have an effect on stock and bond prices. According to certain carefully defined parameters, these prices *may* appear to replicate a random walk. It definitely is to say, however, that the random walk viewpoint is *inadequate* because capital market prices *also* follow certain general forms and patterns regardless of the timing or content of spasmodic economic news releases. Therefore, it is extremely important to investigate empirically the existence and nature of these hypothesized market patterns. Fortunately, a great deal of this natural history, or data collecting, work already has been completed. It is quite noteworthy, though not necessarily surprising, that many of the empirically derived forms of technical analysis are identical to the deductively derived forms of Greek thought.

The forms and proportions that Greek thought held most primary were the harmonic ratios of the musical scale and the Golden Mean (which in a few cases are one and the same). Expressed mathematically, the Golden Mean (also called *phi*) is 1.618 to 1 to .618. This proportion also describes the limit ratio between consecutive numbers in the Fibonacci sequence. In geometry, this proportion governs the Golden Section, Golden Rectangle and Golden Spiral (see Chapter 3 in *Elliott Wave Principle)*. Both Pythagoras and Plato apparently felt that this proportion somehow contained "The Secret of the Universe." Newton had the logarithmic spiral engraved on the headboard of his bed, and Kepler, one of the grandest minds ever known, felt that this proportion described virtually all of creation. It is this very proportion that Elliott wave theory claims describes virtually all significant movements in the capital markets.

The history of science provides numerous examples of such "mathematic curiosities" eventually proving to have a very profound real-world basis. Kepler, for example, related the ratio and proportions of the vibratory rate of the notes of the musical scale to the rate of orbit and eccentricity of all the known planets. Not only did this musical model accurately predict every planet's orbit, but because there was a missing "note," Kepler claimed that there was a missing heavenly body. Nearly two centuries later, Ceres, the largest asteroid, was discovered precisely where this quaint ratio analysis suggested it would be.

Similarly, a century ago, Dimitri Mendeleyev noted that the elements, when numbered according to the ratios among their atomic weights, tended to repeat fairly similar properties at every seventh element, just as the notes of the musical scale. Because there were a few gaps, or "missing notes," in the sequence of ratios, he predicted the existence of three completely unknown elements, and described their characteristics. Within a decade, this ratio-based prophecy was fulfilled exactly by the discovery of gallium, germanium and scandium.

Similarly, "Balmer's Ladder," a sequence of harmonic ratios developed more than a century ago by an obscure Swiss mathematics teacher, was considered nothing more than numerology until Niels Bohr demonstrated that these relationships correspond exactly to the intervals of electron shells within the atom. Thus Balmer's ratios, this "quaint mathematic curiosity," became the foundation of modern quantum mechanics.

This story merits some elaboration here because of certain additional similarities between the Balmer sequence and the Fibonacci sequence. Leonardo Fibonacci originally presented the Fibonacci sequence in *Liber Abaci*, the treatise which in 1202 introduced Arabic numbers to the Western world. In this historic work, Fibonacci asked, "How many pairs of rabbits placed in an enclosure can be produced in a single year from one pair of rabbits if each pair gives birth to a new pair each month, starting with the second month?" The answer is 144 pairs, the number of pairs each of the twelve consecutive months being 1, 1, 2, 3, 5, 8, 13, 21, 34, 55, 89 and 144. Each number in the Fibonacci sequence is the sum of the previous two numbers. Once the sequence gets underway, the ratio of any number to the previous one always approximates 1.618. Thus the Fibonacci sequence is the archetype of *gnomonic* expansion — that type of growth that always retains its basic proportionate form irrespective of the magnitude of change. It is, in modern parlance, the ultimate fractal.

A similar, if much less pervasive, fascination attended the sequence of ratios that Balmer discovered in 1885. What fascinated Balmer was the fact that the spectral lines of the element hydrogen followed a music-like sequence of ratios. For example, measured in angstroms, the lines demonstrated a curious, music-like sequence; viz., 5/9, 12/16, 21/25, 32/36, 45/49, 60/64, 77/81. Note that each denominator is a cardinal square in natural succession, and that each numerator is equal to four (4) less than its own denominator. Physicists of the day held that Balmer's sequence was nothing more than meaningless numerology, or a quaint mathematical coincidence. However, this skeptical position was exploded when quantum theorist Bohr proved that these ratios corresponded precisely to the quantum intervals of the electron's "gravic shells" within the atom. Not only did Bohr show that all three of Kepler's Laws of Planetary Motion hold for the electron, but he also demonstrated that electrons can move only in those specific areas pre-identified by Balmer's ratios. Whenever an electron absorbs or emits sufficient energy, it will leave its contemporaneous "shell," or "orbit," but irrespective of *how much* energy it loses or acquires, it must make a quantum jump precisely to another theoretic orbit. It can never meander in between the potential orbits described by Balmer's ratio. This Balmer phenomenon is quite similar to the Fibonacci phenomenon frequently observed to attend market prices. For example, once sufficient energy is built up or dissipated in the market, prices will be forced from their contemporaneous level. But they apparently cannot go just anywhere; instead they tend to jump to the next "quantum" level as described by the Fibonacci sequence. Free-market prices are not, of course, simple electrons, but are instead the net result of an infinitude of forces. Hence prices do not behave with either the consistency or the mathematic precision of Bohr's electrons.[2]

Given the predictive results of the ratio-logical thinking of Kepler, Mendeleyev and Balmer, it would hardly be unprecedented if the *phi* (ϕ)proportion and the Fibonacci sequence, which have already proved useful in prediction, are eventually discovered to have a very profound scientific foundation. We find it particularly interesting to note that recent high resolution X-ray studies of the DNA molecule show that the internal structure of the double helix follows this same Golden Ratio (see Figure 11-1 in *The Wave Principle of Human Social Behavior*). Furthermore, recent studies in neurophysiology suggest that the response times of certain cortical potentials of the human forebrain follow this identical ratio. Since the most fundamental form and functioning of the human organism appear to be organized on the basis of the *phi* proportion, it is not surprising that various human activities, such as bond price behavior, reflect this same property.

Why the *phi* proportion should be ubiquitous in the marketplace and throughout the animate and inanimate universe remains an open question. Conceivably, the formula *a=1.618d* might describe some fundamental attribute of the electrodynamic fields that impose order on living and nonliving systems alike, just as the formulae $F_g = \dfrac{Gm_1 m_2}{d^2}$ and $\dfrac{P_1^2}{P_2^2} = \dfrac{R_1^3}{R_2^3}$ do for gravitation and planetary motion. That question need not concern us now; our concern here is the *fact* that this proportion has been shown to have predictive significance in the capital markets.

Perhaps when we learn more of nature's secrets, the logic behind these observed market phenomena will likewise become clear. The new discipline of chaos theory, with its observations concerning "fractals" and "self-similarity," seems to be addressing much the same phenomena that Elliott theory addresses. Also, the recently emerging science of "complexity" theory, among other things, deals with the phenomenon of "Increasing Returns" in economic systems as opposed to the conventional Law of Diminishing Returns, which underwrites classical theory but which fails to account for significant amounts of capital market behavior. Furthermore, its stated attempt to discover *"the general law of pattern formation in non-equilibrium systems,"*[3] as Goerner explores in Chapter 10, is to a significant degree a formal attempt to explain the verities that market technicians have been describing and applying, if not altogether rigorously, for decades.

Some have argued that while the existence of non-rational forces within the marketplace may be a fascinating premise, actually pursuing such a will-o'-the-wisp is too "unscientific" to be of interest to serious market scholars and money managers. However, the verities of "science" are logically prior and temporally previous to man's discovery of them. Furthermore, the attitude that all these efforts are "unscientific" betrays a fundamental misunderstanding of the true nature of scientific inquiry. Scientific inquiry does not properly begin, as some would tell us, with the collection of hard facts and pure data. Nor does it begin with the projection of indubitable hypotheses, as others would have it. Proper scientific inquiry rather begins with the observation of *a problematic situation,* since it is the nature of the particular problem at hand that must determine what types of data are relevant to the situation and what sorts of hypotheses are appropriate to its solution. It follows that there are as many proper "scientific methods" as there are fundamentally different types of problems. The problem under consideration here— capital market behavior— has been so unsatisfactorily addressed to date as to require particularly unconventional scientific methods. As noted in Chapter 7, the entire modern scientific enterprise is possible only because the Law of Conservation of Momentum applies to physical systems. Since mental states do not obey this law, traditional economic approaches, which are based on it, have severely limited application within an investment context and often are logically untenable.

While the laws that mental states *do* obey are largely unknown, one principle that the human nervous system clearly does follow is the "all-or-none law." This law describes the fact that a neuron will not fire unless its threshold potential is met; but if and when this threshold is reached, the neuron will fire with its maximum potential, irrespective of the absolute energy brought to bear on it. Perhaps something analogous to this all-or-none phenomenon in collective behavior accounts for the tendency of market prices to make quantum leaps from one Fibonacci level to the next. Or perhaps something even more fundamental is at work here. For example, maybe this ratio describes some basic attribute of the electromagnetic fields that maintain order in both living and non-living systems.

The investment problem is different from many other scientific problems. Money management constitutes a perpetual forced option among imperfect alternatives, because even when a manager does nothing, since he is not redeploying his assets, he is implicitly making an active decision to hold them, which is equivalent to a passive decision to repurchase them. Therefore, the money manager must, by definition, act continually, and he must do so in the face of constant, awesome uncertainty. This being the case, incomplete empiric data and partially developed concepts — even probabilistic principles — that would be quite unacceptable in the exact sciences, are unavoidable aspects of investment decision making. Another related aspect of the investment problem is similar to the "multi-body problem" of physics, wherein there is such a tremendous number of constantly changing variables impinging upon a point that it becomes virtually impossible to ascertain the specific effect of any one factor at any one time. The investment problem is unique in that even when the absolute values of individual variables are known, the precise *significance* of these variables at any particular time is never known. So the fact that non-rational market factors are as yet not fully quantified can hardly disqualify them from serious consideration. *Most* of the variables in the investment equation are by their nature nebulous and difficult to quantify.

Another distinctive characteristic of the investment problem—somewhat analogous to what physicists refer to as the Heisenberg Uncertainty Principle—is the fact that the very act of observation affects the result. In the exact sciences, for example, the more often a particular procedure has given a particular result, the greater the probability that the same result will obtain in the future. In the capital markets, however, the very fact that a particular procedure has been successful in the past may increase the probability that this particular procedure will *fail* in the future. The most brilliant stratagems can be rendered counterproductive if a significant number of competing professionals simultaneously attempt to profit from their application. This being the case, exclusively conventional approaches are likely to lead us into an analytic cul-de-sac, because no matter how accurate our calculations or how flawless our logic, if everyone else is making similar deductions at the same time, we are *all* likely to be on a fool's errand. Only if we develop *original* approaches, or apply conventional principles in an *unconventional* way, are we likely consistently to generate excess returns.

Furthermore, and contrary to presumption, highly original notions are often much *safer* than conventional ones because even if these original notions prove false, since the expectation of their being correct has not already been reflected in contemporaneous market prices, the worst likely result would be average returns. However, if a highly *conventional* notion should misfire, the result could be devastating, inasmuch as the belief in its validity has presumably already been incorporated into the price structure of the capital markets.

Because of these and other unique aspects of the investment problem, unique approaches are required. Classic economic theory and traditional fundamental analysis *do* properly address certain aspects of the investment problem. However, they are totally unscientific when dealing with *other* vital aspects of the problem, much as classical mechanics, while providing a valid description of some aspects of physical reality, is incapable of dealing with either its subatomic or macrocosmic aspects. The nature of the investment problem is such as to suggest that rather than being dismissed out of hand, unconventional approaches are precisely where one must direct his attention if he aspires to consistently superior returns. The success of certain technical approaches to market analysis suggests that the adoption of the Greek view of the primacy of formal causes[4] is a prerequisite to achieving those returns.

A Reply to Purported Critiques of Technical Analysis

The appropriate *empiric* position of economic science on technical analysis would seem to be to require tests of the actual success of this methodology. The failure of the professional and academic communities to take this methodology more seriously may be due in part to the impression that the proper tests already have been made and the discipline found wanting. Unfortunately, however, the appropriate tests have not been made, and the prevailing opinion that technical analysis is worthless appears to be based on highly impertinent evidence and grotesquely faulty logic.

For example, one of the alleged bits of evidence against cycle theory is the oft-cited observation, "with two dice you can manufacture what looks like a business cycle." While many seem to believe this pronouncement is saying something meaningful, it is in fact merely an analytic statement, i.e. a statement whose truth follows from the definition of the words that occur in it. By the terms "dice" and "random" numbers, we mean numbers that *can* occur in *any* sequence, and eventually *will* occur in *every* sequence. So, to say that dice can produce a sequence of numbers that mimics the sequence of numbers in an actual price cycle is true by definition. Since the only information this statement contains relates to certain linguistic conventions, it is logically impossible to conclude therefrom anything at all about real world matters of fact. So, this putative criticism of cycle theory is devoid of any scientific significance. A more rational approach to cycles would be to ignore such emotive tautologies and instead to critique those empiric studies that claim to have found statistically significant cyclical patterns in economic data series. Until such analysis is performed and all alleged cycles shown to be spurious, cyclic forecasts of economic data such as interest rates cannot be dismissed.

While there has been relatively little empiric study of temporal patterns in the capital markets, there is voluminous literature regarding the possible existence and potential use of price patterns. Originally, various price filters, serial correlations, runs, autoregressions, first differences of the logarithms, etc. were tested, and the conclusions generally have been that any such patterns that may exist are not of sufficient magnitude to permit investment strategies based thereon to be more profitable than a buy-and-hold strategy. While these early studies were very worthwhile inasmuch as they identified certain investment rules that do not work, the methodologies tested generally were foreign to the actual procedures of technical analysis. Attempts were made to rectify this deficiency by testing some of the principles actually used by market technicians, such as moving averages and relative strength. Even these more nearly pertinent studies, however, are vitiated by the fact that generally only one parameter was tested at a time. Testing various technical measures in isolation is inadequate, because they occur in combination, and the significance of most technical measures derives from their context. For example, many momentum gauges, relative strength parameters, price/moving average disparities, over-bought/ sold oscillators, etc. have contrary implications in bull and bear markets. Therefore, using the same parameters to test a technical rule over several market cycles might indicate the tool to be worthless, whereas the addition of an appropriate independent filter might show it to be quite puissant.

Thus, the validity of most of these academic studies notwithstanding, they imply nothing about technical analysis as actually practiced by competent professionals. Unhappily, many have made the erroneous inference from these studies that technical analysis is not valuable, apparently by applying logic of the following sort:

> Studies prove that following some price patterns is a worthless investment strategy; technical analysis invests by following some price patterns; therefore, technical analysis is worthless investment strategy.

This is an invalid argument, being an example of what logicians call *The Fallacy of the Undistributed Middle*. Clearly the fact that certain price patterns have not proved profitable implies nothing whatsoever about the price patterns technical analysis follows, which might be—and in fact are—something entirely different.

There is, however, one paper that did attempt to address a price pattern that technicians do use and which is important enough to merit special attention here. This paper is Harry V. Roberts' oft-cited and oft-reproduced classic, "Stock Market 'Patterns' and Financial Analysis," which is recognized as one of the cornerstones of the Random Walk Theory. Its aim was to demonstrate that one of the cornerstones of technical analytic theory, the "head-and-shoulders" pattern, can be approximated quite easily by merely randomizing numbers. Based on this exercise, the author suggested that considerable research was called for into alleged market patterns, and this historic work did in fact stimulate unprecedented interest and precipitate voluminous studies. Unfortunately, however, many professionals have mistakenly concluded that Roberts' classic work constitutes some sort of evidence against technical analysis. This is a most egregious error, for several reasons.

In the first place, most technicians would claim that Roberts' random numbers did not produce a technical pattern at all. Since both the preceding sustained trend and the idiosyncratic volume patterns necessary to define a head-and-shoulders formation are missing from Roberts' figure, to call it a technical pattern is to commit the logical fallacy known as *Partis per Toto* i.e. confusing the part for the whole. One could nevertheless argue that even if Roberts' randomized numbers did not actually produce a classic technical pattern, randomized numbers *could* do just that. Unfortunately, such an affirmation would be an analytic statement and, as discussed earlier, necessarily devoid of any factual content at all.

Even if one were to ignore these two logical problems and concede that head-and-shoulders patterns are randomly generated statistical artifacts, it still would not be possible to conclude anything at all about the myriad other technical patterns and methods. To draw such a conclusion would be to fall prey to the *Fallacy of the Undistributed Middle* mentioned above. Unfortunately, however, even a severely limited negative conclusion regarding head-and-shoulders patterns is invalid. Many have concluded that this pattern is a statistical artifact by reasoning roughly as follows:

> Randomizing numbers produces classic technical patterns; capital market price sequences produce classic technical patterns; therefore, capital market prices are random.

This entire line of reasoning is fallacious, as it is an example of the illogical argument known as *The Fallacy of Affirming the Consequent*. The above reasoning is identical to the argument that: *Men are mortal; Socrates is mortal; therefore, Socrates is a man*. Such logic is obviously faulty, since *Socrates* could be a woman or a house cat, or any living system. Just as obviously, *capital market price sequences* logically could be produced by any number of principles other than randomization.

Therefore, to conclude anything whatsoever about the usefulness of technical patterns from Roberts' random numbers is invalid, and the "long tradition" that this exercise "meet(s) academic standards of evidence" and provides a "plausible and persuasive" demonstration "that changes in stock prices (are) random" is incorrect. As discussed earlier, the bulk of the random walk literature, while worthwhile in and of itself, cannot properly be adduced as evidence against the discipline of technical analysis. The prevailing academic belief that "there is now overwhelming evidence to suggest that...technical analysis cannot provide any guidance to the investment manager" may be entirely correct, but it is well to remember that it is just that: a belief. It is a philosophic or religious position, a statement of negative faith. That statement may or may not eventually prove to be correct, but since it derives from improper evidence and false inference, it has no scientific or logical status at all.

[*Editor's Note*: In support of the utility of technical analysis, Montgomery attached to his essay 33 published short-term calls for bond prices dating from March 17, 1981 through September 2, 1983. His table, reproduced below, constitutes his full track record as of the publishing date of the essay. Twenty-nine of his signals were profitable, one produced a loss, and two broke even. He also reported two long-term signals: From an initially bearish position on bond prices, he issued a buy on October 1/2, 1981 and a sell on June 20, 1983.]

RECORD OF SHORT TERM SIGNALS°						
+	SELL	March 17, 1981	+	SELL	August 18, 1982
+	BUY	May 5, 1981	+	BUY	September 2, 1982
+	SELL	June 1, 1981	-	SELL	October 1, 1982
N	BUY	August 3, 1981	+	BUY**	November 1, 1982
+	BUY*	September 9, 1981	+	SELL	November 12, 1982
+	SELL	September 21, 1981	+	BUY	December 13, 1982
+	BUY	September 28, 1981	+	BUY*	January 31, 1983
+	SELL	October 13, 1981	+	SELL#	March 2/3, 1983
+	BUY	October 27, 1981	+	BUY	March 14, 1983
+	SELL	November 12, 1981	+	SELL	April 19, 1983
+	BUY	December 19, 1981	N	BUY	May 31, 1983
+	BUY*	January 21, 1982	+	SELL	June 23, 1983
+	SELL#	March 5/8, 1982	+	BUY**	July 8, 1983
+	BUY	June 7, 1982	+	BUY*	August 11, 1983
N	BUY*	June 21, 1982	+	SELL	August 25, 1983
+	SELL	July 21, 1982	+	BUY	September 2, 1983
+	BUY	August 12, 1982			
			+	Profitable	29
			-	Loss	1
			N	Break-even	3
*Repeat signal		#Signal for futures and cash occured on different days.			
°Based on nearby Treasury Bond Futures, repeat signals ignored.					
**Clients were advised not to trade these signals.					

NOTES

[1] Burr, H. S. and F.S.C. Northrup. (1935). "The Electrodynamic Theory of Life." *Quarterly Review of Biology*, no.10, pp.332-333.

[2] It is premature to assert that prices do not move precisely, as one must be sure to have exhausted all avenues of inquiry along those lines. To the extent that imprecision is found to exist, we would then have to determine whether it resulted from a robustness or variability in collective thought or an imprecision in aggregate market prices as a tool for expressing it.—Ed.

[3] Waldrop, M. Mitchell. (1992). *Complexity: The Science at the Edge of Order and Chaos,* New York: Simon and Schuster, p.299.

[4] See also the discussion of "formological systems" in *The Wave Principle of Human Social Behavior* (1999, New Classics Library).

Chapter 9

FANTASIES AND FRICTIONS
OF FINANCE

by John L. Casti

*A portion of this chapter appeared in a collection of winning
essays sponsored by American Express, London, 1991.
It is reprinted by permission of Oxford University Press.*

Summary

Virtually all conventional theoretical models of economic phenomena and, perforce, all mainline academic models of finance, rest
upon a metaphor drawn from classical physics. The discussion given
here shows why such mathematical and computational pictures of the
world of finance — including even the newest metaphors from modern physics involving such things as chaotic processes — are forever
doomed to fail as valid portrayals of the way *real* investors behave and
the way *real* financial markets operate. The conclusion emerging from
these deliberations is that financial modelers would be far better off
consulting a biology book than a physics text for their metaphorical
inspirations — finance is just too complex for physics.

1. Models, Muddles and Money

It's one of the small ironies of history that in 1699 Isaac Newton
was appointed Master of the Royal Mint, a position from which he
ferociously pursued counterfeiters for many years. Ironic, since were
Newton alive today, there's little doubt that he would be equally relentless
in hunting down the business-school professors who have so debased
Newton's own mechanistic view of the world by assuming that that's how
the world's financial markets operate. When you read *The Wall Street
Journal* and then turn to the *Journal of Finance*, it doesn't take much of

a genius to realize that there's a Grand Canyon-sized gap between what the professors are saying and what's actually happening out there on the street. So let's face reality: There's something dramatically wrong with the conventional wisdoms of academic finance. In this chapter I want to argue that the root cause of this gap is the unhealthy preoccupation of market modelers with the paradigms of physics-classical and modern.

The Newtonian assumption from which everything else flows is that all observable phenomena emerge as the result of the interaction of material particles. So Newton's world is a world of particles and forces. Since an understanding of this world is crucial to the theme of this essay, let me briefly sketch the outline of the *Weltanschauung* bequeathed to us by Newton.

Assume we have a system Σ consisting of N material particles. Let's agree to let the quantity $x_i(t)$ represent the position of the ith particle at time t, with the velocity of this particle then being just $\ddot{x}_i(t)$, the time derivative of the position. Suppose now that we are interested in some property Q of the system, say its temperature, color, shape or whatever. Newton made the astonishing claim that *any* such property Q could be expressed as a function of the positions and velocities of the particles, i.e.,

$$Q = Q(x_i(t), \dot{x}_i(t)), \qquad i = 1,2,..., N.$$

In particular, if our property Q happens to be the acceleration of, say, the first particle, then we are immediately led to Newton's Second Law, $a = \ddot{x}_i(t) = F/m$, where m is the particle's mass and F is a force. Cagey as ever, Newton never really specified the exact nature of this mysterious "force" F, stating simply "I make no hypotheses."

Let's look for a moment at some of the not-so-hidden assumptions built-in to this wildly simplistic view of the way and why of things.

• *Conservative:* As the particles career about on Newton's billiard table, the overall system neither gains nor loses energy to/from the external environment. In particular, there are no frictional effects and the system runs-on forever.

• *Homogeneous:* The Newtonian particles are indistinguishable from one another and, in fact, have no observable attributes whatsoever other than their mass, position and velocity.

• *Indestructible:* Particles are neither created nor destroyed.

• *Path Independent:* The value of any quantity Q at time $t + \Delta t$ depends only on the value of Q at time t. In other words, the system has no memory.

- *Absolute:* There is no built-in upper limit to the velocity of a Newtonian particle; neither is there any lower limit to the "action" of a particle.
- *Equilibrium-oriented:* While not explicitly built-in to the Newtonian setup, there is a strong presumption that the kind of systems described by Newton are stable. In fact, the presumption is that the long-run behavior of these Newtonian systems is either a periodic orbit or, if frictional effects are introduced, a single global equilibrium point to which all motions are drawn as $t \rightarrow \infty$. A consequence of this assumption is that the system always moves so as to arrive at a state of minimal energy. In particular, the particle trajectories remain bounded, much like balls on a billiard table, and don't fly off to infinity.

So these are the ground rules in Newton's game of particles and forces. And, in fact, it has become something of a cottage industry and a prescription for Nobel prizes in the physics community to relax one or another of these constraints. For example, imposing a finite universal speed limit on particle velocity led Einstein to the special theory of relativity. Similarly, Max Planck assumed a finite lower bound on a particle's action, which led to quantum theory. In yet another direction, Ilya Prigogine dropped both the conservative and equilibrium assumptions, the end result being his theory of far-from-equilibrium dissipative processes — and a Nobel prize in chemistry.

With these successes, it's hard to argue with Newton's intellectual treasure chest, at least in physics. And it's certainly defensible to probe the limits to which this billiard-ball paradigm can be extended to other areas of life. But in the case of finance, what's good for the goose is definitely not good for the gander, too. What works for physics, sad to say, just doesn't seem to work for finance — despite what the professors say. To see why, let's first see how the current conventional wisdom in academic finance matches up to this Newtonian setup.

2. The Physics of Finance

To paraphrase Oscar Wilde, jargon is the last refuge of scoundrels. More specifically, it's the barrier behind which every special-interest group hides the poverty of its message. And the academic financial community is no exception to this venerable principle. So let me briefly go over the primary buzzwords forming the backbone of the conventional wisdom in academic finance. We'll then see how these watchwords of finance are simply translations of the same concepts sketched above for the Newtonian paradigm of mechanics.

• *Efficiency:* By an efficient stock market, financial theorists mean one in which any piece of new information coming into the market is immediately assimilated and reflected in stock prices. Depending on the assumptions made about the nature of the information, various "random walk" theories (RWT) of price behavior have arisen. If the information available is only past and current prices, then we have what's called the *weak RWT.* On the other hand, if the information set consists of any *publicly-available* information, we then have what's called the *semi-strong RWT.* The semi-strong RWT more often goes under the rubric the *efficient markets hypothesis (EMH).* Finally, if *all* information, public or private, is admissible, then we come to the *strong RWT.* Each of these random-walk theories holds that there can be no trading system based upon the corresponding type of information that will allow one to systematically outperform the market, taken as a whole (measured by, say, something like the Dow Jones Industrial Average).

• *Rationality:* Perfect rationality — finance style — means not only that all information relevant to the price of a stock is processed objectively, instantaneously and without error, but also that investors act so as to maximize their marginal utility. So in arriving at a decision to buy or sell, a rational investor has "properly" taken into account all relevant information (we'll see later what that *might* mean).

• *Homogeneity:* This assumption means that all investors are alike; they have the same desires (to maximize their take) and the same attitudes toward risk.

• *Stability:* The standing stability presumption in finance is that price of any security is always moving toward a single, stable equilibrium price at which all the buyers and sellers in the market are satisfied.

• *Memory-free:* "The market has no memory" is the catch-phrase describing this assumption. It means simply that the path the stock's price took in getting to its current level is irrelevant in assessing what tomorrow's price will be. In mathematical terms, such a process is termed "Markovian," implying that the stock price at the next moment is determined solely from its current price. In short, whatever information about the past is relevant to the future is already built-in to the current price.

Table 1 shows how these properties of the world of finance match-up to the features of Newton's world presented earlier.

Finance		Physics
efficiency	↔	conservative, path-independent, absolute, minimal energy
rationality	↔	path-independent, absolute
homogeneity	↔	homogeneous, indestructible
stability	↔	conservative, minimal energy
memory-free	↔	path-independent

Table 1. Finance versus Physics

From the above table, it's evident that the boundaries between the concepts finance theorists find useful and those employed by physicists are not an exact match. So, for instance, we find the single (and singular) finance concept of "efficiency" tied-in with both path independence and absolutism in physics. This is because efficiency assumes that all relevant past information is already reflected in the current stock price. So, in principle, an unlimited amount of past information has been processed by the market, and how the price arrived at its current level is irrelevant to determining where it will go next.

It goes without saying that gurus of academic finance continue to cling to one or more of the fantasies outlined above. Since the natural forum in which disagreements on such matters are debated is the academic conference and symposium, let me now shift into my own fantasy mode for a bit. The following imaginary dialogue[1] states far better than any dry, pedantic account what's at issue in this paradigm crisis in finance and what I think needs to be done to resolve it.

3. A Dialogue on Two World Systems

The Scene

EVENT: The annual meeting of the Transworld Society for Science, Truth and Beauty in Modeling

DATE: Sometime in the very near future

SETTING: A panel discussion on "Mathematical and Computer Modeling of Economic and Financial Processes — Science or Alchemy?"

THEME: Is physics a suitable metaphor upon which to base models aimed at explaining and/or predicting the behavior of price movements on speculative markets?

Dramatis Personae

• **Prof. Ransom ("Randy") Walker:** guru of mainline academic finance and devotee of efficient markets and rational expectations; renegade theoretical physicist turned financial analyst

• **Mr. D.O.W. Jones:** representative from the Association of International Investment Fund Managers; training in philosophy, with an MBA in finance

• **Prof. Max U. Till:** Viennese-born and educated behavioral psychologist; well known for his experimental work on the identification of how real people make real financial decisions in real market environments

• **Col. Hy R. Fees:** big-time stocks-and-commodities broker; a man with no formal academic training whatsoever, but an expert in making "the right connections" (and lots of money)

• **Dame Bea Wright:** avant-garde systems thinker, modeler, intellectual gadfly and general iconoclast; originally trained as a mathematician and computer scientist, but now working as a theoretical biologist and philosopher of science

• **Panel Moderator**

The Panel Discussion

Moderator: Near the end of the Second Epilogue of *War and Peace,* Tolstoy remarks that, "Only by taking an infinitesimally small unit for observation (the differential of history, that is, the individual tendencies of men) and attaining to the art of integrating them (that is, finding the sum of these infinitesimals) I can we hope to arrive at the laws of history." Of course, in writing this passage Tolstoy was merely echoing the scientific attitude of his day, one anchored firmly in the clockwork picture of the progression of worldly affairs bequeathed to us by Newton, and enshrined in Newton's famous laws of motion governing the behavior of material bodies. But to my eye it looks as if by substituting the word "finance" for "history," Tolstoy's statement would serve equally well as a research manifesto for the mathematical and computer modeling branch of the academic finance community. Perhaps Professor Walker would care to open our discussion by commenting on this?

Prof. Walker: I don't think any of us here would deny that all economic activity ultimately rests on the "individual tendencies of men," to use the phrase from Tolstoy's elegant formulation. And it is certainly a truism that the sum total of all these individual decisions and actions is exactly what ends up determining the price of a share of stock or a barrel of oil. But financial modelers have come a long way since the time of Newton — and since the time of Tolstoy, too, for that matter.

In the 1960s financial theorists discovered earlier work by the Frenchman Louis Bachelier, who around the turn of the century was the first to study mathematically the properties of price changes of a speculative commodity. Bachelier's ideas led to what we now call the "random walk hypothesis." This is the claim that price changes for any commodity fluctuate randomly. As a result, theorists claim that a history of such price information cannot serve as the basis for any kind of trading scheme, or rule, that can consistently outperform the market as a whole, measured by, say, something like the S&P 500 index of stock prices on the New York exchanges. "Souping up" the random-walk theory by adding the notion of an "efficient market," essentially a behavioral assumption about the way investors make decisions, modern financial theorists have strengthened Bachelier's ideas into the so-called *efficient markets hypothesis* (EMH). Put simply, the EMH states that no publicly-available information of any kind can form the basis for a trading rule that will regularly beat the market over a long period of time.

Moderator: But doesn't the EMH rest on assumptions that are just translations into financial terms of many of the very same assumptions underlying the Newtonian models of how material objects like planets and billiard balls behave?

Prof. Walker: Speaking as a former physicist, I can hardly deny that. The hypothesis of market efficiency is basically an equilibrium assumption, saying that investors behave so that any imbalance in supply and demand generated by new information coming into the market is immediately counteracted. This kind of negative feedback effect then acts to generate price movements that tend to push prices toward a single, global, stable equilibrium level at which both buyers and sellers are satisfied. And such a single, stable equilibrium is definitely a central aspect of the Newtonian picture of the movement of material bodies.

Furthermore, the EMH assumes that all investors act in a purely rational manner on the basis of their expectations of future prices. More specifically, the assumption is that each investor forms an estimate of tomorrow's price, and then acts today so as to maximize his or her expected marginal return. So, speaking loosely, you might say that the rational expectations assumption is a finance-world version of the principle of minimal energy governing the behavior of a system of Newtonian particles.

And, of course, the essence of the whole EMH idea is that finance is not a historical process, in the sense that the particular path taken in arriving at today's price has no influence whatsoever on what will happen tomorrow- just like tomorrow's position of the Moon is determined only by where it is today and not how it came to be in this location. So if you want to think that these features of the EMH suggest a kind of physics-envy on the part of academic finance theorists, you have my blessing. After all, why shouldn't we base our models on those of physics? They are by far the most well-developed, coherent and successful set of theories we humans have ever created for describing in scientific terms the way the world seems to work.

* * *

Remarks

Put more technically, Bachelier's results focused on the properties of the *differences* in stock prices rather than the absolute price levels themselves (the logarithms of these differences, actually). So if we let P_t represent the stock price at time t, what Bachelier considered was the quantities $s_t = \log P_{t+1} - \log P_t$, $t = 0, 1, \dots$ These logarithmic differences give rise to the time series of numbers $S = \{s_0, s_1, s_2, \dots\}$. Bachelier drew three principle conclusions about this time series:

A. *Independence.* The individual entries in the series S, the numbers S_i, are statistically independent of each other. Thus, knowledge of the numbers $\{S_j\}$ for all $j < t$ is of no help in predicting the value S_t. This conclusion forms the basis of what Professor Walker called the "random-walk hypothesis." In our earlier terminology, it is actually the weak RWT since the available information is assumed to be only past prices.

B. *Stationarity:* This means that the statistical properties of any sufficiently long subsequence from S will look the same as the properties from any other subsequence of similar length. So the particular point in time when you start taking data is irrelevant, as over a fixed time interval the market will look exactly the same regardless of when that interval begins. An important implication of this conclusion is that the underlying market price-setting mechanism remains the same at all times. In short, there are no structural changes in the way the market goes about setting prices. Of course, the reader will note that this conclusion flies straight in the face of the idea that the future behavior of prices depends on the particular path the prices took in arriving at their current level.

C. *Normality:* Bachelier claimed that if you plot the set of numbers S in a histogram, what will come out is the familiar bell-shaped curve of the Gaussian distribution. Moreover, this curve will have its peak, i.e., mean, at zero. So the most likely price change is no change at all! Moreover, since the gaussian distribution is perfectly symmetric, the likelihood of a boom or bust of a given magnitude is exactly the same.

So these were Bachelier's conclusions. But it should be noted that they were not arrived at as the end result of an air-tight mathematical *proof*. Rather, they were more in the way of empirical relations distilled from Bachelier's studies of actual price histories of government bonds on the Paris Bourse. And, in fact, part of the indictment against mainline finance is that each and every one of Bachelier's conclusions is contradicted by the way actual markets seem to behave. But more of this later.

It's also of interest here to note Professor Walker's observation about the negative feedback tending to push the market to an overall equilibrium. This is exactly the kind of reaction that in physics corresponds to what we normally call "friction." That is, a force that tends to oppose the system's current direction of motion. I'll return to this point below. But now let's get back to the debate.

* * *

Mr. Jones: Maybe these theories do a good job of describing the worlds of black holes, planets, quarks and billiard balls. But if you'll pardon the neologism, those Newtonian notions don't seem to fit my world of *Realfinanz,* at all. In this world I see as much irrationality and 'groupthink' as I do cool, calculated, rational behavior. Personally, I think this rational expectations business is a lot of abstract "p in the sky" invented by you professors of finance to debate at academic conventions and write scholarly articles about. I don't think it makes one bit of contact with the way things actually work on the floor of the exchange.

Col. Fees: Hrumph! Hrumph! I dare say old boy I'm forced to agree with you. Some of my clients are real boffins, frightfully good chaps with numbers, formulas and that sort of thing. And some of them have told me about various stock market anomalies, things like the Value Line enigma, the low price/earnings effect and the small-firms phenomenon, each of which certainly seems to put the lie to the EMH. Why, one of my American clients even says he can forecast the long-term movement of the market using the outcome of their Super Bowl football game, whatever that is. Some sort of American rugby I gather, not real football at all. The fellow's slightly barmy, if you ask me. Nevertheless, he swears that this Super Bowl indicator works over 90 percent of the time. But even if it doesn't, I can hardly think of a more irrational scheme for betting, err...I mean investing, on the market. How can football scores have anything to do with stock prices? Sounds like a lot of claptrap to me. Complete rubbish!

* * *

Remarks

Here we come to a second appearance of what might be termed "friction" in the business of finance. Implicit in the EMH are the assumptions that: (1) information is processed without error or mis-interpretation, (2) information is processed instantaneously, (3) all information relevant to a stock's price is taken into account, and (4) investors act rationally. *All* of these hypotheses are open to question, especially the last, as Colonel Fees's remarks about the Super Bowl Indicator illustrate. Thus, if we think of friction as being that which acts to generate inefficiency in the market, then the failure of anyone of the foregoing assumptions constitutes a type of friction in the market.

Consider, for a moment, the assumption of rationality. The bedrock assumption upon which academic finance rests is the so-called *rational expectations hypothesis.* This principle states that, *on the average,* the investor's subjective estimate of a market indicator like the S&P 500 will equal its true value. So the rational investor asks himself, "What price can I expect that will make everything correct, on the average, if all investors anticipate that price?" He then makes his decision to buy or sell on the basis of this estimate of the price. Since this rationality hypothesis is so important in academic finance, let's dress it up in slightly more formal clothes.

Let I_t be the information available at time t, and let X_{t+1} be a random variable representing the level of the S&P 500 index at time $t+1$. We want to form a rational expectation of the quantity X_{t+1}. Since a rational investor will use the information available to form this estimate, let $E\,[X_{t+1}\mid I_t]$ denote the expected value of the S&P 500 at time $t+1$ conditioned on the information available at time t, i.e., conditioned on I_t. Then we can write the error in our forecast as

$$\text{forecast error} = e_{t+1} = X_{t+1} - E\,[X_{t+1}\mid I_t].$$

The rational expectations hypothesis connects the above conditional expectation generated by using the true (but unknown) probability distribution governing the market with subjective estimates of the same quantity made by investors. If we let X_{t+1}^{exp} denote the subjectively-derived estimate, then the entire rational expectations idea can be compactly expressed as

$$\{\text{subjective expectation} = X_{t+1}^{exp} = E\,[X_{t+1} \mid I_t] = \text{true}$$
$$\text{conditional expectation}\}.$$

In particular, using these ideas about conditional expectations, we can conveniently rephrase the weak random-walk theory as

today's price = the conditional expectation of tomorrow's price.

Thus, we see that the change in price between today and tomorrow is analogous to a forecast error. We'll see more about the rationality hypothesis later. But from what has been said already, I think it's clear that any kind of irrationality in the market acts analogously to friction so as to impede the orderly progression of prices to the level that the rational expectations hypothesis dictates.

* * *

Moderator: Hmm, yes. Ah...thank you very much, Colonel Fees. Let me shift the discussion for a moment to one of the most exciting new scientific ideas to hit the world of theoretical finance since the random-walk theory. Of course, I'm referring to the claim that price changes follow what the mathematicians call a "chaotic" rule. A lot of edge-of-the-frontier financial thinkers currently seem to believe that there really do exist definite rules, or recipes, according to which price histories are generated in a fixed, even deterministic way. But the problem is that whatever the precise form of these rules may be, the result of applying such a rule to past prices leads to a chaotic, "incompressible" sequence of numbers. So, although a definite rule for price changes may indeed exist, we could never hope to make use of it in any practical way to predict the future course of price movements.

Mr. Jones: Why not? If we know the rule, then it should be straightforward to employ it to calculate what the markets will be doing next.

Moderator: The reason why such a chaotic rule cannot be applied to past price changes in order to predict future ones is that the outcome of following such a rule is pathologically sensitive to any errors we make in measuring the past price information or in carrying out the computations called for by the rule. In the language of physics, this kind of prescription for price changes is unstable in the worst possible way. So even if we knew the exact form of the rule (which we most assuredly do not), since data is almost always known imprecisely and computations are carried out only to a fixed degree of precision, the predictions obtained from following this kind of chaotic rule rapidly degenerate to meaningless nonsense. Ironically, this unpredictability of price changes is just what the random-walk theory claims, too — but for very different reasons. However, even if there is some magical chaotic rule that really is the one true mechanism by which market prices fluctuate, I still wonder how it fits in with the deeper issue of whether physics —classical or chaotic — is a suitable metaphor upon which to build valid models of the behavior of financial markets. I know that Dame Wright holds some rather definite views on this matter.

Dame Wright: Indeed. To mathematically represent price changes with a model displaying chaotic behavior, thereby thinking you're making progress in financial modeling, is like thinking you're making progress in getting to the Moon by going out into your garden and climbing a tree. Both show the same singular lack of understanding of the basic nature of the problem.

Chaotic dynamical processes depart in no essential way from the Newtonian paradigm of a clockwork universe. Their only novel feature, and the source of all the recent brouhaha about "chaos" in the popular and scientific press, is that they display a new type of long-run behavior quite unlike that shown by more traditional dynamical processes.

Classical Newtonian systems have two types of long-run behavior: (1) an equilibrium point of the type a marble rolling around inside a soup bowl ends up at, or (2) a periodic orbit like the path the Earth takes in its annual tour around the Sun.

In addition to these classical types of "attractors," which were known even in Newton's time, chaotic processes can show a third type of long-run behavior called a "strange attractor." Instead of being points or closed orbits, strange attractors look a lot like a bowlful of spaghetti. This means that small, perhaps unmeasurable — or even unknowable — disturbances to the system can push the system trajectory from moving along one strand of spaghetti to motion along another. And in this way the process goes off onto an entirely different course of behavior. As our moderator already mentioned, it's this almost pathological type of sensitivity to disturbances that gives rise to the great difficulties we have in predicting what a chaotic system will do next. But the underlying framework is still resolutely Newtonian — and in exactly the sense we spoke of earlier. All that's been added to Newton's picture is this third type of attractor.

* * *

Remarks

Suppose for the sake of argument we have a market in which the price P_t of a stock at time t is give by the following rule:

$$P_{t+1} = P_t + x_t - \tfrac{1}{2}$$

where the quantity x_t satisfies the logistic equation

$$x_{t+1} = ax_t(1 - x_t), \quad 0 \le a \le 4, \quad t = 0, 1, \dots .$$

So in this market tomorrow's price just equals today's price plus a deterministic fluctuation represented by the quantity x_t (the factor $-\tfrac{1}{2}$ is thrown in to ensure that the price changes are always between $\pm \tfrac{1}{2}$ It's well known that if $a > 3.82...$, the logistic equation displays behavior that is observationally indistinguishable from a purely random process.

In that case, the price fluctuations in this market will also be observationally random. Now we can ask if knowledge of the price history for this security in any way helps predict the movement of future prices. If so, the market is not efficient.

Applying standard statistical tests to a price history $P = \{P_0, P_1, P_2, ...\}$ from the above market, we are led to the conclusion that the market is efficient. Clearly, we can make a lot of money in such a market. If we know that the fluctuation mechanism is the deterministic logistic law above and not a true stochastic process, then we can use that knowledge to predict future prices with great accuracy. The question for real markets is the following: Given a price history P, can we determine whether or not P was generated by a deterministic mechanism as above or is stochastically random?

The jury still seems to be out on the matter of whether chaos is lurking in these kinds of financial time series. In extensive summaries of the situation up to 1991, William Brock and Blake LeBaron have concluded in [1-3] that while there appears to be some structure in the data P that conventional statistical tests are missing, the evidence for predictability of returns is still rather weak. This conclusion supports Dame Wright's claim that chaos in the cause of stock-price prediction is still a very dicey business indeed.

* * *

Prof. Walker: Perhaps Dame Wright would care to enlighten us by spelling out just what she thinks a proper, 21st-century non-Newtonian framework for modeling financial processes should look like?

Dame Wright: I'm glad you asked that question, Professor Walker. Earlier you told us that EMH-oriented financial theorists regard finance as a non-historical science. I often wonder how professors of finance can make such statements with a straight face. It doesn't take much by way of deep analysis of the literature or detailed study of the behavior of actual markets to see that this can't possibly be the case. Future price changes are dramatically affected by the particular path a market has taken in getting to its present level. For example, if the S&P 500 index stands at 370 today, it's ludicrous to think that tomorrow's level doesn't depend in crucially important ways on exactly what path events took leading up to the index being at this level. I think anyone with even a modicum of street smarts will tell you that if the 370 level is reached in a climate of steadily rising interest rates and unemployment, that's a totally different story than seeing the index at 370 against a background of declining interest rates and increasing consumer confidence. The big run-up in stock prices in early 1991 following the Gulf War is a perfect example illustrating the point. Of course, EMH advocates have constructed many devious schemes to try to circumvent this glaring deficiency in their financial *Weltanschauung*. But you can't sweep the dirt under the rug forever. Eventually you've got to toss it into the trash barrel. And that means creating a modeling paradigm that's specifically designed for the peculiarities of financial markets and human beings, not billiard balls and planets. So the first feature a non-Newtonian modeling paradigm for finance should display is some kind of provision for path-dependence in its descriptive framework.

Mr. Jones: But what about things like market crashes, tulip manias and all the other situations in which rapid, discontinuous shifts in prices occur? Don't you think something like the chaos-type models might be the best way to account scientifically for these kinds of booms and busts?

Dame Wright: Not necessarily. Any dynamical process, chaotic or otherwise, that admits both stable and unstable long-run behaviors can give rise to such rapid, jerky kinds of shifts under appropriate circumstances. And, in fact, if you give me a set of price changes, I'll give you back an infinite set of rules (i.e., models), *all* of which will reproduce your price history exactly. Good models of reality give us genuine *insight* into that reality, not just good agreement with what's been observed. And the business of science is knowing the why of things, not just the what or even the when. So any type of recipe for price movements that merely agrees with observed past price histories is very far from being a "good" model, at least in a scientific sense.

Prof. Walker: But, but...

Dame Wright: Please allow me to finish. I'm not saying that these chaos-based models are necessarily on the wrong track; I'm saying simply that they don't as yet make explicit provision for the sort of *explanatory* features that a good mathematical reflection of market reality should display. Or, at least, what a model should contain if it's to give us any genuine insight into what's happening in these markets and why. For example, not only are the current models inherently non-historical, they are also pitifully inadequate when it comes to their built-in assumptions about the psychology of market participants, as both Mr. Jones and Col. Fees have already mentioned in connection with the rational expectations fairy tale.

* * *

Remarks

The claims advanced here regarding the path-dependence of price changes can be taken as a refutation of Bachelier's stationarity assumption. In short, the claim is that it does matter when you start taking data in creating a prediction scheme. Market structures and fashions *do* change, and if you want to outperform the market your scheme cannot ignore these facts.

We can illustrate this point by noting, first of all, that the kind of discontinuities we see in stock prices imply a system with multiple equilibria. But this fact, in turn, strongly suggests a system with positive feedbacks. Furthermore, once random events select a particular path, like on the 'bowlful of spaghetti' strange attractor mentioned by Dame Wright, the choice may become locked-in regardless of the attractiveness of alternatives.

A good example of this "lock-in" phenomenon noted by W. Brian Arthur [4-5] is the videocassette recorder. Initially, the VCR market had two comparably-priced formats: Sony Betamax and VHS. Each format could realize increasing returns as its market share increased, since large numbers of, say, VHS recorders would encourage video stores to stock more VHS films, thereby enhancing the value of owning a VHS recorder and leading more people to buy one. So in this way a small increase in market share would improve the competitive position of VHS, helping it further increase its share. In short, positive feedback.

By way of contrast to the unstable, multiple-equilibria systems generated by positive feedback like that above, we have the classical single-equilibrium, stable systems of classical economics and finance. Economic theory says that two competing technologies in such a system will eventually move so as to share the market in a predictable proportion that best exploits the potential of each. It's manifestly evident, I think, which of these two possibilities offers the best paradigm for financial markets.

The matter of which equilibria the market is trying to move toward also sheds light of a different color on the matter of frictional effects. In physics, it's the frictional forces that cause the dissipation of energy that ultimately results in the system state moving onto one or another of the possible attractors. The classical supply-demand picture governing the How of prices would see the frictional force as being just the counter-balancing effect of a buyer and a seller negotiating a price at which each would be satisfied.

But the positive feedback effects noted above tell a quite different tale. In such a market, the forces driving the system from the domain of attraction of one equilibrium to another are nothing as substantial as a buyer-seller negotiation. Rather, they can be (and usually are) such evanescent events as a publicly-visible guru pontificating on the state of a certain stock or the public becoming disenchanted over the state of a country's economic situation. Or it could even be something as capricious and short-lived as a comment by the Chairman of the Federal Reserve or a rumored assassination attempt. In short, almost any snippet of information, however minor, could act as a trigger to set the market off onto an entirely different course, depending on whether the market is poised on the boundary separating one domain of attraction from another.

As for the matter of models and explanations, Dame Wright has hit upon the crucial point that a good model of the behavior of speculative markets would be more than a "machine" for making predictions. Such a model must somehow encapsulate what we see as the causal pathways leading from the way investors process information in arriving at an investment decision to the way those decisions actually get transformed into a change of price in the security. It is definitely *not* sufficient just to have some kind of rule like the Super Bowl Indicator, that's merely *correlated* with shifts in the market. Unless we can trace out the causal path leading from the football field to Wall Street, such a rule fails completely as an explanation of market behavior.

* * *

Moderator: You've raised a vitally important point regarding the way real-life investors behave when faced with real financial decisions. Professor Till is well known for his ingenious experiments aimed at determining just exactly how these real investors do in fact behave when hard cash is on the line. Could you please tell us about some of your findings, Professor?

Prof. Till: Ja. It is my pleasure. We have built a mini-exchange in our laboratory mit students playing on this market with real money. What we have discovere is that speculative "bubbles" come always, even when traders know the market price is far above the fundamental stock value. These bubbles, they are caused by inexperienced and overeager traders. When we try to remove these bubbles by adding futures trading, margin buying, short selling and rules to stop trading when the market falls by a certain amount — what the press calls "circuit breakers" — we find that only futures trading reduces the size and duration of these bubbles. It is funny that circuit-breaker rules actually make these bubbles bigger and last longer — before the big crash.

Col. Fees: Jolly good, Professor. Maybe your results will convince the SEC and other market meddlers that the brokers were right after all, and that these circuit-breaker rules only make markets more volatile, not less.

Mr. Jones: Tell us, Professor, what have you discovered about the behavior patterns of individual traders?

Prof. Till: We have discovered that traders get carried away in rising markets, bidding prices up instead of buying on fundamentals like price/earnings ratios or expected dividends.

We also made a very important empirical discovery. We discovered that individuals do not maximize utility in the way economists think. Standart theory tells us that an individual makes choices to maximize marginal utility. This means that choices are made so that we tend toward an equilibrium state in which equal margins of satisfaction come from each possible activity. This is the principle of maximal marginal utility. We find this assumption is completely wrong.

Our experiments show that traders tend to maximize *average* utility, not marginal. What this means is that they use a non-standard formula to discount time. Standard theory says time is discounted at a constant rate; we find that time is discounted at a *hyperbolic* rate. So rewards not only take on different values at different times in the future, they lose value at different rates too. This kind of discounting predicts that traders will initially act rationally; but eventually they will fail to do so.

Mr. Jones: But why would traders follow such a discounting rule? It seems that by doing this they are acting against their own selfish interests, giving up gains that they could have received through maximizing marginal returns in favor of the lower returns they get from this hyperbolic discounting scheme, which maximizes only their average utility.

Prof. Till: Ja. This is the key question. Hyperbolic discounting is nonoptimal — maybe! The problem is with how you measure what is optimal. We think that the solution is that it is much easier to calculate average utility than marginal. So we believe that while marginals are needed for truly rational behavior, they are hard to compute. Most people lack the information and analytical power to compute them reliably. Also, these marginals, they are very unstable; a small mistake in the data or in the computation, it leads to a big error in the end result. So we think that over the millennia evolution has favored the computation of average utility, not marginal. This means that investors, they do not act like rational expectations theory says.

Moderator: So would you conclude, Professor, that another crucially important feature that a new framework for financial modeling should incorporate is some replacement for the rational expectations hypothesis?

Prof. Till: Jawohl! What we need is some new way to represent how traders really form expectations of the future.

* * *

Remarks

To re-state Professor Till's point, empirical evidence shows that real people just do not behave in the way standard economic theory says they should. Not only do they not act so as to maximize their marginal utility, they also place undo emphasis on short-term payoffs. To illustrate, suppose the winner of a lottery is given the choice between a $100 prize to be received today and a $120 prize to be received in one week. Empirical study shows that a large number of people when faced with this choice take the immediate $100 prize, even when it is guaranteed that the money will be put in escrow and delivered faithfully in one week.

A person who chooses the $100 prize is implicitly using a discount rate of at least 20 percent per week. But now suppose the same person is asked if he will take $100 today or $1,300,000 a year from today. Almost without exception, people choose the larger amount. But rational-choice theory would argue that the right choice is still to take the $100, since $1,300,000 discounted at 20 percent per week for a year is only $99.20.

The problem with standard utility-maximization theory stems from its formula for discounting time. Since the theory assumes that behavior is always consistent with underlying preferences, it requires that time be discounted at a constant rate. But experience with lottery winners and others shows that people don't discount time this way, at all. Rather, rewards have different values at different times. Constant-rate discounting says that if the perceived value of a future reward declines by 20 percent next week, then it must do the same for *every* week. A hyperbolic discounting scheme, however, predicts that next week's 20 percent rate will give way to progressively lower rates as time goes on.

So to return to the lottery example, when the lag between the prizes is only one week, then the large prize shrinks by 20 percent while the small one has not shrunk at all. On the other hand, if the lag is one year the two prizes will have effectively the same value. Thus hyperbolic discounting says that the right choice is to go for the larger prize.

So what Professor Till is trying to tell us is that the single hyperbolic discounting scheme predicts the lottery winner's preference for the larger of two deferred prizes, as well as explaining his quick grab for the smaller of two more-or-less immediate payoffs. Thus, in this one discounting rule we can account for both an initial determination to act rationally as well as for the eventual failure to do so.

* * *

Dame Wright: Perhaps a helpful way to think about this matter is to say we need to inject a form of self-reference into the paradigm for finance. I think even Professor Walker would agree that every trader has some kind of internal mental model of both the market and himself, which he runs on a time scale faster than real time in order to generate his individual expectation for the future. Our non-Newtonian view of financial markets should explicitly incorporate these self-referential models somehow, as well as include learning procedures by which these models get updated. The rational expectations hypothesis neatly does away with this problem by the crude expedient of just assuming that all traders use the same maximal-marginal-return model for the future and, moreover, that the model is never updated. But we know that not everyone has the same attitudes toward risk, nor do people fail to learn from past experience. So again we find the conventional wisdom of the EMH being more of an academic fantasy than an account of how the players act in any real financial market.

Prof. Walker: Naturally, we always simplify real-life situations for the sake of arriving at a formulation of the problem that we can work with. It would be totally impractical, if not impossible, for our models to account explicitly for every trader's personal picture of the market and himself. Scientific theories and models are always simplifications of the real thing. And the rational expectations hypothesis is just such a simplification.

Dame Wright: I think it was Einstein who once remarked, "A theory should be as simple as possible — but no simpler." By this, I think what he meant was that what separates a good theory from a bad one lies in the choice of the features of the real situation to include in the theory and what aspects to leave out. In my opinion, the traditional EMH-based models of financial markets, including the ones based on chaotic dynamics, end up throwing out the baby with the bathwater.

Moderator: Well, I see our time is running short. So I'm afraid I'll have to bring this very thought-provoking discussion to a close. But before doing so, let me try to summarize what's been said here today.

My sense of the discussion is that the conventional physics-based paradigm for modeling the price changes on speculative markets is in deep trouble, epistemologically speaking at least. Some radically new framework, or paradigm, seems to be called for that would, at the bare minimum, incorporate the following features: (1) positive (i.e., deviation-amplifying) feedbacks, thereby admitting the possibility of processes having both stable and unstable modes of long-run behaviors, (2) path-dependence of price changes, (3) new behavioral assumptions replacing the notion of strict rationality, and (4) the self-referential, anticipatory models of individual traders.

When I look at this list of desiderata, I can't help thinking that what we're talking about here is a modeling metaphor that's a lot closer to something we might see in a biology book than what's on offer between the covers of a physics text — classical or modern. Somehow it seems as if the physics-based frameworks are just too simple, in Einstein's sense, for the real world of finance. If we're ever going to get a scientific handle on the ways of financial markets, let alone on the larger universe of social and behavioral phenomena, it looks as if we'll be forced to move away from the realm of the simple systems of physics, and confront complex systems head-on. From what we've heard from the panel today, finance is just too complex for physics.

Now let me thank the participants for taking time today to give us their views on this fascinating topic. Perhaps we can continue this discussion at next year's TSSTBM meeting. Hopefully, by then some of today's discussants, or even some of you in the audience, may have new ideas and research results to share with us about how to deal with the complexities of finance. So until then, I wish you all the best of luck in your individual gropings and copings with complexity — wherever and whenever you stumble over it!

* * *

Remarks

What the Moderator seems to be driving at here is a paradigmatic framework for speculative markets that recognizes explicitly the fact that finance is a game that's *created* by the players. Moreover, finance — unlike physics — is a game in which the observers cannot pretend that they are insulated from the phenomena they observe. There is a direct effect not only of the players on the market, but also of the market on the players. This is exactly the kind of symmetric interaction that's commonly encountered in biology, where organisms exist in a kind of symbiosis with their environment. It's also exactly the kind of interaction that's ignored in physics. But to make progress in modeling processes like price changes on speculative markets these factors must be taken into account.

It's far from clear, at present, what kind of modeling framework we need in order to encompass things like the observer-environment interaction and self-referential features of the investor. One thing is clear, however, and that is that the metaphor upon which such a modeling paradigm should be based is far more likely to be biology than physics. What's needed is to add to the particles and forces of Newton the features characterizing living systems. This means a framework that takes explicit account of things like self-repair and replication, as well as the pure metabolism that distinguishes the Newtonian view. The theory of metabolism-repair systems as outlined in [6-8] is a start in this direction. But only the future will tell if it is the path with heart — or a cul de sac.

NOTES

[1] Casti, J. (1991). "Money is Funny, or Why Finance is Too Complex for Physics." *Finance and the International Economy*: 5, The AMEX Bank Review Prize Essays. R.O'Brien, ed. Oxford: Oxford University Press, pp. 148-161.

REFERENCES

1. Brock, W., "Causality, Chaos, Explanation and Prediction in Economics and Finance," in *Beyond Belief: Randomness, Explanation and Prediction in Science,* J. Casti and A. Karlqvist, eds., CRC Press, Boca Raton, FL, 1991, pp. 230-279.

2. Brock, W., "Nonlinearity and Complex Dynamics in Finance and Economics," in *The Economy as an Evolving Complex System,* P. Anderson, K. Arrow and D. Pines, eds., Addison-Wesley, Redwood City, CA, 1988, pp. 77-97.

3. LeBaron, B., "Empirical Evidence for Nonlinearities and Chaos in Economic Time Series: A Summary of Recent Results," SSRI Workshop Paper 9117, Social Systems Research Institute, University of Wisconsin, Madison, WI, August 1991.

4. Arthur, W. B., "Positive Feedbacks in the Economy," *Scientific American,* February 1990, pp. 94-99.

5. Arthur, W. B., "Self-Reinforcing Mechanisms in Economics," in *The Economy as an Evolving Complex System,* P. Anderson, K. Arrow and D. Pines, eds., Addison- Wesley, Redwood City, CA, 1988, pp. 9-31.

6. Rosen, R., *Life Itself,* Columbia University Press, New York, NY 1991.

7. Casti, J., "Newton, Aristotle and the Modeling of Living Systems," in *Newton to Aristotle,* J. Casti and A. Karlqvist, eds., Birkhauser, New York, 1989, pp. 47-89.

8. Casti, J., "The Theory of Metabolism-Repair Systems," *Appl. Math. & Comp.* 28 (1988), 113-154.

Chapter 10

UNDERSTANDING THE ORDER-PRODUCING UNIVERSE

by Dr. S.J. Goerner

originally published in November 1993;
adapted from presentations to the
Third Annual Elliott Wave Conference
Buford, GA, 1993 and the
Second Annual Chaos Network Conference
Santa Cruz, CA, June 1992

Chaos is part of a much bigger and more important revolution in understanding than has currently been popularized. We stand at a turning point in human civilization the magnitude of which we are only barely aware but whose importance cannot be doubted. The changes in thinking will affect every segment of the culture. The key factor is an understanding of how order emerges and change is driven. Specifically, science is in the process of developing the physical understanding of an order-producing universe. Suddenly "science" suggests that humankind is embedded in and part of a vast interconnected process that created and is still creating all the intricate order we see about us and the order we have yet to envision.

Swenson's (1989a,b) Principle of Maximum Entropy Production (MEP) crystallizes the physical understanding of order production by adding a rate factor to the second law of thermodynamics, the very law that has long been viewed as an anti-order principle. The net result is a fully physical understanding of ordering that can be traced from the mechanical to the biological.

The concept of nonlinearity is key because order-building is primarily a product of nonlinear dynamics. The first thing to know about nonlinearity is that, despite its distressing name, it is utterly simple. Technically, a nonlinear system is any system in which input is not proportional to output, that is, an increase in x does not mean a proportional increase or decrease in y. A simple example of a nonlinear system is the headache system. If you have a headache and you take one aspirin, it will reduce your headache by a certain amount. If you take two aspirin it will reduce it somewhat more and eight aspirin somewhat more. But it is quite obvious that 64 aspirin will not reduce your headache 64 times as much as one. A headache is therefore a nonlinear system.

Nonlinearity is as simple as that. It is everything whose graph is not a straight line, and this is essentially everything. The second thing to know about nonlinearity is that, from a linear perspective, it is quite a paradoxical beast. Humankind's first-position thinking is linear. In linear thinking, if something works well, then more of it is better; if something has a bad effect, less is better. And while this is an extremely reasonable place to start, one quickly learns that the world is much more subtle than this. The rise of nonlinear models means the rise of a more subtle and consequently a more realistic vision of the world. For example, nonlinear modeling has helped engineers see why adding a new road sometimes increases traffic congestion. This and similarly contrary phenomena have long been observed, but without nonlinear models they seem to defy logic, law and reason. Time and again nonlinear models show that apparently aberrant, illogical behavior is, in fact, a completely lawful part of the system. Nonlinear models make such behavior more concrete, and, consequently, it seems more reasonable. They make nonlinear behavior logical. Nonlinearity is simple, non-magical, lawful and yet extremely versatile. Everything is fundamentally nonlinear, and nonlinearity has the potential for behavior quite out of line with linear expectations. When you broaden science with insights of the nonlinear world, you get a very different picture of how the world works.

There is another concept that is also critical to the nonlinear revolution: interdependence. A conversation is an interdependent (also called interactive) communication between two people. Both people are affected, and the exchange becomes a reciprocating mutual-effect system. In theory, a soliloquy is an independent (uni-directional) communication; one can speak of the message having an effect only on the receiver. Independent systems like linear systems are actually just useful idealizations. In the real world, there are no truly linear systems and there are no truly independent systems, not even soliloquies. The notion of truly independent systems has also tended to create erroneous assumptions about how the world (versus our models) works. Interdependence is important because it, too, is a critical part of chaos, self-organization and order-building. The nonlinear revolution, then, is about exploring the nature of nonlinear interdependency, which in the final analysis is what all real world systems are.

The classical injunction against order has forced scientists to invoke accident, anomaly or various mysterious makers of order (for example, selfish genes, the human brain, life) as the origin of the particular directed orderly phenomenon that they examine. An order-hostile universe makes it hard to explain where coordination comes from. It also tends to make human beings see themselves as separate from the world. The nonlinear revolution, from chaos to general evolution, supports a very non-Newtonian image of the world. The first message of chaos is that physical and lawful does not mean predictable, controllable or completely knowable. This alone shakes the classical firmament. Thus, an evolving ecological universe is lawful, physical, but not completely predictable, controllable or knowable. It is a bit more elusive, more endlessly mysterious than a Newtonian world. Chaos' second message is that there is order hidden in complexity. When nonlinear interdependence is restored to the world, the miracle of order-production is made part of the world, not some kind of accident.

Self-organization and the thermodynamics of evolution expand the vision of order that chaos implies. Thus, an evolving ecological universe is also active, creative, goes in a direction, and is capable of producing both order and disorder. It is not regular, but it is lawful and patterned. Change is not gradual, but punctuated; it moves through periods of stable sameness and qualitative change. Above all, the universe is a vastly more integrated, holistically interconnected unity than was previously realized. The order in chaos is holistic order and results from mutual effects. The order in chaos is a result of interdependent variables co-affecting each other, push-me pull-you fashion, into a coherent pattern. The result is a hidden holistic pattern. It does not come from any one variable, it doesn't go in a straight line, nor does it imply a fixed sequence. It is order of the whole.

The order in chaos provides a mechanical explanation for "mysterious" hidden global ordering (an "invisible hand"). Adam Smith spoke of an invisible hand at work behind the operation of economies. Hegel described the world evolving through dialectics and order hidden beneath surface vicissitudes. The activity of the elements of a mutual-effect system creates global order, and this mutually-created global order creates a pressure on each individual element towards conformity to the global pattern. Nonlinear interactive dynamics have a penchant for creating wholes out of parts.

Nonlinear systems may exhibit qualitative transformations of behavior (bifurcations). A single system may exhibit many different forms of behavior, all the result of the same basic dynamic. The classic example here is a horse's gaits: walking, trotting, galloping and running. Each gait represents a completely different organization of leg motion. The transition between gaits occurs in a sudden reorganization. Generally, the horse goes faster and faster within one gait and then suddenly shifts to a new type of organization that allows a faster speed —walk to trot, trot to gallop, gallop to run. This list exhibits another phenomenon, that bifurcations frequently occur in a series as a particular parameter is increased. In the case of a horse, gait bifurcations occur in a series as speed increases.

Chaos provides a completely mechanical understanding of ecological dynamics. Self-organization theory adds the dimension of energy flow (usually couched in terms of distance from equilibrium). The growth of complexity (evolution) is an energy-flow-rate phenomenon. One need think only of boiling water. You have a lot of heat, first you get little bubbles, then strings of bubbles up the side, ripples, undulations and finally a full rolling boil. Each stage sets the stage for the next, and each transfers energy a little faster. This same acceleration of energy flow has been observed over the evolution of life on earth, the succession of ecosystems (grass plains to oak forests) and the evolution of the universe (atoms to galaxies). Thus, increasing levels of "ordered complexity" are intricately tied to increasing rates of energy flow. The idea that evolution follows a serial pattern of organization and reorganization is in fact quite old. Herbert Spencer (1862) noted the "instability of the homogeneous... the transformation of the incoherent into the coherent hold uniformly from the earliest traceable cosmic changes down to the latest results of civilization." Similarly, land plants emerged through symbiotic coupling between lichens and photosynthetic algae. Maturana and Varela (1987) similarly describe biology via coupling: from single cells to multi-cellular animals to families to herds to civilizations.

Self-organization found in nonliving systems provides both a metaphor and a conceptual model for living systems and supra-living systems (for example, cities). Even in simple physical self-organizing systems such as whirlpools and tornados, one finds the basic elements of a "self," a figure distinct from its surroundings. One finds boundaries, ordered activity that maintains the system's form (identity), and energy exchanges with the environment that maintain its distance from equilibrium. Prigogine described how self-generated, self-maintaining self-organizing dynamics produce and maintain these phenomena spontaneously.

Thermodynamics is the science of energy-flow. Like classical mechanics, classical thermodynamics grew up around its first-accessible cases, in this case, closed, near-equilibrium systems. Like linear/independent systems, closed near-equilibrium systems are an extremely limited idealized case. Here, too, assumptions derived from this early work were inappropriately extrapolated and have become insidiously woven into everyday thought. Goldstein (1990), for example, has outlined how equilibrium thinking affected the work of Sigmund Freud and Kurt Lewin.

Illya Prigogine (1980, 1984) is the person most singly attributed with self-organization theory. A chemist, Prigogine detailed far-from-equilibrium systems that had certain amazing characteristics: they self-organized. His systems were not life, but they behaved much like life. Self-organizing, self-maintaining dynamic organizations spontaneously occur far-from-equilibrium. They do not occur at or near equilibrium. Various other authors have developed the notions of co-evolution and the invisibly ordered context. Eigen and Schuster's (1979) notion of hypercycles describes how self-sustaining cycles develop, increase in coherence, and spread their interconnections. Chemical hypercycles can be seen in living (the Krebs cycle) and nonliving (the carbon cycle) systems and at scales from the microscopic to interplanetary. Like Prigoginian self-organization, such cycles have many behaviors that mirror life. For example, Csanyi (1989) describes how cycles begin to reproduce themselves, creating widespread replicative networks. The spontaneous emergence of replicating cycles, self-maintained boundaries, self-maintained internal coordination, and internal/external exchanges in nonliving systems makes life seem like a much more natural thing. Even origin-of-life work is beginning to be re-cast as a coupling of independent forms into a cooperative with qualitatively new survival enhancing properties (see Dyson, 1987). To sum up, the image of an intricately interwoven ecological universe — self-ordering and built of nonlinear dynamics — is already well supported. MEP fits into this rather pregnant context like a kind of keystone.

Whenever there is a concentration of energy, there is a force, a pressure to flow. Resistance in its many forms (barriers, weight, momentum, density, inertia) constrains flow. When the pressure to flow is small, inertia wins out, and the system runs downhill (energy flows slower and slower). When the pressure is large, it overcomes resistance, and the system runs uphill (energy flows faster and faster). Whether the system goes downhill, uphill or creates new order all depends on the pressure to flow. At first, if pressure is greater than resistance, energy flows faster and faster within its current form. However, there is a limit to how fast any particular type of flow can transfer energy. If the pressure to flow is still greater than resistance when that limit is reached, a crisis occurs, and the system will drive a new more efficient form of flow into being. It opportunistically amplifies some randomly-occurring, minutely-more-efficient fluctuation into a new form of flow. A bifurcation occurs. Massive disequilibriums create a cycle of evolution. Each new form comes into being, accelerates, reaches its limits, and is succeeded by a yet more efficient form of flow. Such systems or, more accurately, such fields, will exhibit punctuated equilibrium, periods of sameness followed by sudden change. Such fields will exhibit an accelerating pace of change, accelerating energy-flow efficiency and increasing complexity. The earth being between the sun and the cold sink of space is in such a massively far-from-equilibrium field. The universe itself, expanding from the big bang, is also a massively far-from-equilibrium field. The biological record exhibits a punctuated equilibrium pattern (see Gould, 1980, and Zeeman, 1986). In addition, such a recursive cycle of order-production would help account for the commonness of fractal geometry in nature. Fractals are quintessentially an outcome of recursive processes. Moreover, energy-driven evolution is a phenomenon of the *whole* field. Complexity grows and flow accelerates in the field as a whole, not necessarily in any given locale. Particular locales may evolve in relative isolation for a while, but, in the final analysis, all smaller fields are part of the larger fields. As locales become more and more tightly integrated, they spread and press outward. In the background, subtle organization (the Gaian type) acts as a hidden connection. Everything affects everything, eventually.

The field's pressure to flow brings us and all other things into being in co-evolving ecological interconnectedness. This is the basic picture of evolution and the order-producing universe. Nonlinear dynamics explains the mechanics, self-organization explains particular locales, the thermodynamics of evolution explains why it goes in a series and is interconnected, and biology bears it out.

Practical Human Organization

The difference between a mechanistic and an ecological vision is striking. In an ecological view, people are intrinsically motivated, self-organization will occur spontaneously if the environment is conducive, emphasis on control is bad for structurally sound growth, and the future is not an extrapolation of the present. In an ecological world, competition is a survival phenomenon. All self-organizations must compete for enough energy (resources) to hold their boundary intact and maintain their internal coordination. Self-organization needs energy to survive. Cooperation is also a survival phenomenon, but of a different type. All major increases in efficiency are a result of cooperative effects. Because evolution is a matter of increasing efficiency, increasing levels and intricacy of *cooperation* enhance survival. Thus, competition keeps an organization intact, but cooperation is the route to long-term continuation. We are embedded in an on-going evolutionary process that moves inexorably and opportunistically towards increasing levels of ordered complexity. There is a the distinct possibility that there is more than metaphor here. Carneiro (1967, 1987), for example notes that the surface/volume rule holds for the growth of villages and cities. They hit the 2/3 power ratio and either stop growing, fall apart, or reorganize. Real (1990) shows that decision making in lower animals (for example, bees selecting flowers) follows standard energy-flow curves. The distinct possibility is that we are guided by a more physical invisible hand than we currently imagine. If the evolving ecological metaphor is the real model of the world, it has profound implications.

Chapter 11

METAPHYSICAL IMPLICATIONS OF THE ELLIOTT WAVE PRINCIPLE

by Jordan E. Kotick
originally published in the MTA Journal[1]
Spring/Summer 2001

> With earth's first clay they did the last man knead,
> And there of the last harvest sowed the seed.
> And the first morning of creation wrote
> What the last dawn of reckoning shall read.
> — Omar Khayyam

Introduction

It strikes me that a philosophical discussion of the Elliott Wave Principle is a worthwhile and relevant pursuit, especially since some of its most noted practitioners, such as A.J. Frost and Robert Prechter, do not hesitate to discuss philosophical issues in their writing nor do they fail to quote various philosophers in connection with their own advocations. I believe that Frost was the first to specifically articulate the connection between philosophy and the Wave Principle as evidenced by his observation, "It is possible to read into stock market behavior a philosophical significance under the basic tenets of the Elliott Wave Principle."[2]

There is no shortage of philosophical issues that can be discussed in relation to the Wave Principle, but the limitations inherent in this paper force me to zero in on a select few. As such, I have decided to examine determinism and specifically whether it should be said, from a philosophical point of view, that the Wave Principle is inherently deterministic. This consideration also seems to have occurred to Frost: "It is an open question whether or not man is a puppet on a string. In the short term he is not, but over the longer period he may be"[3] and Prechter, "the Wave Principle form shows that a collective system is... deterministic."[4]

This paper is not about the persuasiveness of any particular form of determinism nor the validity of the Wave Principle. Instead, my intent is to investigate the compatibility, or lack thereof, between the two. Deciding whether the Wave Principle is deterministic is a challenging task since it requires a metaphysical examination of a theory that by its nature was not directly intended to address metaphysical issues. There is an important difference between the determinism of a particular theory and the more enveloping, less precise notion that the world is itself deterministic. This latter view embraces a much bolder metaphysical view, and while it can be supported, it requires more than just the consideration of the determinism of a particular theory.

As is the case with any philosophical undertaking, precisely defining the beginning precepts is a daunting, yet not insurmountable, task. However, a discussion of the semantics of determinism is not the primary focus of this paper, and as such, I will use determinism in a general philosophical way while admitting at the outset that there are various versions of determinism that I will omit due to the limitations of this paper. For the purposes of this paper, I will examine scientific determinism and show why I believe that a case can be made that it is compatible with the Wave Principle.

The Elliott Wave Principle
Ralph Nelson Elliott

Ralph Nelson Elliott (1871-1948) developed a theory of stock market behavior, which he detailed for the public in a series of twelve articles written for *Financial World* magazine in 1939. In 1946, Elliott wrote what he considered to be his definitive work, *Nature's Law — The Secret of the Universe.* The grandiose title reflected the confidence Elliott had in his theory, which he believed not only encompassed the action of the stock market averages but also the much larger natural law that he believed governed all of man's activities.

As articulated by Frost and Prechter in their work, *Elliott Wave Principle,* "The Wave Principle is Elliott's discovery that crowd behavior trends and reverses in recognizable patterns. Elliott named and illustrated thirteen patterns, or 'waves,' that recur in markets and are repetitive in form but not necessarily in time or amplitude. He further described how these structures link together to form larger versions of the same patterns and how those in turn become the building blocks for patterns of the next larger size and so on." Regardless of the size, the form remains constant.

Prechter further explains, "The Wave Principle is the pattern of progress and regress in which progress occurs in specific patterns of five waves and reaction occurs in specific patterns of three waves or combinations thereof. Progress ultimately takes the form of five waves of a specific structure. The three waves in the direction of the trend are labeled 1, 3, 5, and are separated by two countertrend interruptions, which are labeled 2 and 4.

"The essential form is five waves generating net movement in the direction of the one larger trend followed by three waves generating net movement against it, producing a three-steps-forward, two-steps-back form of net progress."

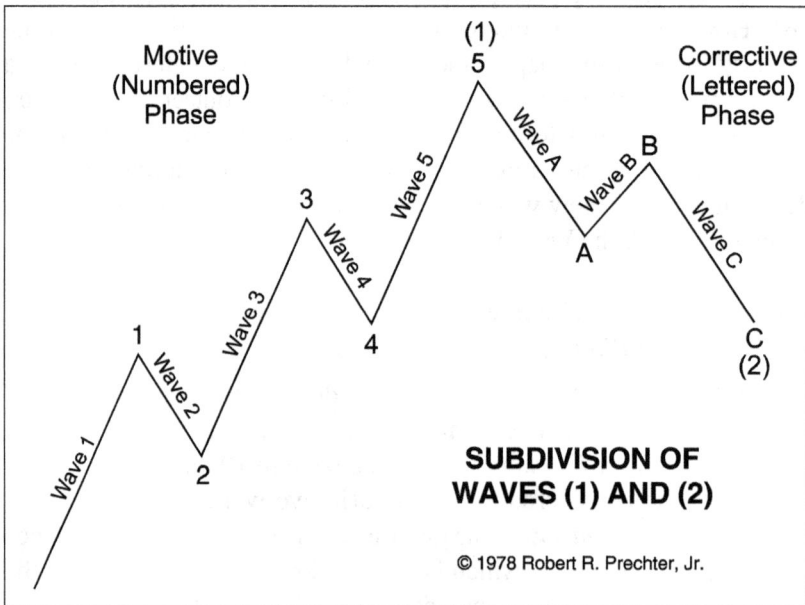

SUBDIVISION OF WAVES (1) AND (2)

© 1978 Robert R. Prechter, Jr.

Leonardo Fibonacci da Pisa

Leonardo Fibonacci da Pisa was born between 1170 and 1180. He was the son of a shipping clerk named Bonaccio (for writing purposes, Leonardo nicknamed himself Fibonacci, short for *filius Bonacci* which means son of Bonacci).

Fibonacci wrote three major mathematical treatises; *Liber Abaci* (Book of the Abacus) in 1202, *Practica Geometriae* (The Practice of Geometry) in 1220 and *Liber Quadratorum* (Book of Square Numbers) in 1225. Of the three, *Liber Abaci* is his monumental work. Fibonacci continued to expand his mathematical insights and later re-released an updated version of *Liber Abaci* in 1228. While the stated purpose of the book was to introduce Hindu-Arabic numerals to Europe and explain their usage, it is within the pages of the *Liber Abaci* that he introduced the famous sequence.

Leonardo Fibonacci discovered (or more accurately rediscovered) what is now commonly referred to as the Fibonacci sequence of numbers: 1, 1, 2, 3, 5, 8, 13, 21, 34, 55, 89. It begins with the number 1, and each new term from there is the sum of the previous two. The ratio of any two consecutive numbers in the sequence approximates 1.618, or its inverse, .618 after the first several numbers. The higher the numbers, the closer to .618 and 1.618 are the ratios between the numbers. The number .618034... is an irrational number that has been referred to historically as the "golden mean," but in this century as *phi* (ϕ).

Elliott unified his theory in 1940 when he recognized that the Fibonacci sequence was the mathematical basis for the Wave Principle. The Fibonacci sequence and its corresponding ratios govern both the numbers of waves in a completed Elliott pattern and the proportional relationships between the waves.

Determinism

This metaphysical principle has been understood and assessed in various ways over the centuries. Discussions concerning determinism are often challenging due to which concept involved, i.e., what "determinism" means in each case. Since the 17th century, it has commonly been accepted as the doctrine/theory that all human thought, action or event is caused entirely by preceding events. This is to say that all physical events and human actions are determined by antecedent factors. Philosophers distinguish between hard determinism (e.g. necessitarianism,[5] fatalism[6]) and soft determinism (e.g. compatibilism[7], libertarianism[8]).

In addressing the validity of determinism, philosophers have often looked to science and scientific theory to represent the best guide to the truth of determinism. Many philosophers have discussed determinism in light of opinions about metaphysical topics such as free will or God. Historically, the principle of determinism applied to both secular and theistic philosophers. While some thinkers, like Immanuel Kant, discussed determinism in terms of the science of the day, others made it part of their philosophy of nature.

Various writers have referred to determinism, causality and natural law as if they were synonymous. They are connected, despite the fact that they are not fully equivalent and the differences between them can be clarified if one wants to make his/her analysis meticulous enough. For the purposes of this discussion, however, I do not find it necessary to attempt to sharpen distinctions to the point of emphasizing all the recognizable differences among the terms. Instead, I shall use them in an essentially common-sense fashion.

Micro or Macro

In the early 1930s, historian Edward Cheney studied various historical events in relation to the seemingly influential actions of certain famous figures. After examining the ostensibly decisive effect exercised by individuals at the time and the role they played in helping to bring about these historical events, Cheney concluded:

> These great changes seem to have come about with a certain inevitableness; there seems to have been an independent trend of events, some inexorable necessity controlling the progress of human affairs...Examined closely, weighed and measured carefully, set in true perspective, the personal, the casual, the individual influences in history sink in significance and great cyclical forces loom up. Events come of themselves, so to speak; that is, they come so consistently and unavoidably as to rule out causes not only of physical phenomena but voluntary human action. So arises the conception of *law in history:* History, the great course of human affairs, has not been the result of voluntary efforts on the part of individuals or groups of individuals, much less chance; but has been subject to law.[9]

Cheney's view strikes me as consistent with the Wave Principle since they both advocate that there is a definite pattern of development in the apparently jumbled story of human history.[10] Further, they both argue that a system's general characteristics can be said to be determined, at least in part, by the structures and characteristics of the constituents of those systems.

Every human event has a definite place in an unalterable and consistent structure of progress and regress as each society passes through a defined series of antecedent changes in order to achieve a subsequent stage. Though individuals are agents that seem to bring about the specific events of social history, they are simultaneously the instruments by which certain laws (Elliott waves) and mathematical principles (Fibonacci) relating to the character of social action become manifest.

Both Cheney's view of history and the Wave Principle share the common premise concerning the impotency of deliberate individual actions to alter the course of social trends. Or as Voltaire poignantly said in the passage on "Destiny" in his *Philosophical Dictionary,* "Everything is performed according to immutable laws...in spite of you."[11] Prechter affords less weight to determinism, asserting that while individuals are powerless to change the character of social mood, they can learn to act independently of it.

This line of thought argues that historical changes are at least to some degree the products of deep-lying forces that conform to fixed, although not always apparent, patterns of development in mass psychology. Didier Somette and Anders Johansen of the Niels Bohr Institute in Copenhagen provided evidence for the existence of a macro intelligence when they wrote in 1997:

> [T]he market as a whole can exhibit an "emergent behavior" not shared by any of its constituent[s]. In other words, we have in mind the process of the emergence of intelligent behavior at a macroscopic scale that individuals at the microscopic scale have no idea of.[12]

Determinism does not necessarily imply that each individual event is causally determined. In spite of the fact that we apparently may not insist upon causality for individual actions or events, it seems that there is some sort of regularity, since the apparently individual actions somehow build themselves into a regular pattern. What is behind this regularity?

The regularity may be formally described by saying that there are *laws* of aggregate behavior, such as the Wave Principle, although there are not always laws for individual actions or events. Elliott clearly believed that he discovered a law of nature. In his previously mentioned work, *Nature's Law,* his first line reads, "No truth meets more general acceptance than that the universe is ruled by law." He goes on to claim, "The very character of law is order...it follows that all that happens will repeat and can be predicted if we know the law."[13]

Frost shared Elliott's sentiments about law and order as evidenced by the following passages: "Law, or Order prevails everywhere and is in and forms part of everything,"[14] "Life is ruled by law and not by accident,"[15] and "Universal law, which asserts itself in our everyday affairs."[16] Clearly, Elliott and many subsequent Elliotticians like Frost believed in both laws of nature and the underlying order of the universe.

The Wave Principle argues that human history illustrates a single, transculturally invariant law of aggregate human mood and activity, and that law is the Wave Principle. Is this law deterministic? It is the purpose of the rest of this paper to find out.

A Brief History of Scientific Determinism

Ancient cultures often attributed reoccurring phenomena such as natural disasters, disease and plague to various gods whose behavior they could neither predict nor comprehend. As time progressed, people began to observe certain regularities in the behavior of nature. One of the first observations was the discovery of the uniform path of heavenly bodies across the sky, thus making astronomy the first developed science. The mathematical foundation for this science was set more than 300 years ago by Newton. His theory of gravity is still used today to predict the motion of celestial bodies. From this example of the birth of astronomy, other natural phenomena were found to obey scientific laws. This led to the advent of scientific determinism, which appears to have been first described by Pierre Simon Laplace (1749-1827). In his *Philosophical Essay on Probabilities* (1814), the French mathematician wrote:

> We ought then to regard the present state of the universe as the effect of its anterior state and as the cause for the one which is to follow. Given for one instance an intelligence which could comprehend all the forces by which nature is animated and the respective situation of the beings who compose it — an intelligence sufficiently vast to submit these ideas to analysis — it would embrace the same formula the movements of the greatest bodies of the universe and those of the lightest atom; for it, nothing would be uncertain and the future, as the past, would be present to its eyes.[17]

By "the forces that animate Nature," I take Laplace to mean the "laws of nature." Laplace's claim is that if one knows the positions and speeds of all the particles in the universe, one could, in principle, calculate their position and motion at any specific time in the past or the future.

This view of determinism holds that the entire future course of the universe has already been determined as a consequence of two factors: natural laws and the state of the universe at any given moment. This is not to say that Laplace held that the course of the universe was entirely knowable, since he did not believe that man was capable of discovering or comprehending the totality of all the natural laws that govern the universe. His claim was intended as an explanation of the principles that govern our existence, not our ability to embrace such a vast understanding. Our inability to perform the computations notwithstanding, the philosophical implications of his view is that our behavior is determined by the laws of nature and the state of the universe at any given moment.

German physicist Max Planck put forth the idea of quantum mechanics in 1900. Its implications for determinism were realized in 1926 by Werner Heisenberg, also a German physicist, through what is now known as the Heisenberg Uncertainty Principle. This principle argues that one cannot measure both the exact position and the exact speed of a particle. Laplace's vision was based on the necessary condition of knowing the exact positions and speeds of particles in the universe at a given time, so it was seriously undermined by Heisenberg's work.

Einstein was not satisfied with the apparent randomness in nature, prompting his famous phrase, *"Der Herr Gott würfelt nicht"* ("God does not play dice"). He seems to have felt that uncertainty was only temporary and that there was an underlying reality where particles had defined positions and speeds that would evolve as Laplace had pointed out, according to deterministic laws.

Scientific Determinism and the Wave Principle

According to scientific determinism, in principle (though not always in practice), whatever happens can be accounted for by citing natural laws and antecedent conditions. Elliott felt that he had formulated a law of nature according to which given events follow from other things: "Even though we may not understand the cause underlying a particular phenomenon, we can, by observation, predict that phenomenon's recurrence."[18]

There are traditional criticisms of determinism, specifically determinism in human affairs, based on the contention that human history does not exhibit the stability and the regular periodicity of science, therefore historical events cannot possibly be elements of a deterministic system. While this criticism may or may not have been persuasive to the idea of historical determinism before Elliott, the Wave Principle seems to provide a system that closely mirrors the mechanical explanations of many other sciences.

Newton provided a deterministic system since he compiled in his mechanics a schema for mechanical explanation of the physical world (for example, his 2nd law that force on a body is equal to its mass times its acceleration). If one knew both force and mass, one could calculate the acceleration. Thus, in order to find out the mechanical explanation of given phenomenon, one had only to fill in the schema by finding the variables involved. If you know the laws, and you know the present conditions, you can predict the future. The precision in Newton's formulations offers an unnecessarily narrow application of what a deterministic system *must* be like. After all, if one knows the current wave position, one can persuasively extrapolate the forthcoming patterns that are likely to unfold. He/she can deductively reason, based on deterministic patterns, what the fractal structure will look like, and this forecasting will be based on the correct identification of the fractal pattern alongside the current position of the pattern. I believe this paralellism rebuts those who might claim that only "traditionally scientific" systems can be deterministic.

To understand the limited extent to which determinism is implied by the Wave Principle, it is important to understand the type of fractal pattern it reflects. Traditionally, it has been assumed that fractals are either self-identical (each component of the pattern is exactly the same as the whole) or indefinite (self-similar to the extent that it is similarly irregular at all levels). Based on Elliott's discovery of a third type of self-similarity, Prechter introduced the idea of a new type of fractal, a "robust fractal." This pattem has highly variable components that fall within a certain defined structure. As Prechter notes, "Component patterns do not simply display discontinuity similar to larger patterns, but they form, with a certain defined latitude, replicas of them."[19] This "latitude" reflects nature's robustness and variability within overall de-termined forms. While it may be an open question whether every nuance of this "latitude" is determined, the Wave Principle unquestionably rests on the premise that certain essential aspects of the design always prevail.

Consider the following example: Assume that you believe a wave four has finished and that wave five is about to begin. Why should this occur? According to Laplace, there are two ingredients in the explanation:

Ingredient One: Natural Laws.

1. Stock market prices trend and reverse in recognizable patterns.
2. The patterns are repetitive in form.
3. Progress takes the form of five waves of a specific structure.
4. Three of these waves, which are labeled 1, 3, 5, actually effect the directional movement.
5. Waves 1, 3, 5 are separated by two countertrend interruptions which are labeled 2 and 4.
6. Wave 2 never moves beyond the start of wave 1.
7. Wave 3 is never the shortest wave.
8. Wave 4 never enters the price territory of wave 1.

Ingredient Two: Antecedent Conditions

1. Wave four has unfolded in three waves.
2. Wave a and wave c have traced out five completed waves.
3. Waves a and c are equal in length.
4. Wave four has not broken the price territory of wave 1.

Of course, this is not an exhaustive list of either the natural laws involved in the Wave Principle nor of the potential antecedent conditions, but the essential point is still made. In terms of the Wave Principle, the natural laws and the antecedent conditions are beyond our control. The pattern of the markets is entirely determined by the laws of nature and antecedent conditions. Natural laws, such as the Wave Principle, account for the way the universe appears to function.[20] On this basis, scientific determinism is compatible with the Wave Principle.

Autonomy and Free Will

It would seem, then, that there is no room for collective free choice or philosophically speaking, free will, in this macro-depiction of the mechanics of the social universe. (The will is philosophically understood as the faculty of choice and decision and figured prominently in the writings of many philosophers such as nineteenth century thinkers Schopenhauer and Nietzsche.) Collective behavior, which is what the

Wave Principle represents, is determined by both the laws of nature and antecedent conditions. The Wave Principle does not address specific acts of individuals within the collective or therefore even of the collective itself, but instead general behavioral proclivities. So while the individuals within the aggregate have autonomy to choose, to the extent that they participate in the collective dynamic, their behavior contributes to the aggregate pattern that is determined.

Prediction and Retrodiction

As argued above, while we cannot predict with any degree of certainty who, for example, the next Prime Minister of Canada will be, we do have strong reasons for believing who it probably will be or who it won't be. While our predictions about the future do not exclude all the conceivable alternatives leaving only one possibility, they rule out a huge amount of possibilities. This leads to the conclusion that even though individuals who participate in the events of human history (such as the election of the Canadian Prime Minister) have free choice in their actions, their collective choice will fall within certain probabilities; the "Wave Principle structurally restricts the number of possible outcomes of social trends."[21] The ramification of this realization is that not everything that is logically possible is necessarily historically possible at a given time in a given place. There are determining factors for both what has happened and will happen throughout human history.

The Wave Principle specifies what the psychological make-up is behind a bull or bear market, impulsive or corrective waves, as illustrated in the next two figures, taken from *Elliott Wave Principle*. If history can be understood (on a macro level) through its wave structure, and if the tenor of the future is also predictable due to its unfolding wave structure, then, in principle, one can specify the circumstances under which certain events will unfold, such as when certain types of politicians, philosophers, scientists and artists are most likely to have creative success or not.

It is undeniable that humans are continual sources of novelties, inventions and creation and that the emergence of individual discoveries or applications are not predictable. No one, for example, could have predicted Count Basie's *April in Paris* or Darwin's *Theory of Evolution*. What the Wave Principle can and does do, however, is ascribe the deterministic patterns that allow for the favourable social conditions that are conducive to both the undertaking of research and the acceptance of innovative discoveries and creations.

Idealized Elliott Wave Progression
© 1980/1999 Robert R. Prechter, Jr.

FINAL ADVANCE
Market performance and fundamentals
improve, but not to levels of wave 3.
Psychology creates overvaluation.

POWERFUL WAVE
Strength. Breadth. Best fundamentals. Increasing
real prosperity. By the end, the underlying trend
is considered up. Wave often subdivides.
Is never the shortest wave.

REBOUND from
undervalued levels.
Recognition of survival.

wave 5

wave 4

wave 3

**SURPRISING
DISAPPOINTMENT**
Signals that best part of growth
phase has ended. Does not
enter price territory of wave 1.

wave 1

wave 2

TEST OF LOWS
Fundamental conditions often as bad as or
worse than those at the previous bottom.
Underlying trend considered down.
Does not carry to new low.

BOTTOM
Large degrees: question of existence; survival; depression; war.
Intermediate degrees: recession; "panic"; limited wars.
Minor degrees: often accompanied by "bad news."

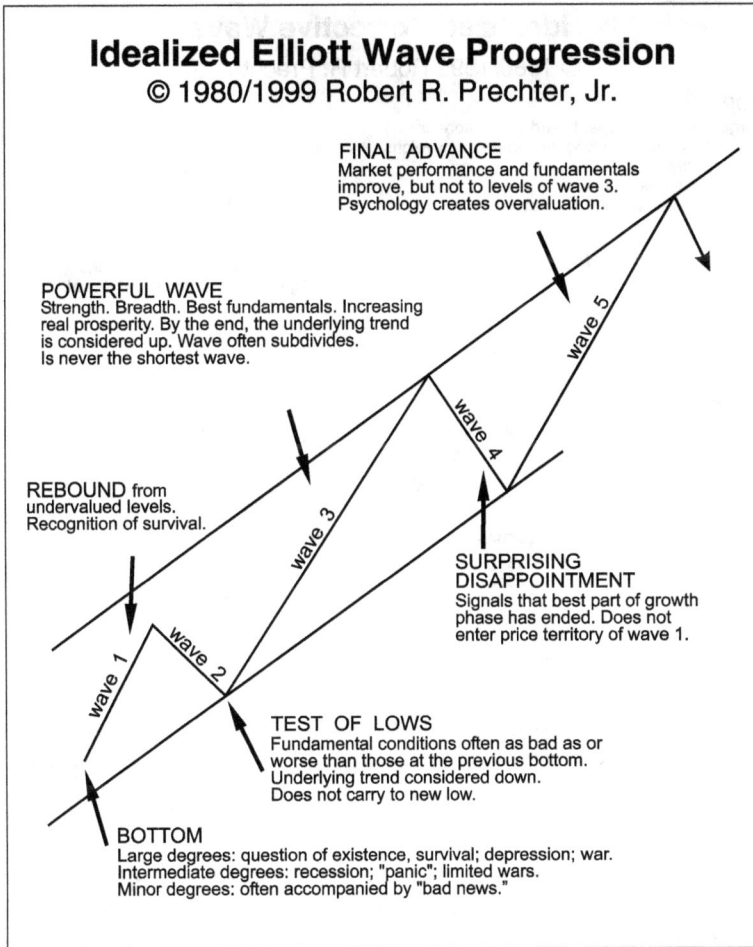

Whether specific events will take place is a question of probability since the Wave Principle dictates only society's coming character changes, not necessarily specific events. This is to say that the aggregate social mood fashions the *character* of history, not the specific manifestations. Even within that realm of determined outcome, variability exists. As Prechter has noted, history repeats in mood, but not necessarily in mode. Or, put another way:

> Because fundamental Elliott wave patterns are limited in number... and because the continual expansion of degree imparts uniqueness to every wave, interactive human mentation and behavior, which produces history, are continually repeated, but not precisely.[22]

Idealized Corrective Wave

© 1980/1999 Robert R. Prechter, Jr.

TOP
Large degrees: prosperity and peace appear
guaranteed forever. Arrogant complacency reigns.
Intermediate degrees: economic
improvement, good feeling.
Minor degrees: often accompanied by
"good news."

NARROW, EMOTIONAL ADVANCE
Technically weak, selective.
Results in non-confirmations.
Fundamentals weaken subtly.
Aggressive euphoria and denial.

TECHNICAL BREAKDOWN
Trendlines broken.
Viewed as buying opportunity.

wave A

wave B

WORST OF BEAR MARKET
Strength. Breadth.
Prices decline relentlessly.
Fundamentals ultimately
collapse in response.

wave C

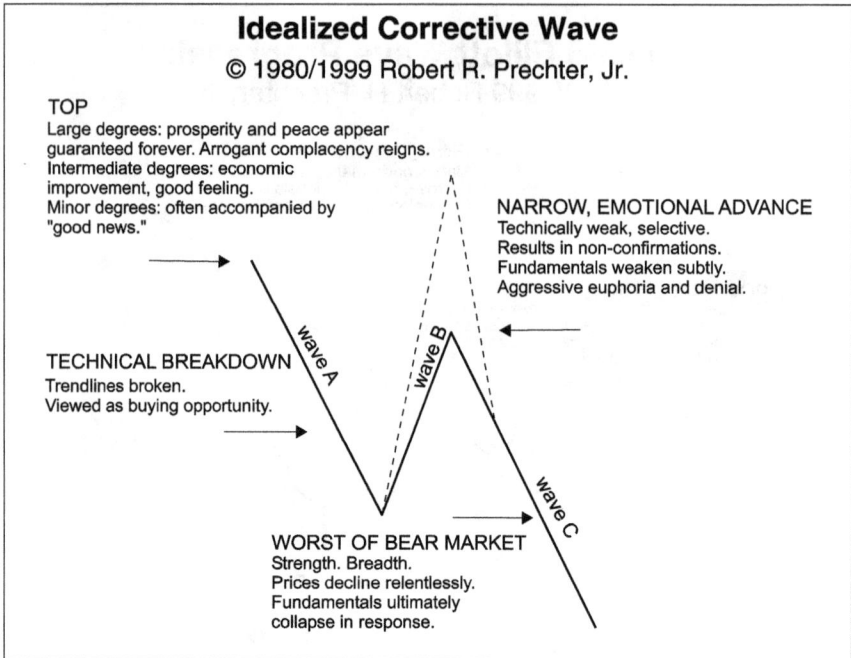

Individual occurrences and events do not follow *deductively* from the wave pattern. While the environment is certain and determined by the wave pattern, the individual occurrences within that environment are not.

Notice in the next figure, for example, that according to this particular wave count, after the Supercycle Wave 2 low in 1859, it was predictable (determined) that Supercycle wave 3 would begin.[23] It was also predictable (determined) that the positive environment that characterizes a wave three (prosperity and optimism) would also occur.[24] Prechter used the social events and conditions of the past to retrodict the position of the waves. The chart is one potential classification of the cultural timeline of Western culture since Roman times. While neither the Industrial Revolution nor the plethora of events that Prechter cites were determined, according to the Wave Principle, the social mood preconditions that gave rise to these events were.

The general pattern of the Wave Principle is universal in form. But in reality, the patterns are rarely, if ever, asserted in precisely the same way (for example, the relative length of each fifth wave is not exactly the same in every pattern even though it is likely to gravitate towards

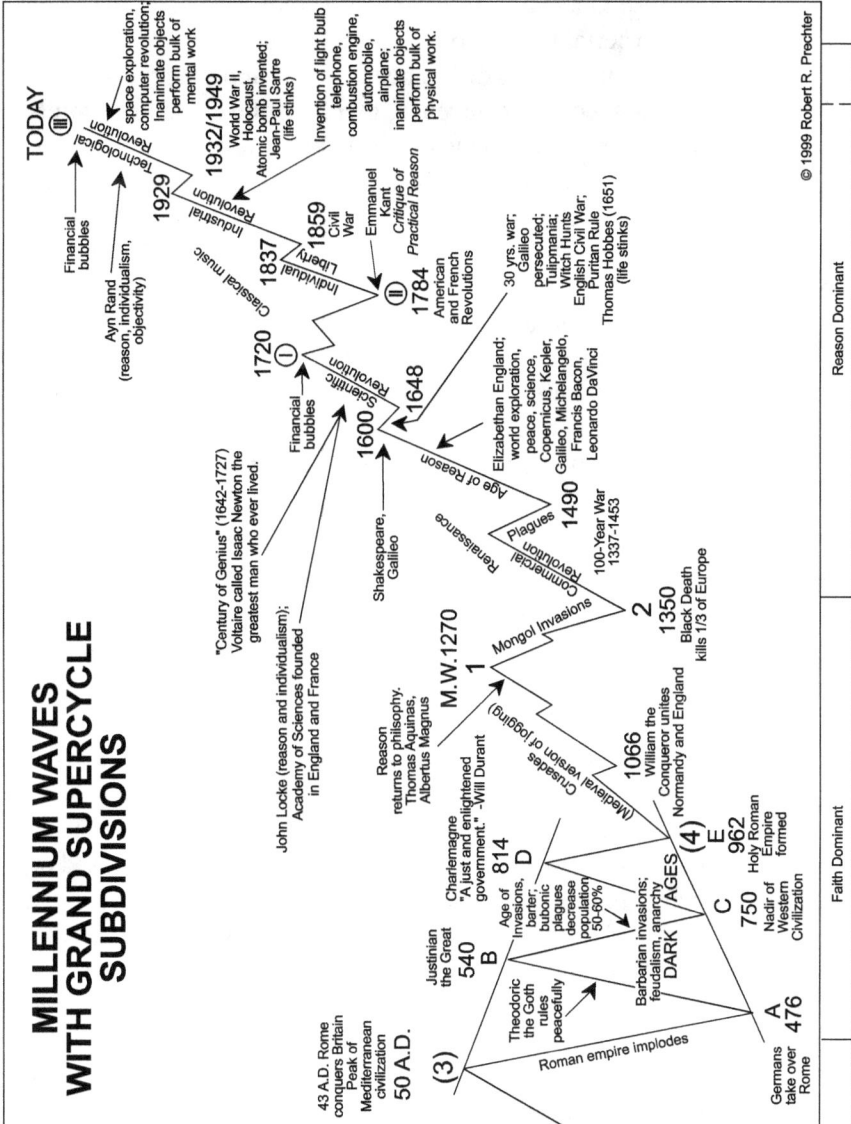

MILLENNIUM WAVES WITH GRAND SUPERCYCLE SUBDIVISIONS

TODAY

Financial bubbles

Technological Revolution (III)

space exploration, computer revolution; inanimate objects perform bulk of mental work

1932/1949
World War II, Holocaust, Atomic bomb invented; Jean-Paul Sartre (life stinks)

1929

Ayn Rand (reason, individualism, objectivity)

Industrial Revolution

Invention of light bulb, telephone, combustion engine, automobile, airplane; inanimate objects perform bulk of physical work.

Classical music

1837

Individual Liberty

1859
Civil War

Emmanuel Kant *Critique of Practical Reason*

1720 (I)

1784 (II)
American and French Revolutions

30 yrs. war; Galileo persecuted; Tulipmania; Witch Hunts; English Civil War, Puritan Rule Thomas Hobbes (1651) (life stinks)

Scientific Revolution

Financial bubbles

1648

1600

"Century of Genius" (1642-1727) Voltaire called Isaac Newton the greatest man who ever lived.

Age of Reason

Elizabethan England; world exploration, peace, science, Copernicus, Kepler, Galileo, Michelangelo, Francis Bacon, Leonardo DaVinci

Shakespeare, Galileo

1490
Plagues
100-Year War 1337-1453

John Locke (reason and individualism); Academy of Sciences founded in England and France

Renaissance

Commercial Revolution

2
1350
Black Death kills 1/3 of Europe

Reason returns to philosophy. Thomas Aquinas, Albertus Magnus

M.W.1270

Mongol Invasions

Crusades (Medieval version of jogging)

1

1066
William the Conqueror unites Normandy and England

Charlemagne "A just and enlightened government." -Will Durant

Age of Invasions; barter; bubonic plagues decrease population 50-60%

814
D

(4)

962
Holy Roman Empire formed

E

750
Nadir of Western Civilization

Justinian the Great

540
B

Barbarian invasions; feudalism, anarchy DARK AGES

C

Theodoric the Goth rules peacefully

43 A.D. Rome conquers Britain Peak of Mediterranean civilization

50 A.D.

(3)

Roman empire implodes

Germans take over Rome

476
A

Faith Dominant | Reason Dominant

© 1999 Robert R. Prechter

predetermined Fibonacci projections), which reflects their aspect of robustness. This situation reflects Einstein's famous expression, "So far as the laws of mathematics refer to reality, they are not certain. And so far as they are certain, they do not refer to reality."

The consequence of this difference is that in applying the generalized patterns to a specific occurrence, there will be some uncertainty concerning the extent to which the given situation adheres to the generalizations. The result is that aside from being unable to give the initial conditions that will result in an exact consequence (the termination of wave five will end at .618 the net of wave 1-3 *if and only if...*), one can only assert that the pattern will *probably* terminate at a certain point, while one can be *certain* only that the pattern will terminate at a time when its required pattern is in place. Just as the form of the impulsive and corrective patterns are determined but the dimensions of the waves within the pattern are not, social-mood conditions attending each wave, and their general results, are determined but the specifics of social events are not.

Conclusion

During this paper, I have attempted to defend neither the validity of the Wave Principle nor scientific determinism. My intention throughout has been to determine whether the Wave Principle was compatible with this version of determinism.

I have drawn a number of conclusions from this work. The Wave Principle seems to be consistent with scientific determinism. Aggregate social mentation and the fundamental fractal pattern of the Wave Principle moves according to a determined yet robust path that is based on natural laws and antecedent conditions. This is not to say that we can equate determinism or the Wave Principle with the potential to predict with unlimited accuracy. At the same time, however, we are directed towards discovering regularities in the operations of systems that will empower us with the ability to formulate various rules that allow for the prediction or retrodiction of the occurrence of events.

I believe that based on the determined path of the Wave Principle, it is reasonable to say that we can predict the future behavior of a large body of people but not the individuals that compose that body. In other words, explanations of aggregate social mood based on wave patterns have the structure of a straightforward deductive argument, while explanations of individual actions in that context do not.

Epilogue

Due to the inherent limitations of this paper, I have had to limit the scope of my examination to specific areas. There remain, however, many other philosophical areas left to investigate.

As we move into the 21st century, technical analysis continues to grow in reputation and stature, so much so that it is slowly being accepted by mainstream academia. Hence, a philosophical look at the some of the techniques practiced and the beliefs held by technicians is an area that I believe holds great potential. It is, in Shakespeare's words, "undiscovered country." If we do indeed stand atop the shoulders of those who came before us, then I believe that some of philosophy's greatest minds have valuable insights for technicians.

When I refer to the dearth in philosophical analysis of the financial markets, I am not referring to Wave Principle specifically (though there is much more to say about philosophy and Elliott Waves) but technical analysis in general. For example, the concept of the herd, central to the technician's view of market movement and market sentiment, was explored in detail by Nietzsche, Kierkegaard and Heidegger. Aristotle had a lot to say about man as a "political animal" and social creature. There is much we can and should learn from these thinkers.

In short, I believe there is a book waiting to be written. This is a book that will look at the greatest philosophical minds and explore what they had to say about the state of nature, human thought and our social condition and compare it to what we know and see in the financial markets. As the layers of market analysis are peeled back and examined, I have every confidence that one will find the footprints of history's greatest philosophers who, if listened to carefully, have something important to tell us.

NOTES

[1] *The MTA Journal* is a publication of the Market Technicians Association, 74 Main St. 3rd Fl, Woodbridge, NJ 07095.

[2] Prechter, Jr., Robert R., ed. *The Elliott Wave Writings of A.J. Frost and Richard Russell,* (Georgia: New Classics Library, 1998), p.401.

[3] *Ibid.,* p.398.

[4] Prechter, Jr., Robert R., *The Wave Principle of Human Social Behavior and the New Science of Socionomics,* (Georgia: New Classics Library, 1999), p.414. Referred to as *Socionomics* for the remainder of this paper.

[5] Necessitarianism holds that humans do not have free will and that actions are entirely determined by antecedent, external causes.

[6] Philosophically, fatalism holds that suffering and despair are the inevitable fate of man. It is often used in conjunction with determinism, since it argues that every event is bound to happen as it does not matter what we do about it. Like necessitarianism, fatalism denies that human actions have any causal efficacy. A determinist may believe that a hangover is the effect of a natural cause, but the fatalist holds that a hangover will occur regardless of whether one drinks or not.

[7] Compatibilism acknowledges that all events, including human actions, have causes. But it allows for free actions when the actions are caused by one's choices rather than external causes.

[8] Metaphysically, the term libertarianism refers to the idea that human beings have free will and thus sees no inherent contradiction between determinism and the proposition that human beings are sometimes free agents.

[9] Nagel, Ernest, "Determinism In History," *Philosophy and Phenomenological Research,* Volume XX, September, 1959. p.291.

[10] Prechter's book, *The Wave Principle of Human Social Behavior,* examines social trends based on the biologically based patterns of fluctuation in collective mood that are formological in that they have consistent Fibonacci-based mathematical properties and produce the Wave Principle. Prechter argues that the patterning of social mood guides and influences the character of individual and social behavior resulting in human actions that in turn cause the trends and events of history.

[11] Voltaire, M. De, *A Philosophical Dictionary,* (London: C.H. Reynell, 1824), p.385.

[12] Prechter, *Socionomics,* p.159.

[13] Prechter, Jr., Robert R., ed. *R.N. Elliott's Masterworks,* (Georgia: New Classics Library, 1994), p.216.

[14] Prechter, *Frost and Russell,* p.378.

[15] *Ibid.,* p.398.

[16] *Ibid.,* p.403.

[17] Pierre Simon Marquis de Laplace. *A Philosophical Essay on Probabilities,* (New York: Dover Publications, Inc., 1951), p.3.

[18] Prechter, *Masterworks,* p.216

[19] Prechter, *Socionomics,* p.56.

[20] This is an epistemological claim, not an ontological one. I do not believe there is any compelling reason to believe that if the Wave Principle is true, it would communicate, as Galileo said, "the language in which the Book of Nature is written." Perhaps *a* language but not *the* language.

[21] Prechter, *Socionomics,* p.414.

[22] Prechter, *Socionomics,* p.285.

[23] Chart on the following page taken from: Prechter, *Socionomics,* p. 345.

[24] Frost and Prechter, referring to the powerful and positive sentiments associated with third waves, called them "wonders to behold." Frost and Prechter, *Elliott Wave Principle,* p.78.

BIBLIOGRAPHY

Bernstein, Peter L. *Against the Gods,* New York: John Wiley & Sons, Inc., 1996.

De Voltaire, M. A. *Philosophical Dictionary,* C.H. Reynell: London, 1824.

Dray, W. H. "Determinism in History." *The Encyclopedia of Philosophy,* Paul Edwards, editor. Volume 2, New York: MacMillan Publishing Co., and Inc. & The Free Press, 1967. pp.373-378.

Frost, A.J. and Prechter Jr., *Elliott Wave Principle.* Georgia: New Classics Library, 1998.

Gies, Joseph and Frances. *Leonard of Pisa and The New Mathematics of the Middle Ages,* Georgia: New Classics Library, 1969.

Hook, Sidney. *Determinism and Freedom in the Age of Modern Science,* New York: New York University Press, 1958.

Marquis de Laplace, Pierre Simon. *A Philosophical Essay on Probabilities.* New York: Dover Publications, Inc. 1951.

McKeon, Richard. *The Basic Works of Aristotle,* New York: Random House Inc., 1941.

Nagel, Emest. "Determinism in History." *Philosophy and Phenomenological Research,* Marvin Farber, editor. Volume XX, New York: University of Buffalo, 1959. pp.291-317.

Prechter Jr., Robert R. *R.N. Elliott's Masterworks.* Georgia: New Classics Library, 1994.

Prechter Jr., Robert R. *The Wave Principle of Human Social Behavior.* Georgia: New Classics Library, 1999.

Prechter Jr., Robert R. *The Elliott Wave Writings* of *A.J. Frost and Richard Russell.* Georgia: New Classics Library, 1996.

Taylor, Richard. "Determinism." *The Encyclopedia* of *Philosophy,* Paul Edwards, editor. Volume 2, New York: MacMillan Publishing Co., and Inc. & the Free Press, 1967. pp.359-373.

PART III

Understanding Investment Manias*

* For another study on this topic, please see Prechter, "Bulls, Bears and Manias" (1997), which has been republished in *View from the Top of the Grand Supercycle* (2001).

Chapter 12

THE STOCK MARKET SCENE TODAY: A JUNGIAN PERSPECTIVE

by Anne Crittenden
originally published December 1997

The mass participation and blind faith in the stock market that we see everywhere today is an astonishing spectacle. I believe that Jungian depth psychology can contribute to our understanding of the phenomenon.

Carl Jung (Swiss psychotherapist, 1875-1961) believed that the psychological foundation we all share as human beings makes us susceptible to "psychic contagion" from those about us. Today, because of electronic communications and mass media, such contagion can rapidly become a full-scale epidemic. When this occurs, we are no longer responsible, sensible individuals, but a herd. This is the situation today in the stock market, particularly in the United States but virtually throughout the world.

The following comments offer a broadly Jungian perspective on three aspects of this mania. Firstly, I outline the depth-psychological processes and events that are taking place, both in individuals and in the collectivity of people; then I look at some of the powerful archetypal symbols that are holding investors spellbound. Lastly, I discuss the psychological reversal that, on Jungian principles, is the mania's inevitable outcome.

The Depth-Psychological Processes Involved in a Mania

According to Jung, the psyche of a human being has three levels or kinds of functioning. The most evident level is the conscious mental ego. This is the rational mind or self that, when it functions in a fully human way, labours to acquire knowledge and to think analytically and critically, both about the external world and about the self. A good education and habits of critical reflection are essential to the advanced development of this part of our mind. Ordinarily, Jung believed, consciousness functions only intermittently at a rational-critical level. People are mostly just processing sensory input in a routine way, and there is little analytical thinking about their own psychology or the outside world. Jung maintained that because of this, most people are largely "unconscious" most of the time. Clearly, he did not mean that they are literally out of their senses, asleep or comatose but that they are not really thinking.

Just beneath the everyday half-conscious mind is what Jung — following Freud — called the personal unconscious, comprising the individual's personal history. Jung regarded this as only a superficial level of the unconscious; it plays little part in mass movements such as manias.

What really drives a mania is the deepest level of the mind: the vast psychological powerhouse that we all share as members of the same species; Jung called this the "collective unconscious." Jung believed that even highly self-aware individuals are far more influenced by this collective psyche than they ever imagine. Our personal individuality, so precious to us (and valued very highly by Jung), floats rather insecurely on an underground psychic sea that is the same in all of us, though it finds varying specific embodiments in different cultures. Most of the time, if we are lucky, this great sea is fairly calm, but if storms arise, the little boat of our individual consciousness can be heaved around like a cork.

Formed over the aeons of our evolution, this collective unconscious comprises our instincts and what Jung called "archetypes" or species-typical patterns of thinking, feeling and reacting. They underlie all our typical life experiences, our typical human hopes and fears. They can be seen, externalized, in the form of mythological and religious motifs that occur throughout the world. I will say more about some particular archetypes relevant to the stock market shortly, but here it should be stressed how much patterns belonging to the collective unconscious influence our individual minds.

As Jung warns, we are most liable to find ourselves at the mercy of the unconscious if we scorn the very idea of an "unconscious" mind. The unconscious, with its highly potent archetypes, needs to be watched carefully if it is not to take us by surprise. The classical world talked about these mysterious psychological forces that could erupt from time to time as deities who must be respected because of their power to suddenly strike us down. Jung, who greatly esteemed the psychological insight embodied in classical mythology, held the same attitude. For him, the supreme task of our inner life — both as individuals and as whole cultures — is to strive to stand in intelligent relation to the unconscious. We must always be aware of the fragility of our rational capacity and must treat the unconscious with great respect and caution. If this is not done, individually, our ego can be seized and enthralled by an archetypal unconscious influence. In the grip of an archetypal idea, our ego becomes charged up by a sense of power. In Jungian terms, the ego becomes "inflated." This is bad enough in an individual, but if the collectivity identifies with an archetype, the result is mass psychic inflation, a populist mania.

Such is the situation today in the stock market, throughout much of the world. There is, alas, nothing new in the phenomenon of mass mania. Throughout history there have been many manias: political, military, religious, financial. The effect is always to over-stimulate the group so that its sense of power and efficacy is abnormally revved up. Social mood becomes supercharged. The collectivity as a whole feels enlarged, energized and empowered. National self-esteem soars. It becomes extremely difficult for any individual to resist this marvellous feeling of elation and godlikeness. Jung never tired of pointing out that only a highly developed consciousness of the power of the unconscious can enable an individual to withstand the power of the psychic flood sweeping everybody along. There is nothing more isolating than maintaining one's individuality in a mass mania. When people succumb, however, they lose the capacity for independent thought and function almost solely as bearers of the prevailing psychological epidemic. Eventually, even previously responsible people can become a mindless herd governed by some collective fantasy.

It is typical of such a situation that people think everything is wonderful, but actually their intoxication is highly regressive. It is a return to what the French anthropologist Levy-Bruhl called "participation mystique," the group consciousness that prevails in tribal societies. Jung often warned of the danger of regressing to this state. Although he never wrote about the stock market (despite having numerous stockbroker patients!) he would, I am sure, have had no hesitation in assessing the stock market mania we see today as a collective psychic inflation. He could point to the giddy level of wish-fulfillment, the mass fantasy of unearned wealth for all, the rapturous state of "participation mystique" and its accompanying irresponsibility and euphoric elation.

Archetypal Symbols Involved in the Mania

The particular archetypal idea or image that enraptures people's consciousness in the stock market today is ascension or magical flight. It is not hard to see why this should be so. The market graphs have been in an overall uptrend since the Great Depression. Then, since 1982, they have been accelerating upwards in a gravity-defying way. The human mind is very susceptible to the allure of this upwardly vaulting line. One of this century's leading scholars of comparative religion, Mircea Eliade, discusses the archetype of ascension in his book *Myths, Dreams and Mysteries* (1957). He argues that the symbolism of ascension, especially ascent far up into the sky, expresses humanity's deep-seated yearning for absolute freedom and for deliverance from the cares and sorrows of earthly life. We long to be able to rise up out of this world of work, suffering and death into a heavenly state of freedom, ease and bliss. World religions, from the most archaic to the most advanced, abound in stories of culture-heroes — spiritual leaders, or embodiments of the aspirations of the group — who ascend to a higher world. The earth, which is the symbol and embodiment of drudgery and hard necessity, is left far below.

Incredible as it may seem, the soaring stock market graphs have activated (Jung would say "constellated") this major archetype in people's minds. The stock market is today's magic stairway by which people imagine they will ascend into a heaven where all their dreams will be fulfilled, and they and their families will live happily ever after.

While the stock market as a whole promises magical ascension, the high-technology stocks embody the archetype of magical flight quite literally. Jung would have been fascinated by the magnetic appeal, to today's investors, of the high-technology stocks. He always held that the presence of what he called the "cosmic element" was a sure sign of the activation of an archetype of the collective unconscious. By cosmic element he meant anything that suggested the attainment of infinity, such as extraordinary angles of flight, enormous speed, or vast extension. In today's mania, the high-tech stocks obviously exhibit such "cosmic" qualities, embodying fantasies of unlimited power. The vast amount of money committed to these stocks certainly testifies to the power of this particular archetype. (A recent PBS television program interviewed a suburban lady who has put the family fortune into two technology stocks whose names she cannot quite recall. There can be little doubt that the collective unconscious is in the driver's seat there!)

The ego-inflation that causes the mass throwing-off of any and all caution, under the influence of the ravishing archetype, is most evident in people's attitude toward mutual funds. This phenomenon exhibits several unhealthy psychological features in addition to the prevailing ascensional fantasy. One is the activation of the "saviour" archetype. In the funds, people are giving their life savings to certain financial wizards who will supposedly save their clients' financial lives via an ever-ascending stock market. To their followers, these money-management heroes radiate numinous power; they are regarded as semi-divine, awesome, because they possess enthralling access to the hidden financial mysteries that govern all life. While they are flying high, these heroes have intense charisma. The tendency to archetypal projection is so strong that as soon as one idol disappoints by failing to perform magically, he is denounced as a mere mortal; the faithful then shift their hopes to the next supposed genius. The most famous investors on whom saviour expectations have been projected are Warren Buffett, John Templeton and Peter Lynch. As psychic inflation is so extremely contagious, it is impossible to say whether these luminaries or any of the other top investment superstars can resist believing that their followers' worship is justified. Jung stressed that archetypal projection of the "saviour" archetype is almost always shared by the supposed saviour. Everyone ends up inflated. (Jung was writing about this archetype in 1936. He had in mind what today we might well call "Fuhrer-mania." That was the last great political mania seen in a western country, though lesser ones occur frequently.)

The investment scene as a whole is so archetypally excited at present that deep emotions that we would normally consider religious now flow into, and add great power to, financial longings. Wall Street itself has become a place of numinous power, a "World Center" where people worship the gods who decide human fate. It is as much a sacred precinct as were the great temple-complexes of ancient Mesopotamia, with their ziggurats climbing into the heavens. For the first time since the great Crash of 1929, Wall Street once again radiates what anthropologists call "mana" — an almost supernatural aura of prestige and power.

The irrationality of this situation is evident to a detached observer. However, the collective consciousness is so dominated by unconscious projections that people will not accept that there is anything irrational about their rapturous faith in the financial markets. They justify themselves by pointing to past performance — about which they know virtually nothing beyond a few slogans provided by Wall Street. They believe they are acting rationally, but reason is in fact just the dazzled dupe of the whole mana-messiah-ascensional flight archetypal complex that holds the populace transfixed.

Of course, the yearning for magical access to wealth is always with us, being archetypal. Gambling is endemic in most human societies. However, gambling is too prevalent to qualify as a special mania or psychological epidemic. Stock market manias erupt periodically in modern societies. Charles Kindleberger's *Manias, Panics and Crashes* (see Acknowledgments) brings home just how often they appear. Robert Prechter has recently graphed some of the most spectacular manias in his Special Report, "Bulls, Bears and Manias." [See *View from the Top of the Grand Supercycle.*—Ed.] He includes the Tulip Mania, the South Sea Bubble and the Japanese stock market boom of the 'eighties. Mention should also be made of the 19th century gold rushes. Like stock market manias, these were mass psychological epidemics. All around the world, people abandoned their families, quit their jobs and "rushed" out to California and then on to Australia. Later, they rushed north to Alaska ("Klondike Fever") and to the West Australian desert. (During this last, my own great-grandmother stomped out West and hauled her man back home.)

All these examples show that human beings are extremely susceptible to anything that promises magical deliverance from a life of poverty and toil. It is not hard to see why the populace today should be caught up in an ascensional mania. Despite a long economic expansion, many ordinary people find that their future prospects are contracting; at the same time, all about them they see favoured individuals soaring up to stupendous wealth and fame. Leading entertainers and sports people, often only in their twenties, are able to live like emperors. Adulation of the rich and famous pours from the media. In this atmosphere, surrounded by this conditioning, ordinary people can become nearly mad with frustration over their own inability to rise. They are desperate for a way to tap into all that wealth, to enjoy self-respect and security. Finding that they are going down, not up, exacerbates their credulousness to anything that seems to offer guaranteed ascension.

Another mass outbreak of the magical-wealth fantasy comparable to today's stock market scene was the "Cargo Cult" of Papua, New Guinea. In the first half of this century, indigenous New Guineans, just emerging from a Stone Age way of life, viewed with heartfelt awe and yearning the planes that descended from the sky to unload endless wealth in the form of "cargo" for the European settlers and officials who bustled about. In several different regions, the local people secretly constructed little airstrips, burned all their old huts and their now-despised traditional possessions, then lined up expectantly at their strips. (On the coast, they built "ports" and awaited cargo boats.) Surely the ancestral spirits, source of all largesse, would now redirect the cargo to their descendants? It was only right and just. Why should the whites get everything and them nothing? Anthropologists are all too familiar with these outbreaks of mass frustration and compensatory magical-wealth fantasy. The views of today's ordinary people resemble those of the Cargo Cult. The gods have brought wealth to the Buffett-Templeton-Lynch tribe; why not to us as well? They seem to share a belief with the New Guineans, perhaps covertly, that it is not rare talent and immense effort (not to mention in this case a convenient multi-decade bull market from low values) that brought the riches, but magic: anyone can have it, any time they want. "The market always goes up long term" is all one has to know.

The Inevitable Outcome

The despair that followed the Cargo Cult is a good illustration of the likely outcome of the present stock market mania. Discussing ascensional yearning, Mircea Eliade stresses that people do not normally try to live everyday life in a condition of "magical flight." However, all great financial manias — whether Cargo Cult, gold rush or stock market stampede — show that if people become frustrated in their too-high expectations of wealth, they can succumb to acting out their archetypal longing with no regard for the possibility of failure. In Jungian terms, when that happens, the psychological balance between conscious and unconscious forces is lost. The unconscious has triumphed; one-sidedness prevails.

Jung always stressed that one-sidedness is the greatest psychological danger faced by people, both as individuals and collectively. To avoid it, people have to learn to endure what Jung called "the tension of the opposites." If they buckle under the pressure of this tension, and flee into one-sidedness, disaster ensues. The number of opposites we must hold in balance is legion, but the most fundamental one, in Jungian thinking, is the tension in our lives between archetypal patterns of response on the one hand and rational consciousness on the other. To take refuge in either of these "opposites" is to become one-sided. Living wholly in archetypal fantasies is madness, but equally, excluding the unconscious from one's conception of life and personality means barrenness. Jung insisted that people must learn to tolerate and value their struggle with these opposites.

All this may seem a long way from the stock market, but it is not. The "opposites" that investors must deal with are the market's opposing forces: up/down in direction, positive/negative in sentiment — in short, bull and bear. As Prechter's extensive work applying the Elliott Wave Principle has demonstrated, a healthy market is engaged in continuous dynamic interplay between these two poles or opposites. Rises are corrected by falls; falls build up the energy to generate rallies. Jungian depth psychology would condemn (as Prechter did in his "Mania" report) a unidirectional market as unhealthy and dangerous, because anything unidirectional eventually reaches an extreme that generates an extreme reversal. Jung called such a reversal an "enantiodromia."

Enantiodromia means a drastic reversal or swinging over to the opposite. Jung took the term from Heraclitus, the 6th c. B.C. Ionian (Greek) philosopher. Heraclitus, whom Jung respected greatly, viewed all existence as flux. Everything about existence is dynamic, changeable. The changes are not random, but are governed by enantiodromia, the principle of "running to the opposite." This is an iron law of life. Heraclitus saw the interplay of opposites in everything in nature: life-death; waking-sleep; generation-decay. In antiquity, his nickname was "the weeping philosopher" because of his perception that the brightest light always presages a turn towards darkness.

Jung realized that the principle of enantiodromia applies to human psychology as well as to the physical universe. He saw enantiodromia as a potentially terrifying problem for human societies. He stressed that the consequences of one-sidedness are so damaging that we must never allow any attitude or value to take over our consciousness entirely. It was essential, if huge swings to the opposite were to be prevented, that people always keep both poles in sight.

The psyche, Jung believed, does its best to keep people in balance; therefore, whenever any particular pole is excessively valued by the conscious mind, the unconscious will begin to activate ("constellate") the opposite pole. Jung called this the "compensatory" (i.e. corrective) role of the unconscious. If the neglected opposite is relentlessly ignored by consciousness, it either causes chronic neurotic symptoms or builds up massive force until it bursts out in an explosion that shocks everybody. The previously reigning conscious attitude is then completely overthrown.

Jung did not live in a dream world; he was an experienced psychiatrist who was very concerned about current political and social developments, which he saw as resting on group-psychological foundations. His 1936 comments on the saviour archetype, referred to above, reflected his disgust at the then-current psycho-political situation in Germany. As far back as 1928, he had foreseen disaster ahead for Europe. In "The Spiritual Problem of Modern Man," written in that year, he deplored the elated optimism he saw everywhere: the smug sense of superiority over previous benighted generations, the delusion of having arrived at the culmination of world history, the universal certainty that peace and harmony can be made to prevail in the world. In 1928, of course, a Supercycle degree Elliott wave was ascending to a great peak. The stock market and social optimism were sky high, exactly as they are now, at the top of the ensuing Supercycle, which is also ending an even larger Grand Supercycle wave. (On stock market cycles and their relationship to history I am heavily indebted to Robert Prechter's brilliant Elliott Wave analyses.)

Jung had history as well as psychological insight to draw on in his expectation of disaster. The euphoria of 1928, he wrote acidly, was a repeat of the mindless optimism he remembered from before 1914 and would inevitably end the same way. A fearsome enantiodromia was building up in the unconscious of the peoples of the world. The situation was just like that prevailing towards the end of the French Enlightenment or "Age of Reason," the eventual outcome of which was revolution and the Reign of Terror. (This last was Jung's favourite example of a great historical enantiodromia.)

Granting the law of enantiodromia, what can we expect at the end of the current stock market mania? The best guide is to expect the opposite of whatever now reigns in the public consciousness. The following are some likely features of the future landscape.

1. The present psychic inflation will reverse to psychic deflation. This will probably not happen overnight. The 1914-18 precedent referred to by Jung shows that the prewar optimism carried over into the war

situation for a while. Each side declared war believing that (a) it would win; and (b) the fighting would be over in six weeks. Inspired by the upbeat mood, thousands enlisted voluntarily. It took the mud, rats and carnage of the trenches to disillusion these unfortunates.

2. The present archetypal fixation on ascent will give way to its opposite, a fixation on descent; magical flight will reverse to a sickening plummet from the sky. This event conforms to another great mythological archetype of the collective unconscious. According to the Bible, our first parents "fell" and were ejected from Eden when they became arrogant and careless. Instead of living in an earthly paradise, they and their descendants were condemned to a life of toil, suffering and death. In early myths, numerous angels "fell" from Heaven when, becoming frustrated and resentful of their subservient position, they attempted to usurp the Deity's place. In Greek myth, Daedalus, master of technology, made wings for his son Icarus. He warned Icarus that the glue would melt if he flew too high, but Icarus ignored the danger, his wings fell off, and he crashed to earth. The present stock market situation is homologous to all these visions. It is all too likely, therefore, that the next great archetypal experience of the world's investors will not be the joy of arriving in Heaven, but the horror of a universal "Fall."

3. In terms taken from Buddhist myth, instead of entering Nirvana, investors will find that they have fallen back into Samsara, the endless cyclical round of earthly existence. (The Buddha's key teaching was that earthly suffering arises from the fact of "dukkha," or unsatisfactoriness, and that our efforts to escape dukkha invariably make our sufferings worse.)

4. The current egotistical social self-esteem will vanish. Confidence will reverse to fear, elation to depression, manic hyperactivity to numbness and, eventually, confidence to utter prostration.

5. The present universal good feeling will be replaced by rage and despair, fraternal goodwill by hostility to all and sundry. The investment heroes who are now adulated as saviours will be reviled as traitors. In retrospect, their present charisma will seem demonic. It is all too likely that the mutual funds, now so easy and attractive to get into, will appear as towering infernos from which it is impossible to escape. Some will be falsely accused of having caused the disaster. Even those who have had the good sense to avoid it may be regarded with bitterness.

6. Wall Street's current aura of mana will be replaced by loathsomeness. It will be regarded as a world center of everything evil and corrupt.

7. All this would be bad enough, but unfortunately the Fall will be so deep and the losses so far-reaching and destructive that a quick return to either the previous manic condition or to an outlook of chastened sobriety is most unlikely. Near the bottom, another dangerous enantiodromia will be forming in the collective consciousness. People will be longing for deliverance from their suffering. One can only speculate, but on the basis of past history and archetypal patterns, we can expect that a political "saviour" of some sort will be demanded by the population. No doubt there will be numerous candidates stepping forward to fill this high office.

8. Looking further ahead, one can foresee a long succession of enantiodromias. The present situation is so extreme that a single swing of the pendulum has virtually no chance of settling it down. If we take the Dow Jones Industrials graph since the beginning of the manic upswing (for instance, Fig. 9 of Robert Prechter's "Bulls, Bears and Manias"), tip it toward the side, then flick its uptrend line down so as to set off a pendulum, we get some idea of what may lie ahead. In general, the Jungian-Heraclitean principle of enantiodromia supports Prechter's case that the pattern of the Great Bear Market will be a contracting triangle. That is, the Dow will oscillate in a series of wide swings involving lower highs and higher lows, until everybody is exhausted. Then, of course, the next great Elliott upwave can begin!

BIBLIOGRAPHY

The Portable Jung. Edited, with an Introduction, by Joseph Campbell. Trans. R.F.C. Hull. Viking Penguin, New York, The Viking Portable Library, 1971. Especially "The Relations Between the Ego and the Unconscious" (1928), "The Spiritual Problem of Modern Man" (1928) and "The Concept of the Collective Unconscious" (1936).

Eliade, Mircea. *Myths, Dreams and Mysteries: The Encounter between Contemporary Faiths and Archaic Reality.* Trans. Philip Mairet. Collins/Fontana. 1968 (orig. 1957).

Jung, Carl. *Collected Works.* Published by Princeton University Press, many volumes.

Kindleberger, Charles P. *Manias, Panics and Crashes: A History of Financial Crises.* Third Edition, revised. John Wiley & Sons, Inc., New York, 1996.

Prechter, Robert R., Jr. "Bulls, Bears and Manias," *Elliott Wave Theorist*, Special Report, May 21, 1997. Elliott Wave International, Gainesville, Georgia.

Van der Post, Laurens. *Jung and the Story of Our Time.* Viking Penguin, New York, 1971.

Chapter 13

THE RATIONALIZATION OF
VALUE IN A MANIA

originally published in 1934 and in October 1999

To my subscribers:

This is a special issue of *The Elliott Wave Theorist*, as it is not written by me but by guest contributors Benjamin Graham and David Dodd. I am indebted to veteran analyst Ray DeVoe (*The DeVoe Report*, Legg Mason Wood Walker, 1 Battery Park Plaza, New York NY 10004) for reprinting a long-lost section of Graham and Dodd's classic, *Security Analysis* (1934). This section of their book addresses the change in investors' thinking toward stock valuation that occurred in the late 1920s during the last great U.S. stock mania. This section was *cut from the book* in later printings, apparently to jettison era-specific description and thus maintain the book's universal applicability. Little did the authors anticipate that the discussion did indeed have direct applicability to future investor behavior. The general relevance of insightful commentary about financial market psychology will likely never be outdated because essential human psychology is probably immutable. What is shocking is the specificity with which Graham and Dodd's description of investors' common bases for rationalization in the 1920s applies to the 1990s. I have resisted the temptation to underline and otherwise mark pertinent passages in the attached discussion because there are so many of them. Read this report carefully. If every aspect of its reflection of today's common wisdom does not sink in after the first reading, read it a second time.

Today's investment mania has propelled stock values in terms of dividends and corporate asset values to more than double what they were at the top minute in 1929. Yet the excuse for this historic overvaluation is the same as it was then: Companies whose earnings continue to increase should be bought regardless of both stock prices and the actual level of the companies' earnings, and corporate asset values and dividends are irrelevant and may be sacrificed by companies when chasing the goal of continually higher earnings.

The original excuse for this philosophy was that rising earnings would eventually accrue precisely to asset values and dividends. The irony is that in the process, investors no longer care about either, and as a result, the earnings never so accrue. What is going on here psychologically? The answer is that investors, impelled headlong by the herding impulse to bid stocks to absurdly high prices, must generate a superficially plausible rationalization for their actions in order to satisfy and quiet their reasoning left neocortex, which otherwise might interfere with their actions. It's that simple, not to mention anti-intuitive and profound. For a concurring comment from 1934, see Graham and Dodd's section, "The Justification Offered," on page 190.

This rarely available discussion is nothing less than a large mirror into which baby boomers in the 1990s may look. In doing so, those honest among them will see an image looking back at them and experience a flash of recognition as they exclaim, "Granddad!"

— Robert Prechter, October 1999

Excerpt from *Security Analysis* (1934), by Benjamin Graham and David Dodd, p.306-316:

Investment in Common Stocks Based on Threefold Concept — We thus see that investment in common stocks was formerly based upon the threefold concept of: (1) a suitable and established dividend return; (2) a stable and adequate earnings record; and (3) a satisfactory backing of tangible assets. Each of these three elements could be made the subject of careful analytical study viewing the issue both by itself and in comparison with others of its class. Common-stock commitments motivated by any other viewpoint were characterized as speculative, and it was not expected that they should be justified by a serious analysis.

THE NEW-ERA THEORY

During the postwar [i.e., World War I] period, and particularly during the latter stage of the bull market culminating in 1929, the public acquired a completely different attitude towards the investment merits of common stocks. Two of the three elements above stated lost nearly all of their significance and the third, the earnings record, took on an entirely novel complexion. The new theory or principle may be summed up in the sentence: "The value of a common stock depends entirely upon what it will earn in the future."

From this dictum the following corollaries were drawn:

1. That the dividend rate should have slight bearing upon the value.

2. That since no relationship apparently existed between assets and earning power, the asset value was entirely devoid of importance.

3. That past earnings were significant only to the extent that they indicated what changes in the earnings were likely to take place in the future.

This complete revolution in the philosophy of common-stock investment took place virtually without realization by the stock-buying public and with only the most superficial recognition by financial observers. An effort must be made to reach a thorough comprehension of what this changed viewpoint really signifies. To do so we must consider it from three angles, its causes, its consequences, and its logical validity.

Causes for This Changed Viewpoint.— Why did the *investing* public turn its attention from dividends, from asset values, and from earnings, to transfer it almost exclusively to the earnings *trend, i.e.,* to the *changes* in earnings expected in the future? The answer was, first, that the records of the past were proving an undependable guide to investment; and secondly, that the rewards offered by the future had become irresistibly alluring.

The new-era concepts had their root first of all in the obsolescence of the old-established standards. During the last generation the tempo of economic change has been speeded up to such a degree that the fact of being *long established* has ceased to be, as once it was, a warranty of *stability.* Corporations enjoying decade-long prosperity have been precipitated into insolvency within a few years. Other enterprises, which had been small or unsuccessful or in doubtful repute, have just as quickly acquired dominant size, impressive earnings, and the highest rating. The major group upon which investment interest was chiefly concentrated, viz., the railroads, failed signally to participate in the expansion of national wealth and income, and showed repeated signs of definite retrogression. The street railways, another important medium of investment prior to 1914, rapidly lost the greater portion of their value as the result of the development of new transportation agencies. The electric and gas companies followed an irregular course during this period, since they were harmed rather than helped by the war and postwar inflation, and their impressive growth is a relatively recent phenomenon. The history of industrial companies was a hodge-podge of violent changes, in which the benefits of prosperity were so unequally and so impermanently distributed as to bring about the most unexpected failures alongside of the most dazzling successes.

In the face of all this instability it was inevitable that the threefold basis of common-stock investment should prove totally inadequate. Past earnings and dividends could no longer be considered, in themselves, an index of future earnings and dividends. Furthermore, these future earnings showed no tendency whatever to be controlled by the amount of the actual investment in the business—the asset values—but instead depended entirely upon a favorable industrial position and upon capable or fortunate managerial policies. In numerous cases of receivership, the current assets dwindled and the fixed assets proved almost worthless. Because of this absence of any connection between both assets and earnings, and between assets and realizable values in bankruptcy, less and less attention came to be paid either by financial writers or by the general public to the formerly important question of "net worth," or "book value," and it may be said that by 1929 book value had practically disappeared as an element in determining the attractiveness of a security issue. It is a significant confirmation of this point that "watered stock," once so burning an issue, is now a forgotten phrase.

Attention Shifted to the Trend of Earnings.— Thus the prewar approach to investment, based upon past records and tangible facts, became outworn and was discarded. Could anything be put in its place? A new conception was given central importance —that of *trend of earnings.* The past was important only in so far as it showed the direction in which the future could be expected to move. A continuous increase in profits proved that the company was on the upgrade and promised still better results in the future than had been accomplished to date. Conversely, if the earnings had declined, or even remained stationary during a prosperous period, the future must be thought unpromising and the issue was certainly to be avoided.

The Common-stocks-as-long-term-investments Doctrine.— Along with this idea as to what constituted the basis for common-stock selection, there emerged a companion theory that common stocks represented the most profitable and therefore the most desirable media for long-term investment. This gospel was based upon a certain amount of research, showing that diversified lists of common stocks had regularly increased in value over stated intervals of time for many years past. The figures indicated that such diversified common-stock holdings yielded both a higher income return and a greater principal profit than purchases of standard bonds.

The combination of these two ideas supplied the "investment theory" upon which the 1927-1929 stock market proceeded. Amplifying the principle stated on page 307, the theory ran as follows:

1. "The value of a common stock depends on what it can earn in the future."

2. "Good common stocks will prove sound and profitable investments."

3. "Good common stocks are those which have shown a rising trend of earnings."

These statements sound innocent and plausible. Yet they concealed two theoretical weaknesses which could and did result in untold mischief. The first of these defects was that they abolished the fundamental distinctions between investment and speculation. The second was that they ignored the *price* of a stock in determining whether it was a desirable purchase.

New-era Investment Equivalent to Prewar Speculation.—A moment's thought will show that "new-era investment," as practiced by the representative investment trusts, was almost identical with speculation as popularly defined in pre-boom days. Such "investment" meant buying common stocks instead of bonds, emphasizing enhancement of principal instead of income, and stressing the changes of the future instead of the facts of the established past. It would not be inaccurate to state that new-era investment was simply old-style speculation confined to common stocks with a satisfactory trend of earnings. The impressive new concept underlying the greatest stock-market boom in history appears to be no more than a thinly disguised version of the old cynical epigram: "Investment is successful speculation."

Stocks Regarded as Attractive Irrespective of Their Prices.— The notion that the desirability of a common stock was entirely independent of its price seems incredibly absurd. Yet the new-era theory led directly to this thesis. If a public-utility stock was selling at 35 times its *maximum* recorded earnings, instead of 10 times its *average* earnings, which was the pre-boom standard, the conclusion to be drawn was not that the stock was now too high but merely that the standard of value had been raised. Instead of judging the market price by established standards of value, the new era based its standards of value upon the market price. Hence all upper limits disappeared, not only upon the price at which a stock *could* sell, but even upon the price at which it would *deserve* to sell. This fantastic reasoning actually led to the purchase for investment at $100 per share of common stocks earning $2.50 per share. The identical reasoning would support the purchase of these same shares at $200, at $1,000, or at any conceivable price.

An alluring corollary of this principle was that making money in the stock market was now the easiest thing in the world. It was only necessary to buy "good" stocks, regardless of price, and then to let nature take her upward course. The results of such a doctrine could not fail to be tragic. Countless people asked themselves, "Why work for a living when a fortune can be made in Wall Street without working?" The ensuing migration from business into the financial district resembled the famous gold rush to the Klondike, with the not unimportant difference that there really was gold in the Klondike.

Investment Trusts Adopted This New Doctrine.—An ironical sidelight is thrown on this 1928-1929 theory by the practice of the investment trusts. These were formed for the purpose of giving the untrained public the benefit of expert administration of its funds—a plausible idea, and one which had been working well in England. The earliest American investment trusts laid considerable emphasis upon certain time-tried principles of successful investment, which they were much better qualified to follow than the typical individual. The most important of these principles were:

1. To buy in times of depression and low prices, and to sell out in times of prosperity and high prices.

2. To diversify holdings in many fields and probably in many countries.

3. To discover and acquire undervalued individual securities as the result of comprehensive and expert statistical investigations.

The rapidity and completeness with which these traditional principles disappeared from investment-trust technique is one of the many marvels of the period. The idea of buying in times of depression was obviously inapplicable. It suffered from the fatal weakness that investment trusts could be organized only in good times, so that they were virtually compelled to make their initial commitments in bull markets. The idea of world-wide geographical distribution had never exerted a powerful appeal upon the provincially minded Americans (who possibly were right in this respect); and with things going so much better here than abroad this principle was dropped by common consent.

Analysis Abandoned by Investment Trusts — But most paradoxical was the early abandonment of research and analysis in guiding investment-trust policies. However, since these financial institutions owed their existence to the new-era philosophy, it was natural and perhaps only just that they should adhere closely to it. Under its canons investment had now become so beautifully simple that research was unnecessary and statistical data a mere incumbrance. The investment process consisted merely of finding prominent companies with a rising trend of earnings, and then buying their shares regardless of price. Hence the sound policy was to buy only what everyone else was buying—a select list of highly popular and exceedingly expensive issues, appropriately known as the "blue chips." The original idea of searching for the undervalued and neglected issues dropped completely out of sight. Investment trusts actually boasted that their portfolios consisted exclusively of the active and standard *(i.e.,* the most popular and highest priced) common stocks. With but slight exaggeration, it might be asserted that under this convenient technique of investment, the affairs of a ten-million-dollar investment trust could be administered by the intelligence, the training, and the actual labors of a single thirty-dollar-a-week clerk.

The man in the street, having been urged to entrust his funds to the superior skill of investment experts—for substantial compensation—was soon reassuringly told that the trusts would be careful to buy nothing except what the man in the street was buying himself.

The Justification Offered.—Irrationality could go no further; yet it is important to note that mass speculation can flourish only in an atmosphere of illogic and unreality. The self-deception of the mass speculator must, however, have its elements of justification. This is usually some generalized statement, sound enough within its proper field, but twisted to fit the speculative mania. In real-estate booms, the "reasoning" is usually based upon the inherent permanence and growth of land values. In the new-era bull market, the "rational" basis was the record of long-term improvement shown by diversified common-stock holdings.

A Sound Premise Used to Support an Unsound Conclusion.—There was, however, a radical fallacy involved in the new-era application of this historical fact. This should be apparent from even a superficial examination of the data contained in the small and rather sketchy volume from which the new-era theory may be said to have sprung. The book is entitled *Common Stocks as Long-Term Investments,* by Edgar Lawrence Smith, published in 1924. Common stocks were shown to have a tendency to increase in value with the years, for the simple reason that they earned more than they paid out in dividends, and thus the reinvested earnings added to their worth. In a representative case, the company would earn an average of 9%, pay 6% in dividends, and add 3% to surplus. With good management and reasonable luck the fair value of the stock would increase with its book value, at the annual rate of 3% *compounded.* This was, of course, a theoretical rather than a standard pattern; but the numerous instances of results poorer than "normal " might be offset by examples of more rapid growth.

The attractiveness of common stocks for the long pull thus lay essentially in the fact that they earned more than the bond-interest rate upon their cost. This would be true, typically, of a stock earning $10 and selling at 100. But as soon as the price was advanced to a much higher price in relation to earnings, this advantage disappeared, *and with it disappeared the entire theoretical basis for investment purchases of common stocks.* When investors paid $200 per share for a stock earning $10, they were buying an earning power no greater than the bond-interest rate, without the extra protection afforded by a prior claim. Hence in using the past performances of common stocks as the reason for paying prices 20 to 40 times their earnings, the new-era exponents were starting with a sound premise and twisting it into a woefully unsound conclusion.

In fact their rush to take advantage of the inherent attractiveness of common stocks itself produced conditions entirely different from those which had given rise to this attractiveness and upon which it basically depended, *viz.,* the fact that earnings had averaged some 10% on market price. As we have seen, Edgar Lawrence Smith plausibly explained the growth of common-stock values as arising from the building up of asset values through the reinvestment of surplus earnings. Paradoxically enough, the new-era theory which exploited this finding refused to accord the slightest importance to the asset values behind the stocks it favored. Furthermore, the validity of Mr. Smith's conclusions rested necessarily upon the assumption that common stocks could be counted

Earnings Per Share

Year	Company A (Electric Power & Light)	Company B (Bangor & Aroostook R.R.)	Company C (Chicago Yellow Cab)
1925	1.01	6.22	5.52
1926	1.45	8.69	5.60
1927	2.09	8.41	4.54
1928	2.37	6.94	4.58
1929	2.98	8.30	4.47
5-year average	1.98	7.71	4.94
High price, 1929	86 5/8	90 3/8	35

on to behave in the future about as they had in the past. Yet the new-era theory threw out of account the past earnings of corporations except in so far as they were regarded as pointing to a *trend* for the future.

Examples Showing Emphasis on Trend of Earnings.—Take three companies with the following exhibits:

The 1929 high prices for these three companies show that the new-era attitude was enthusiastically favorable to Company *A*, unimpressed by Company *H*, and definitely hostile to Company *C*. The market considered Company *A* shares worth more than twice as much as Company *C* shares, although the latter earned 50% more per share than Company *A* in 1929 and its average earnings were 150% greater.

Average versus Trend of Earnings. — These relationships between price and earnings in 1929 show definitely that the past exhibit was no longer a measure of normal earning power but merely a weathervane to show which way the winds of profit were blowing. That the *average earnings* had ceased to be a dependable measure of future earnings must indeed be admitted, because of the greater instability of the typical business to which we have previously alluded. But it did not follow at all that the *trend of earnings* must therefore be a more dependable guide than the *average;* and even if it were more dependable it would not necessarily provide a safe basis, entirely by itself, for investment.

The accepted assumption that because earnings have moved in a certain direction for some years past they will continue to move in that direction, is fundamentally no different from the discarded assumption that because earnings averaged a certain amount in the past they will continue to average about that amount in the future. It may well be that the earnings *trend* offers a more dependable clue to the future than does the earnings average. But at best such an indication of future results is far from certain, and, more important still, there is no method of establishing a logical relationship between trend and price.[1] This means that the value placed upon a satisfactory trend must be wholly arbitrary, and hence speculative, and hence inevitably subject to exaggeration and later collapse.

Danger in Projecting Trends into the Future.—There are several reasons why we cannot be sure that a trend of profits shown in the past will continue in the future. In the broad economic sense, there is the law of diminishing returns and of increasing competition which must finally flatten out any sharply upward curve of growth. There is also the flow and ebb of the business cycle, from which the particular danger arises that the earnings curve will look most impressive on the very eve of a serious setback. Considering the 1927-1929 period we observe that since the trend-of-earnings theory was at bottom only a pretext to excuse rank speculation under the guise of "investment," the profit-mad public was quite willing to accept the flimsiest evidence of the existence of a favorable trend. Rising earnings for a period of five, or four, or even three years only, were regarded as an assurance of uninterrupted future growth and a warrant for projecting the curve of profits indefinitely upward.

Example: The prevalent heedlessness on this score was most evident in connection with the numerous common-stock flotations during this period. The craze for a showing of rising profits resulted in the promotion of many industrial enterprises which had been favored by temporary good fortune and were just approaching, or had already reached, the peak of their prosperity. A typical example of this practice is found in the offering of preferred and common stock of Schletter and Zander, Inc., a manufacturer of hosiery (name changed later to Signature Hosiery Company). The company was organized in 1929, to succeed a company organized in 1922, and the financing was effected by the sale of 44,810 shares of $3.50 convertible preferred shares at $50 a share and 261,349 voting-trust certificates for common stock at $26 per share. The offering circular presented the following exhibit of earnings from the constituent properties:

Year	Net after federal taxes	Per share of preferred	Per share of common
1925	$172,058	$ 3.84	$ 0.06
1926	339,920	$ 7.58	$ 0.70
1927	563,856	$ 12.58	$ 1.56
1928	1,021,308	$ 22.79	$ 3.31

The subsequent record was as follows:

1929	812,136	18.13	2.51
1930	*179,876(d)*	*4.01(d)*	*1.81(d)*

In 1931 liquidation of the company's assets was begun and a total of $17 per share in liquidating dividends on the preferred have been paid up to the end of 1933. (Assets then remaining for liquidation were negligible.)

This example illustrates one of the paradoxes of financial history, *viz.*, that at the very period when the increasing instability of individual companies had made the purchase of common stocks far more precarious than before, the gospel of common stocks as safe and satisfactory investments was preached to and avidly accepted by the American public.[2]

NOTES

[1] The new-era investment theory was conspicuously reticent on the mathematical side. The relationship between price and earnings, or price and trend of earnings, was anything that the market pleased to make it (note the price of Electric Power and Light compared with its earnings record given on p.313). If an attempt were to be made to give a mathematical expression to the underlying idea of valuation, it might be said that it was based on the derivative of the earnings, stated in terms of Time.

[2] Graham and Dodd's analysis is wonderfully insightful. Yet it is, we should recognize, an after-the-fact exposition. The publications of Elliott Wave International elucidated the excesses of the 1990s mania as it progressed because the Wave Principle provided the knowledge of the market's environment and long-term position in advance, an immense advantage for a proper perspective on real-time market events. —Ed.

PART IV

Associated Studies in Market Analysis

Chapter 14

PACKET WAVES

by Robert R. Prechter, Jr.
originally published August 3, 1979

The Big Picture

The formation I am going to discuss is beyond a doubt one of the most interesting a market has ever constructed. It is a picture of a huge oscillation, beginning at rest, swinging wider and wider and finally contracting again to a rest point, which is where the Dow stands today (see Figures 1 and 2).

Only two items keep the actual DJIA from tracing a flawless oscillation pattern. First, the low of the seventh swing in 1965 fails by forty points to drop below the low of swing #5, and secondly, the 1968 high falls short of the 1966 high by five points, although it should be noted that all other stock market indexes did clear their 1966 highs in 1968.

There are several points to be made with regard to this formation. First is that the formation has lasted fifteen years, from 1964 to 1979, the same time length as the preceding fifteen-year bull market rise from 1949 to 1964. Second, and possibly most surprising, is that the rest point in March 1964 when the ever-widening swings began was **821** on the Dow (see Figure 3). The July 1979 low, which may mark the final swing in the contracting period, was precisely the same level: **821** on the Dow (see Figure 6c). Why this level? I suspect that a physicist may be able to answer the *why*, but I can certainly answer the what. 820 just happens to be the halfway level between the extreme high of the formation at 1070 in 1973 and the extreme low at 570 in 1974 — a 500-point range, divided in half by its starting and ending points! These considerations lead to the conclusion that we are dealing here with a single formation, a single structure created by changes in mass psychology over a fifteen-year period.

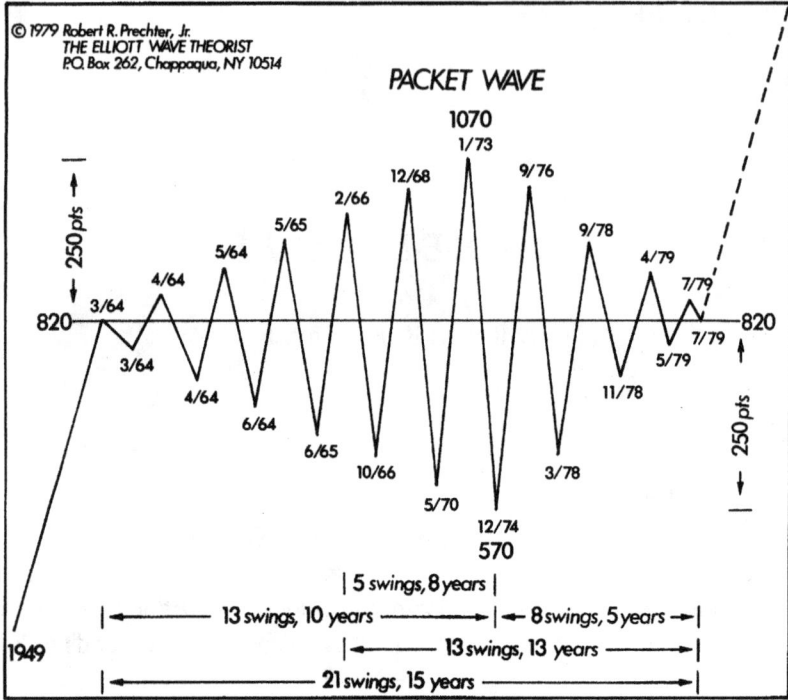

Figure 1

Perhaps this idea of the midpoint explains the surprising results of a computer analysis of total NYSE volume traded within each increment of ten points on the Dow. With a quick glance at Figure 4, you can see that the 830 band clearly accounted for the greatest level of trading volume over the past decade. This study enhances the significance of the oscillation's midpoint, and thus of the oscillation itself.

Fibonacci Phenomena

Briefly, the Fibonacci ratio is the ratio between successive numbers in the Fibonacci sequence and provides the mathematical basis for the Elliott Wave Principle. 5, 8, 13 and 21 are Fibonacci numbers, related to each other by the Fibonacci ratio, .618. I went back to the daily charts to ascertain the total number of expanding swings leading to the 1974 bottom at 570. That number is **13**. The number of contracting swings from 1974 to the present is **8**. The total is **21**. All three numbers are

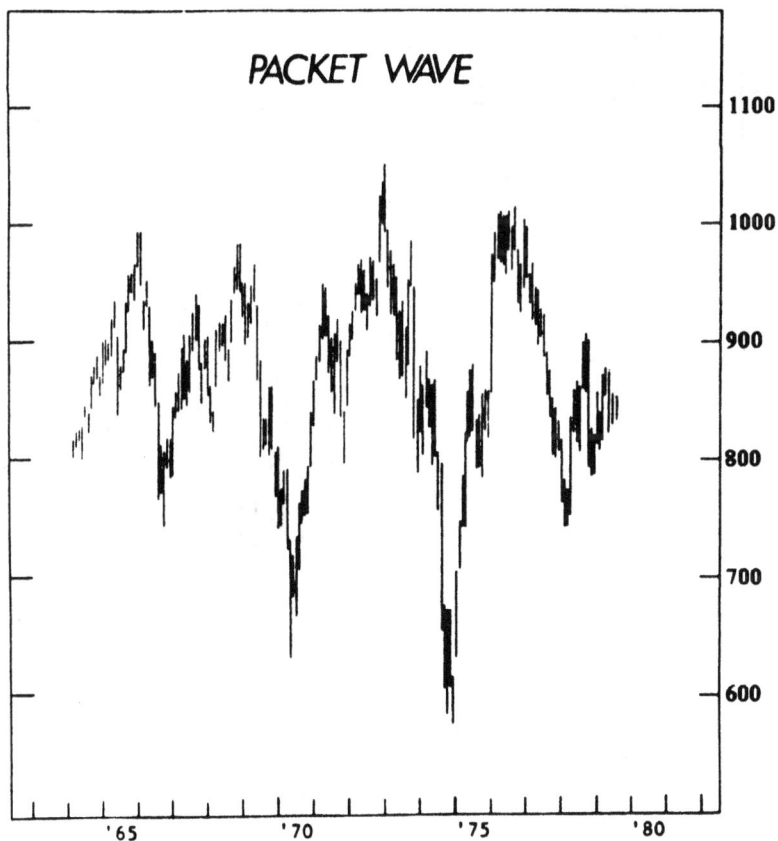

Figure 2

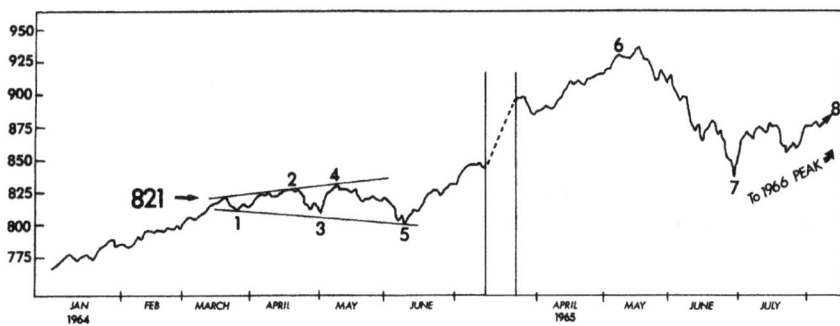

Figure 3

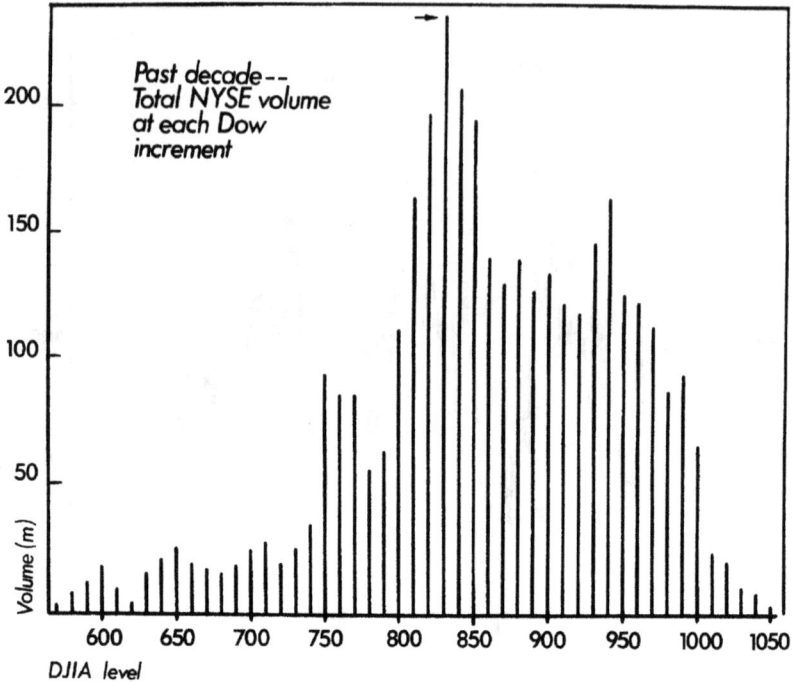

Figure 4

Fibonacci numbers, so that the number of contracting swings is .618 times the number of expanding swings, which is itself .618 time the number of total swings. *This is the typical Elliott relationship between two distinct sections of a single entity.*

The time element is roughly ten years for expansion, five years for contraction, or more precisely, 130 months and 55 months. Since 130 equals 13, a Fibonacci number, times 10, and since 55 is a Fibonacci number, we find that $55 = 130 \times (1.618)^3/10$ or $55 = 130 \times .4236$, where 4.236 is the ratio between second alternate Fibonacci numbers. I find this relationship interesting, but not a necessary element of the thesis.

To further add to the subtlety and complexity of this wave, we might keep in mind that 1966 is the orthodox Elliott Wave peak of the bull market dating from 1942. From that point, the Dow completed **5** expanding swings in **8** years (to 1974) followed by **8** contracting swings in **5** years (to the present), for a total of **13** swings in **13** years. From this perspective, the number of expanding swings is .618 times the number of contracting swings, which is itself .618 times the total number of swings. All these Fibonacci relationships are operating at the same time. Since the 1964 starting point for this formation is open to challenge, we may wish to regard 1966 as the beginning of the phenomenon we are investigating here. Either way, it's a fascinating study in form.

A New Elliott Wave Formation

Now what is really exciting to me as a student of the Wave Principle is that Elliott never saw one of these structures. It is not listed in his extensive catalogue of corrective wave formations, although a corrective wave, at least in this case, is unquestionably what it is.

I feel that this wave structure is a new discovery under the Wave Principle, a new type of correction, basically a combination of an "expanding triangle" and a "contracting triangle." Lots of names suggest themselves: "double triangle," for instance. I talked this formation over with A.J. Frost, who, in his usual poetic way, came up with the name "packet wave" after an illustration in Fritjof Capra's *The Tao of Physics* (Shambhala Publications, Inc., 1975), pictured in Figure 5 below.

The illustration is meant to depict a wave packet in "dynamic equilibrium," a good description of the Dow for the past fifteen years.

The "packet wave" concept explains why some rallies in the Dow during the past five years can be classified as either 3's or 5's, with resulting controversy among Elliotters, or why some rallies look like 3's in the Dow but 5's in the NYSE Composite Index. Since triangle waves always subdivide into 3's, labeled a-b-c, a plausible argument for the unity of this formation can be built upon the easily discernible series of 3's (labeled a-b-c) in the DJIA over the past thirteen years, as illustrated in Figures 6a, 6b and 6c.

WAVE PACKET

Figure 5

By the way, the particular placement of the letters in these figures reflects internal Elliott wave dynamics. Correct counting, for those not familiar with the Wave Principle, often results in placing labels at levels before or after nominal high and low points. Other interpreters may differ slightly. In particular, the 1966 decline and the 1969-1970 decline are clearly seven-wave structures, which have the same interpretive value as 3's under the rules of the Wave Principle, so internal labeling is academic with respect to this discussion.

The Dow, from the perspective of the packet wave, has been in a "bear market" the entire time (although all other indexes have been

Figure 6a

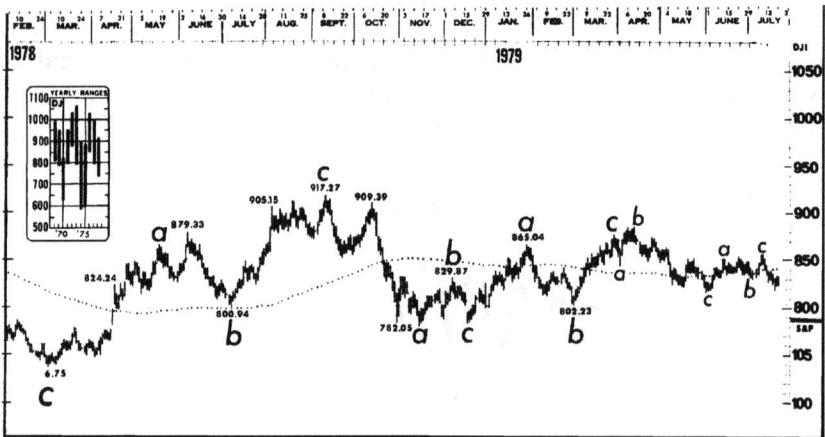

Figure 6b

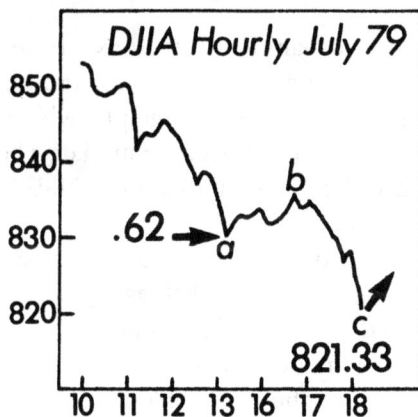

Figure 6c

in bull markets since 1974). Elliott was about the only analyst ever to recognize that sideways motions are bear markets. For evidence of this contention, all one need to do is look at a chart of the "constant-dollar" Dow from 1966 (see Figure 7). Bear market plus raging inflation equals sideways formation.

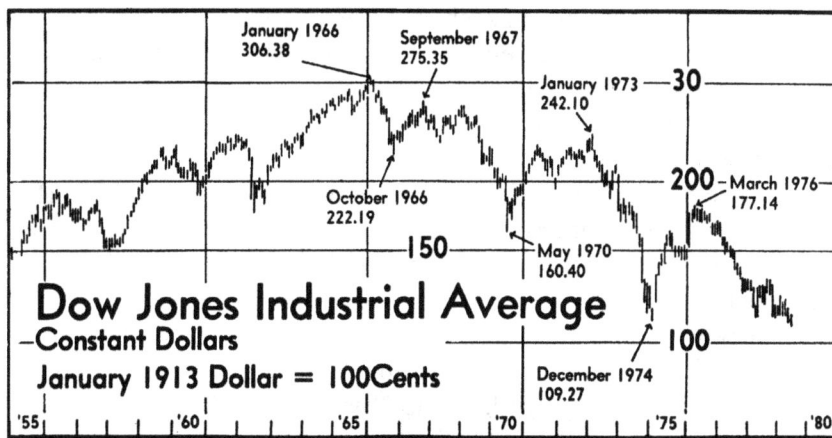

Figure 7

A Bit of History

As far as I know, recognition of the onset or terminus of a *sideways* pattern can be accomplished at or near the time of occurrence only by students of the Elliott Wave Principle, which recognizes them as important events in the progress of the market. The only other such identifications with which I am familiar are R.N. Elliott's conclusions in 1942 and A.J. Frost's in 1964.

In 1942, Elliott called for the end of a 13-year sideways "triangle" and the start of a major new bull market lasting decades. The 1942 low was never broken, and the years after his death in 1948 finally proved him correct. I should point out, though, that the final drop to the 1942 low occurred on a downside break of the long-term triangular formation at just under the level of the previous major low. If that piece of history were to repeat with respect to the current situation, the Dow would soon begin a decline back to just under the 740 level before beginning the extended bull phase. I consider that possibility extremely remote. [Seven months later, the March 1980 bottom occurred at 739, the low of the new decade.—Ed.]

A. Hamilton Bolton later suggested that in retrospect the true end of the "go nowhere" market dating from 1929 was 1949, which marked the end of a 21-year triangle from 1928. Either position is tenable, although Bolton's observation was not made at the time of occurrence.

The second instance of such an observation was A.J. Frost's recognition of a completed five-wave count in 1964 that would mark the beginning of a long period of sideways motion in the Dow. His prediction at that time is recounted in our book, *Elliott Wave Principle — Key to Stock Market Profits*.

I have not lost sight of Elliott's error of the 1930s and 1940s. He recognized so many incredible features of a large triangle, with each swing covering .618 of the previous swing, that he forced himself to call it a "contracting triangle" correction when in reality these phenomena were merely superimposed over the simplest and most acceptable wave count as it is now generally accepted by the major students of Elliott. Actually, the downside break of the "triangle" in 1942 should have alerted him to the correct alternative.

In any case, while I recognize the "packet wave" as a phenomenon, it may not be prudent to begin the orthodox count for the emerging bull market from 1979, but from 1974, as was my previous assumption. In other words, the contracting period in the Dow may be a structure that represents the transition from bear to bull and is superimposed over a wave background which is, in the strict sense of an "Elliott count," a bull market that began in 1974. Similar junctures have existed in the past: 1924, 1942 and 1949, for instance. This is another academic question, of course, since my conclusions regarding the immediate future are identical in both cases.

The Contraction

The period of contracting swings from December 1974 to the present (see Figure 8) is a succession of market moves that are interrelated quite closely by the Fibonacci ratio (see Figure 9). As I followed each of these eight movements, I became more fascinated with the Dow's ability to measure out nearly exact price lengths to satisfy the Fibonacci requirements, and even more fascinated when I could recognize some of these turning points the hour they occurred.

The CONTRACTION

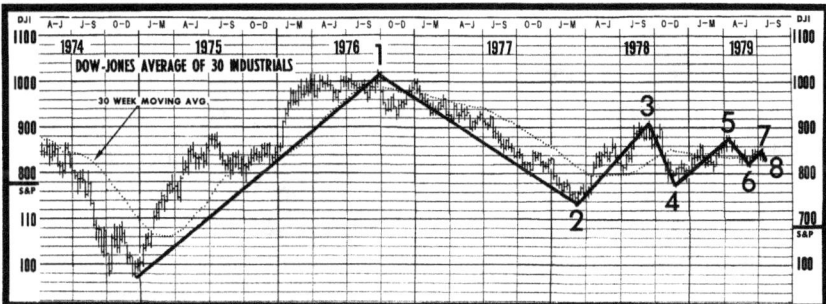

Figure 8

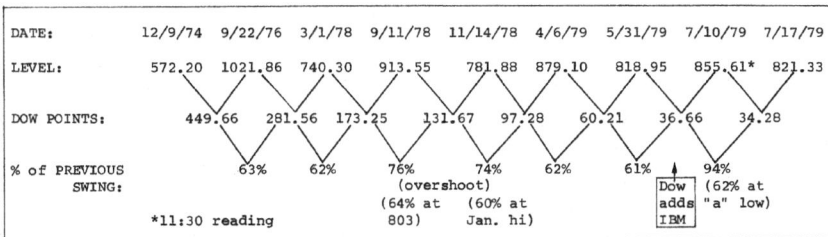

DATE:	12/9/74	9/22/76	3/1/78	9/11/78	11/14/78	4/6/79	5/31/79	7/10/79	7/17/79
LEVEL:	572.20	1021.86	740.30	913.55	781.88	879.10	818.95	855.61*	821.33
DOW POINTS:		449.66	281.56	173.25	131.67	97.28	60.21	36.66	34.28
% of PREVIOUS SWING:		63%	62%	76% (overshoot) (64% at 803)	74% (60% at Jan. hi)	62%	61% Dow adds IBM	94% (62% at "a" low)	

*11:30 reading

Figure 9

Take a look at Figure 10, on which I have marked each rally and decline with a thick dark line. Beside each line is the ratio of the length of that line to the swing that preceded it. I used the exact hourly readings at each peak and trough to drive home the tendency for this average to conform to the .62 ratio during a time which most analysts described as "impossible," "erratic" and even "random." With two important exceptions, the 1978 "October massacre" and its retracement, each swing retraced almost exactly 62% of the previous swing.

The last ratio (94%) was extended quite a bit, although the low at "a" in the a-b-c downswing stopped at exactly a 62% retracement, as shown in Figure 6c. The extended push occurred partly because the final low point was seeking the 821 level, where the entire structure began, and partly because just prior to that downswing IBM and MRK were substituted for C and ESM in the Dow. The extraordinary weakness in IBM during the week following the 855.61 high on July 10 could easily explain why the final downswing was lengthened by ten points. Whether this substitution had anything to do with the outcome or not, the structure did end precisely at 821 immediately thereafter.

The October 1978 Massacre

While the tendency to conform to the 62% ratio is evident, it might be prudent to examine the two back-to-back exceptions. The first retracement that varied significantly from the .62 ratio was the September-November 1978 decline, which retraced 76% (3/4) of the March-September 1978 advance. I remember that juncture particularly because my downside target for that decline was, for a variety of Elliott reasons, 803, a level that also would have been just over 62% of the preceding advance.

I would like to demonstrate that the market appeared to "know" that 803 was a significant level. Each time it was broken on the downside, it was broken in white panic, and when it was penetrated again on the upside, the market generated extreme thrust in order to do it. Figure 11 is an hourly chart of the Dow with those hours within which 803 was crossed left unconnected to demonstrate the enormous moves generated during those hours.

On October 30, the 17-point down opening hour through 803 resulted in a near-record 421 downside gaps in stocks on the NYSE. 803 was penetrated dramatically four times in the next nine trading hours.

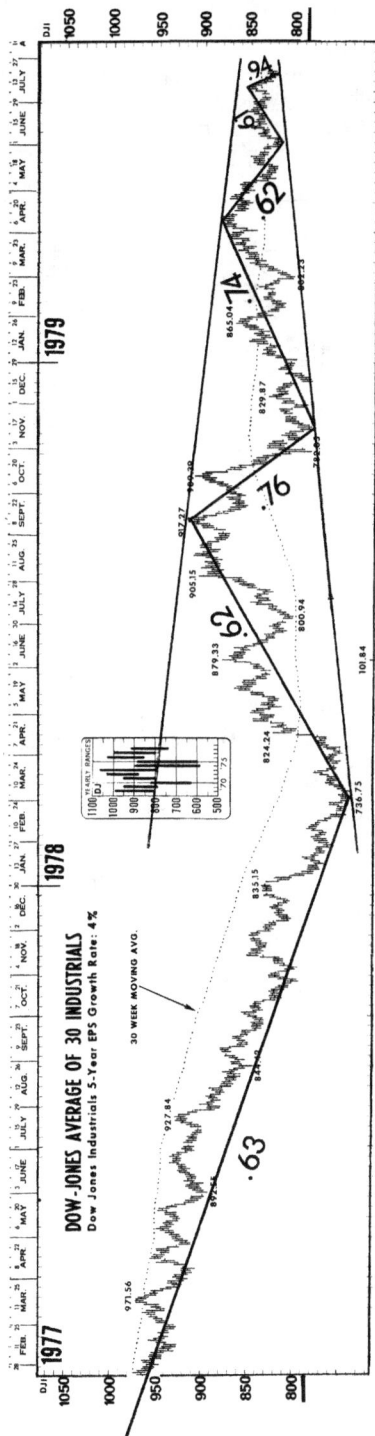

Figure 10

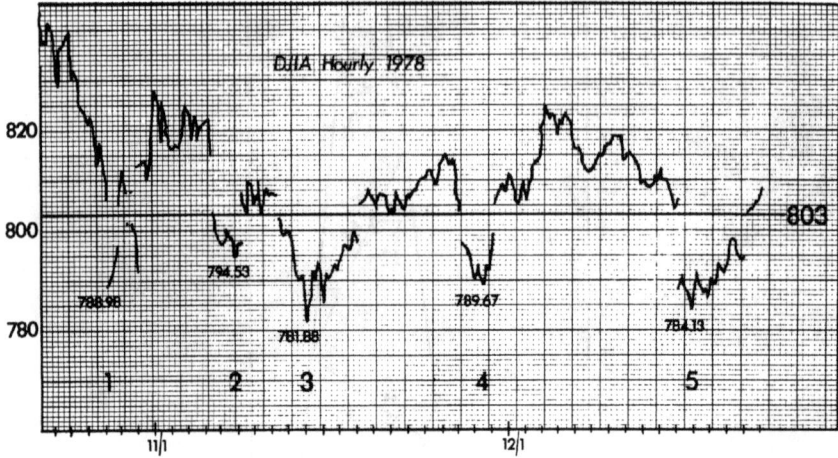

Figure 11

The next morning, it was hurdled again on the 20-point up opening hour of November 11 when the DJIA initiated its largest one-day jump in history. The next two penetrations accompanied 11- and 10-point hours respectively. On November 29, a 0.78-point "intraday" gap crossed 803 on the downside. On December 18, a 17-point collapse in the opening hour broke 803 and left a 6.93-point intraday gap in the Dow, one of the largest ever, as 541 stocks gapped lower, a record one-day number since at least 1972 where my data begins. The thrust on December 22 pushed through 803 on a 9-point up hour, completing a total of five (a Fibonacci number) distinct dips into the upper 700s. Then finally, on the first trading day of 1979, the Dow drifted lightly back to 802, marking the low for the entire year (if my analysis of the future is correct) and then left it behind for the last time. As an additional note, the July 1978 and February 1979 hourly lows were 805, further emphasizing the level's importance both before and after the November-December action at that level.

The second retracement significantly greater than 62% was that *immediately following* the "October massacre" decline. The rally into April 1979 retraced 74% (3/4) of the previous decline, as if to "make up for" the preceding downside overshoot of 76%. Note that before that rally retraced the full 74%, it stopped abruptly in January at 859.75, at 60% retracement, and then fell to test 805 again in late February. Figure 12 shows perfect Fibonacci percentage retracements when we discard

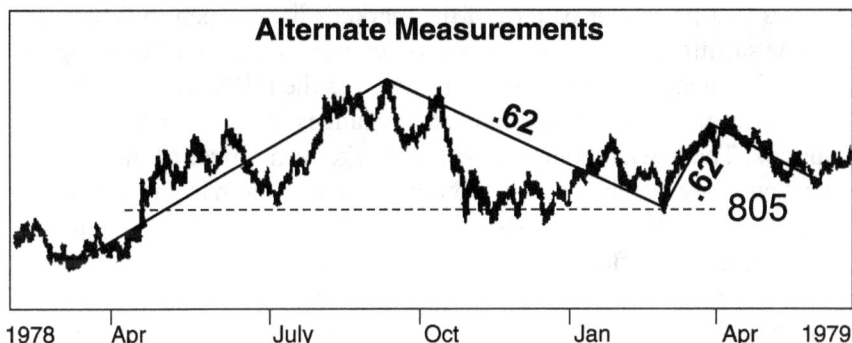

Figure 12

the overshoot period and measure to the late February low. This adjustment would make the first six movements in Figure 10 all Fibonacci retracements.

What's Going On?

Mathematically speaking, it is much more implausible to argue that these numbers are random or coincidence than it is to accept what is happening, that changes in mass emotions, as reflected by the stock market and most especially the Dow Jones Industrial Average, are tied to certain laws of nature, one of which is best expressed by the Golden Ratio, .618, a mathematical relationship that has been considered one of the great secrets of the universe by, among others, Plato, Pythagoras, Kepler, DaVinci, Newton, and the philosopher-mathematician-priests of ancient Egypt.

The "packet wave" structure I have shown here unfolded its pattern quite clearly regardless of wars, energy crises, speeches, assassinations, Watergates, Peanutgates, jawboning, or the weather. To a phenomenal extent, the DJIA appeared to know exactly where it was, exactly where it had been, and exactly where it was going. But *why* is an average of thirty somewhat randomly chosen stocks so reliable in exhibiting over and over again these phenomena of construction?

For a hundred years, investors have noticed that events external to the market often seem to have no effect on the market's progress. With the knowledge that the market continuously unfolds in waves that are related to each other through *form* and *ratio*, we can see why there is little connection. *The market has a life of its own.* Now what ultimately *causes* that particular pattern of the market's life is open to debate. It can be surmised, though, that it is *mass human psychology* that is registering its changes in the barometer known as the DJIA. This idea helps to explain the *cause* of future events: changes in the mass emotional outlook. That's what comes first. The market is a mirror of the forces, whatever they may be, that are affecting humanity both in and out of the market arena. The market doesn't "see into the future" as the discounting idea suggests; it reflects the causes of the future. Increasingly optimistic people expand business; increasingly depressed people contract their businesses. The *results* show up later as a "discounted" future. It's not the politicians who gallantly "save" a bear market by returning to policies of economic sanity, it's the mass emotional environment, as reflected by the market, that forces them at some critical point to do it. Events do not shape the forces of the market; it is the forces behind the market that shape events.

Besides the idea that the emotions of man are tied to the Fibonacci ratio for whatever reason, I think that part of the answer to the Dow's precision lies in the concept of biofeedback. The Dow Industrial Average is the most widely followed market index in the world. It not only *reflects* the pulse of investors, it *affects* the pulse of investors. Not only do our investment decisions force the Dow to go in a certain direction, but the direction of the Dow often causes us to make those very investment decisions. There is a complex emotional involvement there of which we're quite aware but which we don't fully understand. How else can we explain the fact that even though MMM was substituted for Anaconda in the Dow in 1976, the 1976-78 decline still managed to fall exactly to the level that retraced .618 of the 1974-76 advance?

Background, Sentiment and Related Events

I'd like to sidetrack for a bit and ask why the Dow found its initial point of rest in 1964. At that time the United States had no war, no shortages, undisputed world power, cheap energy, a happy populace, a productive economy, and had just lived two decades with relatively competent politicians. [The extremity of positive social emotions that month displayed itself in the orgasmic outburst known as "Beatlemania." —Ed.] The Dow, after climbing a record 13 weeks in a row, took a rest in March 1964 and reflected upon America's positive position in the world and feeling towards itself; it took a look around and liked what it saw.

Now what about 1979? This rest point is the unmotion of impotence. We have "uncontrollable" inflation, labor unrest and violence, slipping world power, shortages, expensive energy, stifling regulation, confiscatory taxes and nearly two decades of dishonest or incompetent politicians. The Dow at this point is looking around and saying "I don't *know* what's going on, so I'm staying put." It has pulled into its shell, waiting for a signal of safety so it can poke its head out above the solid line of resistance we see so plainly on the chart. (That "signal of safety" just may be Carter's appointment of Paul Volcker as chairman of the Fed. The terminations of Elliott Wave structures often correspond to appropriate responses from politicians.) [Six months later, Volcker "slammed the brakes" on inflation.—Ed.]

It is my opinion that within this giant structure, the 1973 high represents a peak of optimism equal to that of the lofty levels of 1964 when the formation began. Moreover, in their own ways, the 1974 low and last Wednesday's low each represent the end of a bear market. Therefore the low on Wednesday, July 17, 1979 (if it is proven to be a low) represents the depths of pessimism equal to that at the low of the structure in 1974. Certainly the recent polls on expectations for the future (a modern record low) and on presidential popularity (a modern record low) bear out this assertion, as do the dire economic predictions and doomsday scenarios emanating daily from the myriad sources, including the government's.

UPDATE: JUNE 29, 1981 *ELLIOTT WAVE THEORIST*

Packet Wave Revisited: A Clue to the Workings of Mass Psychology

Older subscribers to *The Elliott Wave Theorist* will remember my introduction of the idea of a "packet wave" in a Special Report on August 3, 1979. The concept of the packet wave is still valid, but my conclusions regarding subsequent action proved false. After some prompting from Bill Doane of Fidelity Management in Boston, I decided to follow up on that original study.

The packet wave, I am now convinced, operates in and around the Wave Principle, not as a separate part of it. That is to say, wave counts can be made without reference to the occurrence of a packet wave, which is not in itself a separate corrective formation but a pattern that overlays various integrated formations within the Wave Principle. Evidence of packet waves is clear as far back as 1900.

In reference to the packet wave from 1964 to 1979, what *actually transpired* after July 1979 was perhaps more interesting, from a theoretical standpoint, than the "straight up" market I expected. From the *exact hourly point* on July 18, 1979, when the 1964-1979 packet wave contraction ended, another entire sequence of five increasingly violent *expanding waves* got underway, encompassing the October 1979 "massacre" and the March 1980 "massacre" and ending with the August 12, 1980 peak on the Dow (see Figure 14). This intervening half-packet expansion, from July 1979 to the August 1980 peak, held quite neatly within two expanding trendlines. Furthermore, it contained initial swings of 100 points (October 1979 to November 1979 and November 1979 to February 1980) and then 160 points (February 1980 to March 1980), so that the second two swings are related by the Fibonacci ratio to the first

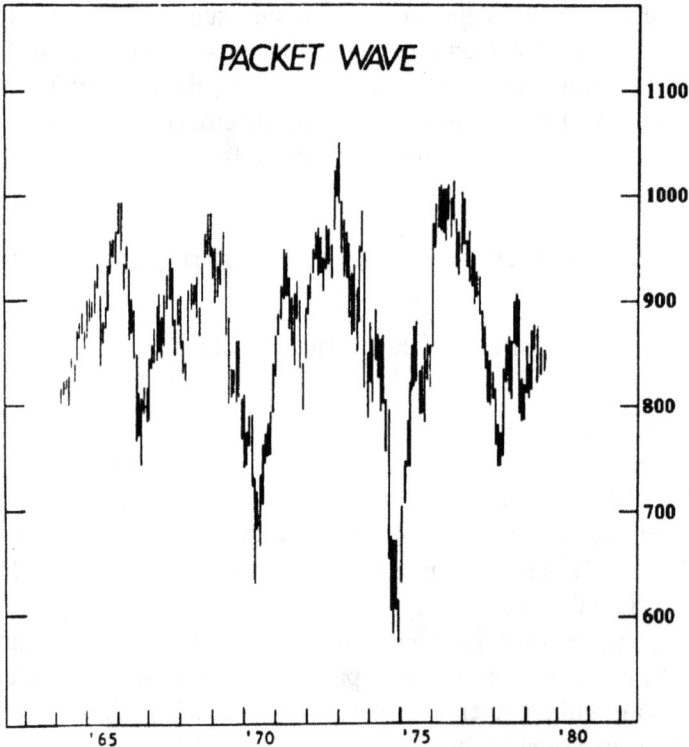

Figure 13

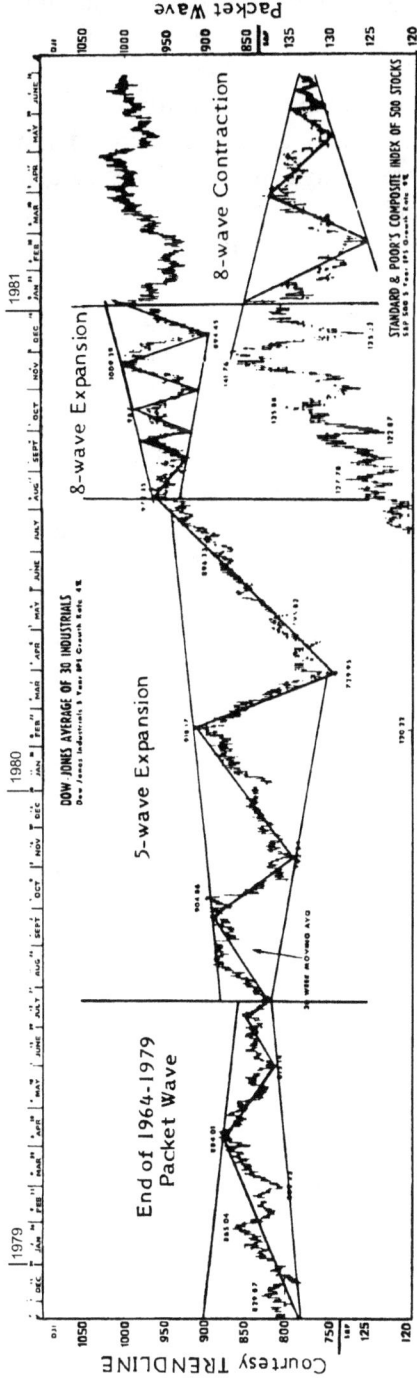

Figure 14

two swings. Its ending point, in turn, was a "point of rest" that ushered in an *entirely new packet wave*, this time of smaller degree.

This new packet wave, extending from August 12, 1980 to the present, has created nearly the same formation in the averages as the 1964-1979 pattern, but in a much smaller degree. The outline of the pattern is best shown by referring to the Dow Jones Industrial Average from August to January and the S&P 500 from January to the present. To get a view of the entire process, take a look at the 10-day rate of change in the NYSE Composite Index, shown in Figure 15. The converging lines show first a dramatic *increase* in volatility, followed by just as dramatic a *decrease* in volatility. It is as if all action during some periods in the market can be accounted for in terms of the model of the Golden Spiral, beginning from a point of rest, spiraling outward, reaching a point of maximum extension, and then returning from whence it came, only to start the process all over again. The only exceptions are first, those periods when unrelenting upside progress is made in the averages, such as the bull period of the 1950s, and secondly, periods such as that from July 1979 to August 1980, a sequence of expanding waves that led abruptly to a point of rest and thence to a new expanding sequence.

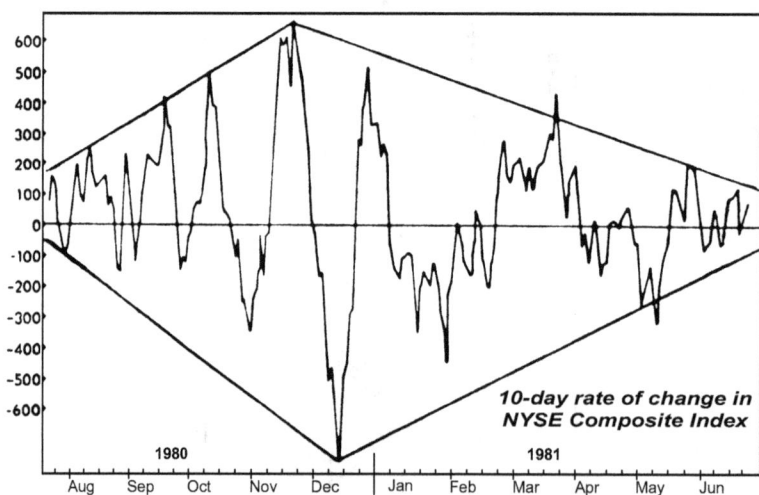

Figure 15

Analytically, what is most thrilling is that the perfection of the packet wave that covered the 1964-1979 period (with its exact center at **821** on the Dow and a maximum upside thrust of 250 points and a maximum downside thrust of 250 points) is again presented in the current smaller version. The beginning of this new packet wave on August 12, at the orthodox ending of the five-wave count from the April 1980 low (see August 1980 letter), occurred at **964** on the Dow. The *lowest* point on the pattern was the **899** low on December 11, 1980, and the *highest* is the **1024** peak of April 27. These two levels mark exactly the same distance, *62 points*, from a center at **962**. In addition, the exact low for what appears to be the last shakeout on the "right" of the pattern so far was the **962** low on May 12. These phenomena appear to establish **962** as the pivot point of the entire pattern.

This fact in itself is quite amazing, but when we remember that the larger packet wave had swings traveling 250 points above and below the center, it also becomes clear that the 500-point height of the larger packet wave is approximately **4.236**, or $(1.618)^3$ times the 124-point height of the smaller! The larger packet wave, furthermore, consisted of **13** expanding swings followed by **8** contracting swings, incorporating Fibonacci numbers. The current formation can be counted as **8** expanding swings and **8** contracting swings, although to get the correct picture, we must use the NYSE Composite or S&P 500 in outlining the contracting phase, as in Figure 14. Perhaps the tug-of-war between the Dow-type stocks on the one hand and the oils on the other has caused the shift of focus from the Dow to the S&P 500 at the center of the packet wave.

I have often noticed the tendency of wave patterns to duplicate themselves on a smaller or larger degree at junctures that portend changes in market behavior. The two packet waves here, of course, are duplicate wave patterns. Moreover, both have the 1000 level as their upside barrier and both managed to break through that barrier briefly, only to fall back precipitously. Could it be that this recent "copycat" packet wave is a launching pad from which the market will break out through 1000, the barrier of *both* patterns, in a spectacular advance? Or are there no implications to be drawn besides an expectation of increased volatility? Undoubtedly we'll know the answer soon.

Point of rest: March 1964.
Expansion: March 1964 - December 1974.
Contraction: December 1974 - July 1979.
Point of rest: July 19, 1979.
Point of rest: August 12, 1980.
Expansion: August 1980 - January 1980.
Contraction: January 1980 - present.
Point of rest: present?

UPDATE: NOVEMBER 29, 1982 *ELLIOTT WAVE THEORIST*

The Packet Wave — A Final Resolution

Sparked by some thoughts from A. J. Frost, I introduced the idea of the "packet wave" in a Special Report on August 3, 1979 and updated the idea in the July 1981 issue of *The Elliott Wave Theorist.* The basic idea is illustrated in this drawing from Fritjof Capra's *The Tao of Physics* (Shambhala, 1975), which is meant to depict a "wave packet" in "dynamic equilibrium," a useful term to describe a market full of sound and fury and going nowhere. It's a sequence of waves, starting from a point of rest, which first expand and then contract, eventually returning again to a point of rest before starting out on a new adventure. There have been several examples of this type of market behavior in the past. This particular occurrence, from 1966, encompassed the entirety of the Dow's wave IV.

I must admit, the final resolution of this model is quite satisfying. For our summation, we can look at this phenomenon from 1966, when the previous trend ended, or from 1964, when the previous advance entered the domain of the packet wave. Here's what we have (see Figure 16):

1) The *expanding* portion lasted from 1966 to 1974, a total of **8 years**.

2) The *contracting* portion lasted from 1974 to 1982, also a total of **8 years**.

3) From 1964, we see a nearly symmetrical pattern, which *begins* at the 800 level and *ends* at the 800 level.

4) Again looking from 1964, we find **5 expanding waves** to 1973 and **5 contracting waves** from there to 1982.

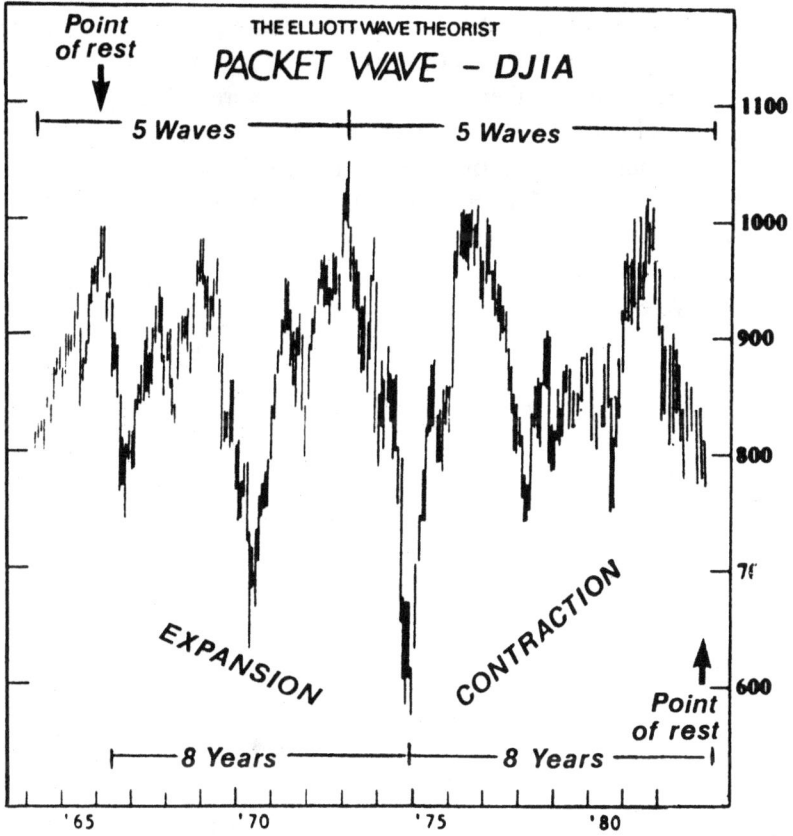

Figure 16

WAVE PACKET

5) Although less compelling, from 1966 we can count **3 waves** (down-up-down) on the left side of the formation, **3 waves** (up-down-up) in the center, and **3 waves** (down-up-down) on the right.

6) The relevant numbers of years and waves are **3**, **5** and **8**, the three key Fibonacci numbers with respect to the Wave Principle.

The beginning "point of rest" was the 1966 peak, which *followed* a long rising wave III. The ending "point of rest" was the August 1982 low, which should *precede* a long rising wave V. The entire formation was an interruption in the main trend, a pause that refreshed. And now it's over. We enjoyed the wonderful performance Mr. Dow, but frankly my sentiments now are, "good riddance!" What follows will be a lot more fun.

Two Decades Later, Another Packet Wave

The figure at right depicts another packet wave, which lasted from May 1999 to February 2001. It began with 5 expanding waves, which were followed by 8 contracting waves on a small scale ending in February 2001. The first contracting wave of that sequence also inaugurated 5 contracting waves (omitting one intraday spike) on a larger scale, ending in February 2001.

We had been intrigued with the sudden flurry of reliable Fibonacci time relationships that appeared in the market and which lasted nearly two full years. By late February, we recognized that the pattern had come to an end because of an overall phi *relationship that suggested a terminal structure. A few weeks later, we published the following report summarizing our observations.*

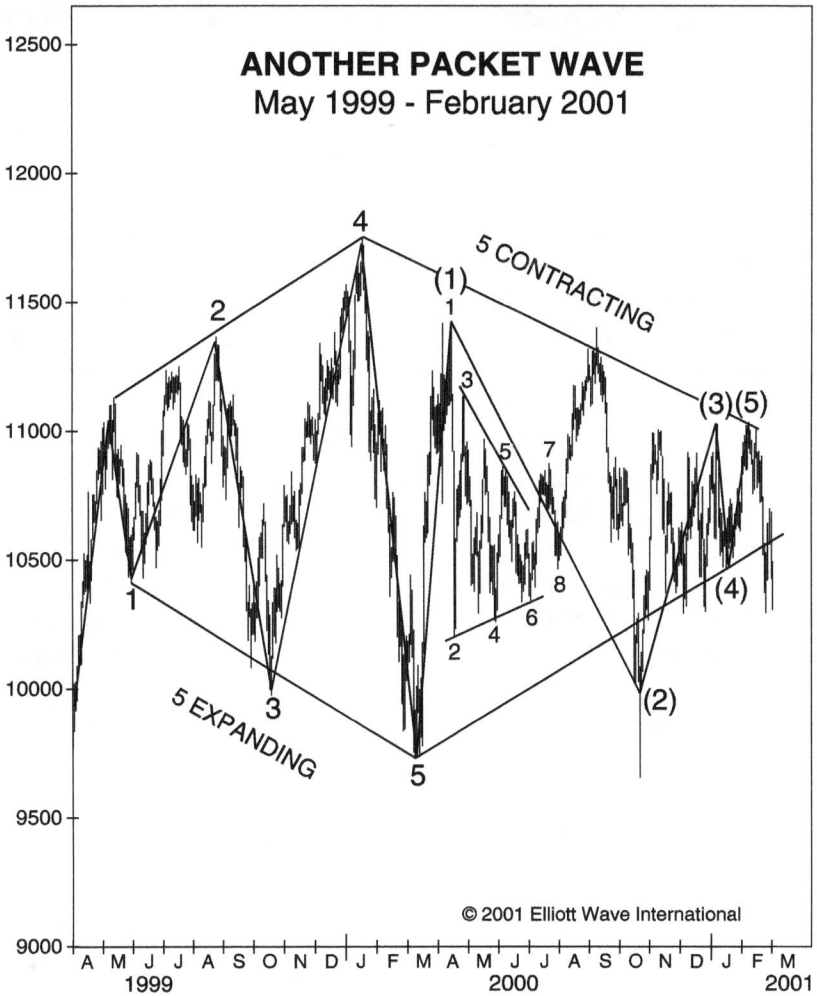

ANOTHER PACKET WAVE
May 1999 - February 2001

© 2001 Elliott Wave International

MARCH 2, 2001 *ELLIOTT WAVE FINANCIAL FORECAST*

FIBONACCI'S BIG TOP
by Peter Kendall

With the stock market's steady decline through February, our January time window can be added to the lengthening list of successful Fibonacci turn dates. By counting Fibonacci numbers of calendar days forward (in this case 377, 233, 144 and 89) from past market turns, *The Elliott Wave Financial Forecast* anticipated another important reversal a month before its occurrence. EWFF did the same thing ahead of significant turns in May, June, September, October and December, using turns extending back nearly two years. Why has this approach been so consistently useful during this time? Our best explanation is that a Grand Supercycle reversal in social mood is a period of tumultuous emotional upheaval. The Wave Principle is nothing less than a mathematical representation of collective human emotion. Since the Fibonacci sequence is the basis of the Wave Principle, Fibonacci has been ruling the rhythm of the 200-year trend change.

In terms of price, another "psychologically significant" aspect of the topping process is Dow 11,000, which has contained the Dow for all but a few brief forays since May 1999. A study of the Fibonacci ratios and the number of trading days around 11,000 shows how thoroughly the topping process has been guided by Fibonacci numbers and proportions.

Figure 1 shows a few of the ratios between highs and lows over this span of exactly 21 months. For instance, the all-time high of January 14, 2000 perfectly subdivides the adjacent highs on August 25, 1999 and April 11, 2000 into .618 and .382 of the whole. The January 14, 2000 peak also bisects the span between the Dow's first sustained closing high above 11,000 on May 13, 1999 and its last touch of 11,000 on February 13, 2001 at .383 and .616, within one day of a perfect .382/.618 relationship.

Fibonacci numbers of trading days also permeate the action above and below 11,000. The sequence has tended to guide the duration of crossings as well as the movement to highs and lows once a crossing takes place. Figure 1 shows just a few of the Fibonacci episodes that connect the first 5 closes above 11,000 in May 1999 to the latest

FIBONACCI RATIOS
AND TRADING-DAY MOVEMENT
DJIA, May 1999 - February 2001

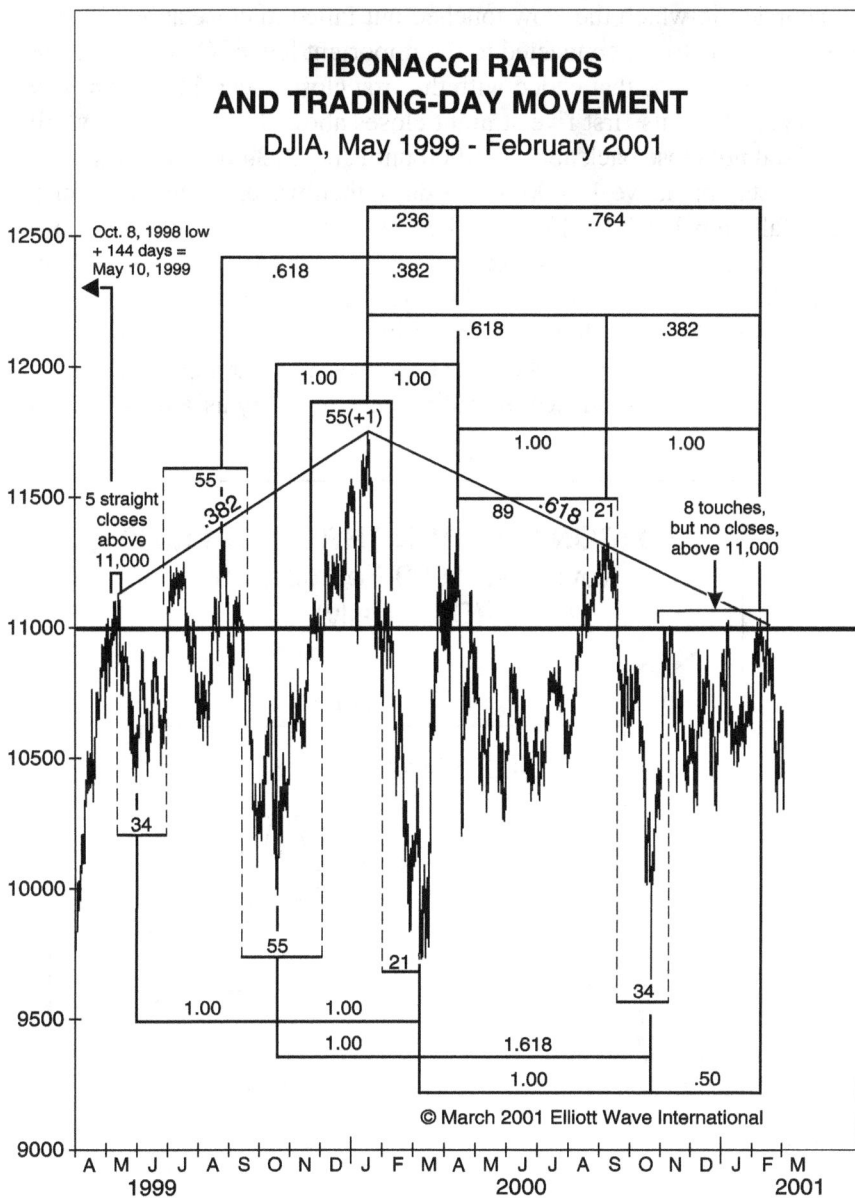

Figure 1

excursion in which the Dow touched but failed to close above 11,000 8 times. The top is connected to the important low of October 8, 1998 by a 144-day rise that ended with the first close above 11,000 on May 7, 1999. After its first five straight closes above 11,000, the Dow fell and did not close back above 11,000 until July 2, 34 trading days later. After staying above 11,000 for 13 days, then wavering across it for 5 and falling below it for 13 more, the Dow rallied past 11,000 for 8 days to a then all-time high close on August 25, 1999. From there, it fell in a definitive break of 11,000 in 13 days. From the last full trading day below 11,000 in late June to the first in mid-September, this summer-long excursion above 11,000 lasted 55 days. The thumbprint is always different, but the sequence of trading days on every assault of 11,000

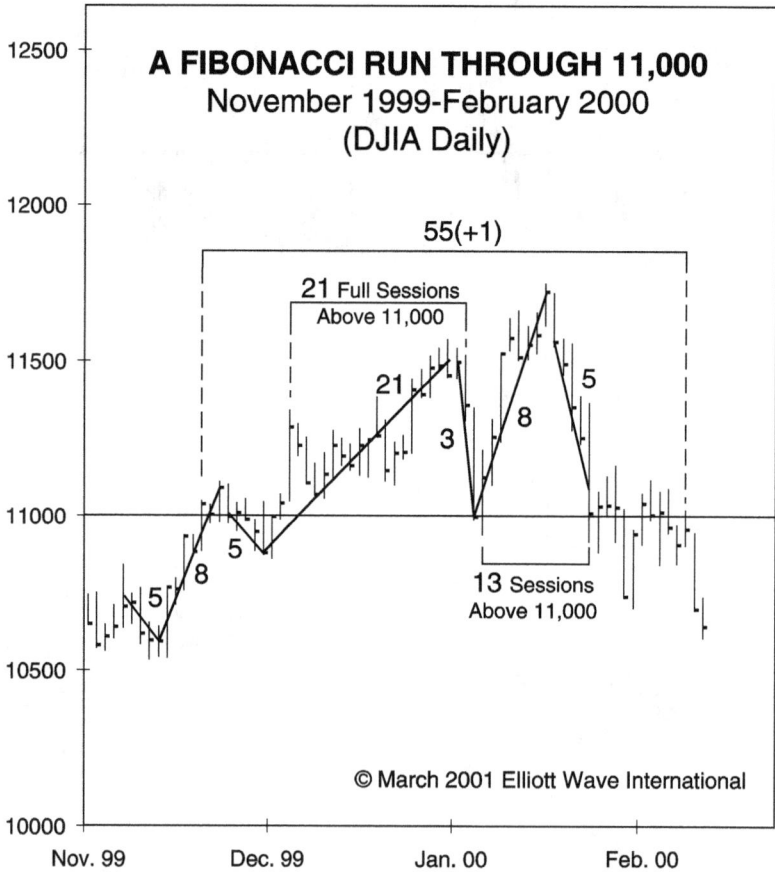

A FIBONACCI RUN THROUGH 11,000
November 1999-February 2000
(DJIA Daily)

© March 2001 Elliott Wave International

Figure 2

bears a distinct Fibonacci stamp. The string of 21 straight sessions above 11,000 in December 1999 is a good example. It started 55 days after the September 15, 1999 break below 11,000 and was followed by a 13-day penetration in which the Dow rose to its all-time high. The close-up in Figure 2 shows the progression.

Notice the resemblance to the peak shown in Figure 3, which depicts the Dow's price action around its high for the 1970s. Like the Dow's recent run past 11,000, the rise through 1000 in 1972-1973 included two thrusts to all-time highs. The first one into late December also included 21 straight sessions above 1000. As in 1999-2000, a second deeper thrust of about 7% followed in the first month of the new year and covered a Fibonacci number of days. The entire event lasted 55

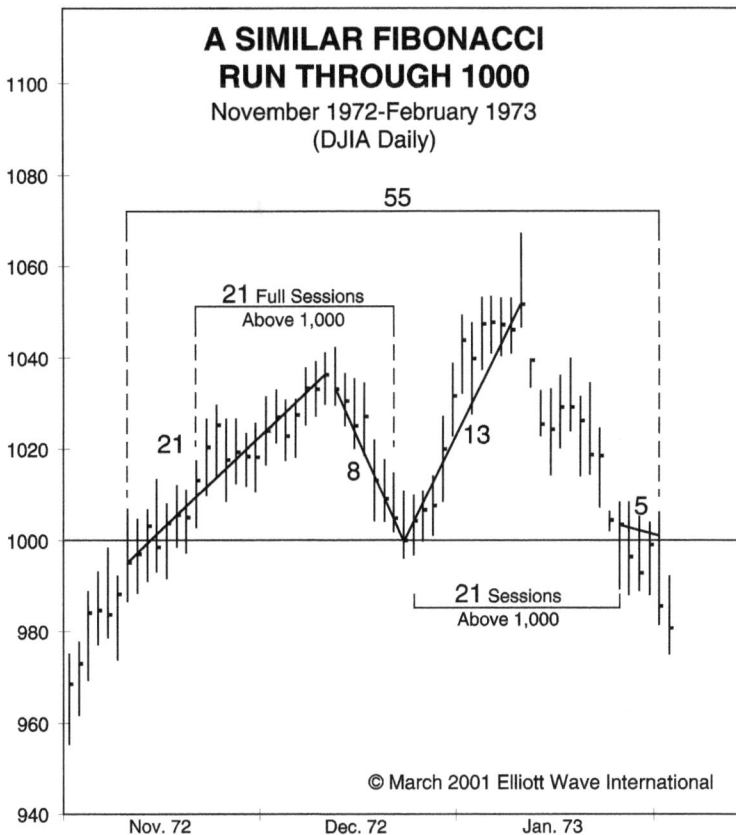

Figure 3

days, one fewer than the move beyond 11,000 in 1999-2000. In fact, an examination of the action around 1000 from 1966 through 1981 shows that four of the 5 failed attempts to surpass 1000 formed patterns in a Fibonacci number of trading days. In 1976, for instance, the Dow made 8 separate stabs above 1000.

There is no fixed pattern, so the forecasting value of the Fibonacci action around 11,000 is limited. It is interesting to note, however, that after its first touch of 1000 in January 1966, the Dow did not materially exceed 1000 for more than 16 years. Likewise, the bullish sentiment that has accompanied the entire episode around 11,000 suggests that it is an emotionally-charged trading range from which the Dow is unlikely to gain any lasting upside detachment.

Chapter 15

RANDOMNESS OR ORDER
IN THE TREASURY BOND MARKET?

by Sam H. Hale, CMT
originally published in August 2000

Preface: Bias, Complacency and Factoids

There is so much we do not know. Astrophysicists tell us that 90 percent of the composition of this wondrous universe is unknown. When presented with information outside the limits of our knowledge, it is natural to be hesitant to accept it, especially if the cause for the observed effect cannot yet be explained. Many who denounce the idea of order in the markets accept other ideas without personal examination to determine their truth, especially if an authority has espoused the theory. For example, it is often claimed that stock prices are earnings driven and that they discount by zero to six months the anticipated earnings reports. There are times when following such a principle has led to financial ruin. Figure 1 depicts the S&P 500 Index (thicker line) and its companies' earnings during 1972-1974. Earnings continued higher throughout this period, and yet the S&P 500 Index declined by 48% between January 1973 and October 1974. Obviously, earnings had nothing to do with the dramatic stock price movement of 1973-1974.

On December 19, 1999, *The Washington Post* quoted analysis by Bob Farrell that showed, "Companies reporting no earnings were up an average of 52 percent (to Dec. 99) in share price. Compare that with companies that do have earnings, which on average lost 2 percent." Obviously, earnings had nothing to do with the immensely diverse stock price movement of 1999. It is doubtful that earnings control stock prices at all.

Certainly, these examples of earnings are simplifications, but they

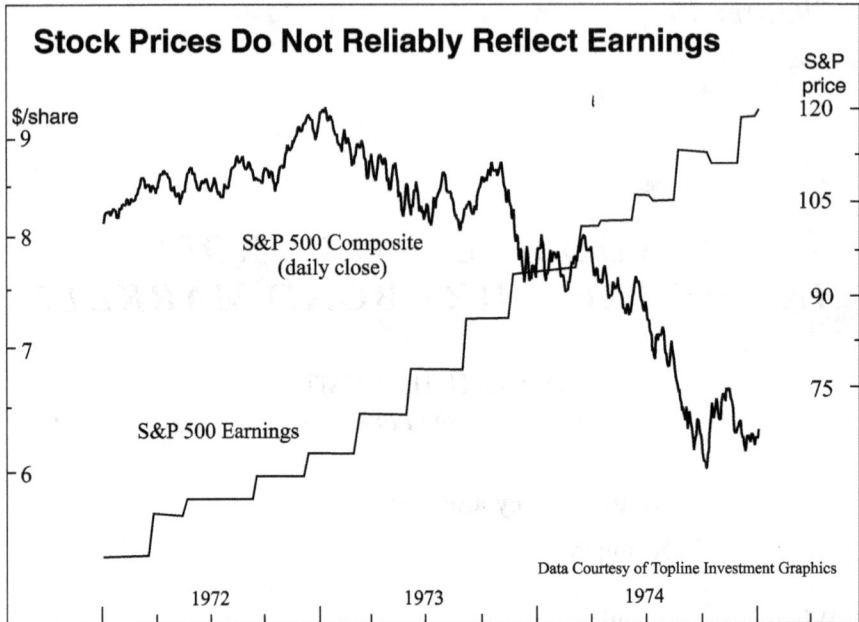

Figure 1

make the point that conventional market wisdom does not describe reality. The following paper presents information that should bring us closer to being able eventually to do so.

Scope of the Study

The purpose of this paper is to present empirical evidence that within one of the largest and most important markets in the world, there are some elements of precise order in measures of both price and time over years of trading and after subtantial price moves. This study encompasses the entire 22-year trading history of 8% U.S. Treasury bond futures contracts (which were replaced by 6% contracts in March 2000).

According to *Barron's* (November 19, 1999), the $13.5 trillion U.S. bond market sees $500 billion in turnover daily in the cash market. The 8% U.S. Treasury bond contract began trading on the Chicago Board of Trade in 1977. It has been one of the world's largest (in terms of the value of open interest) and most active futures contracts during its 22-year existence, with over 112 million contracts traded in 1998 alone. One contract has a value of $100,000. Each point is worth $1000. The smallest increment of trading is 1/32, so the value of one tick is $31.25. The U.S. Treasury bond is an extremely volatile, highly liquid financial market. There is no entity sufficiently large to control this market over any extended period. Thus, it is an excellent vehicle in which to study patterns of human behavior.

Price Considerations

Figure 2 displays the price history of the major moves in T-bond futures. The data consists of each then-current Treasury bond futures contract until its expiration, at which time it displays the price of the new current contract. A cursory glance at this graph reveals nothing unique, just the squiggly lines of a market whose range extends from a low of 55 05 on September 28, 1981 to a high of 135 08 on October 5, 1998.

As bond prices approached their 1993 peak, I observed that the advance from the 1987 low would match the rise from the 1984 low to the major peak in 1986, a length of 1475 32nds, at 122 10. As it turned out, the market did peak exactly at 122 10 and did not exceed that level for over four years. I later observed that the rise from the all-time low in 1981 to the secondary high in 1989, which was lower than the 1986

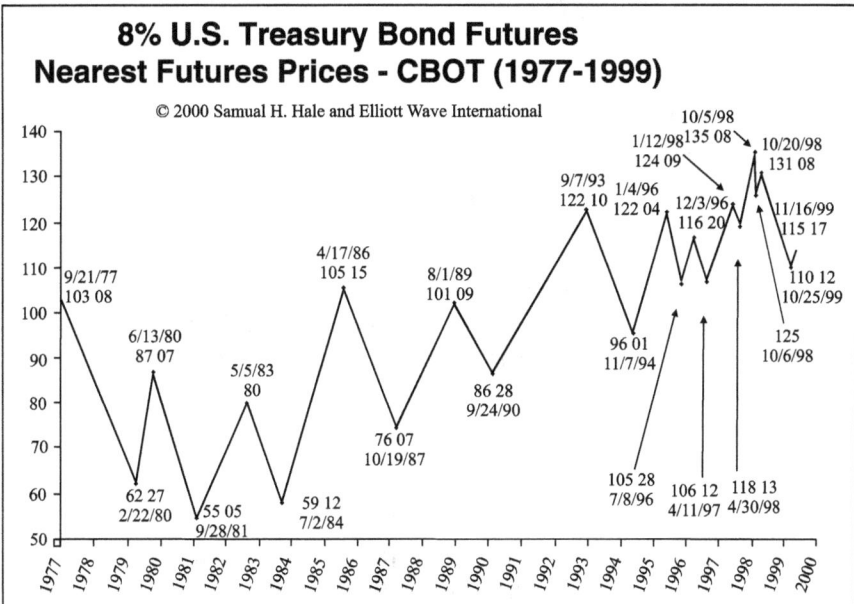

Figure 2

peak, was 1474 32nds. This measure was within a single tick of the two moves of 1475 32nds just discussed. Here is a summary of the three distances, which are displayed in Figure 3:

$$55\ 05\ \text{in}\ 9/28/81\ \text{to}\ 101\ 09\ \text{in}\ 8/01/89 = \mathbf{1474}\ \text{32nds}$$
$$59\ 12\ \text{in}\ 7/02/84\ \text{to}\ 105\ 15\ \text{in}\ 4/17/86 = \mathbf{1475}\ \text{32nds}$$
$$76\ 07\ \text{in}\ 10/19/87\ \text{to}\ 122\ 10\ \text{in}\ 9/07/93 = \mathbf{1475}\ \text{32nds}$$

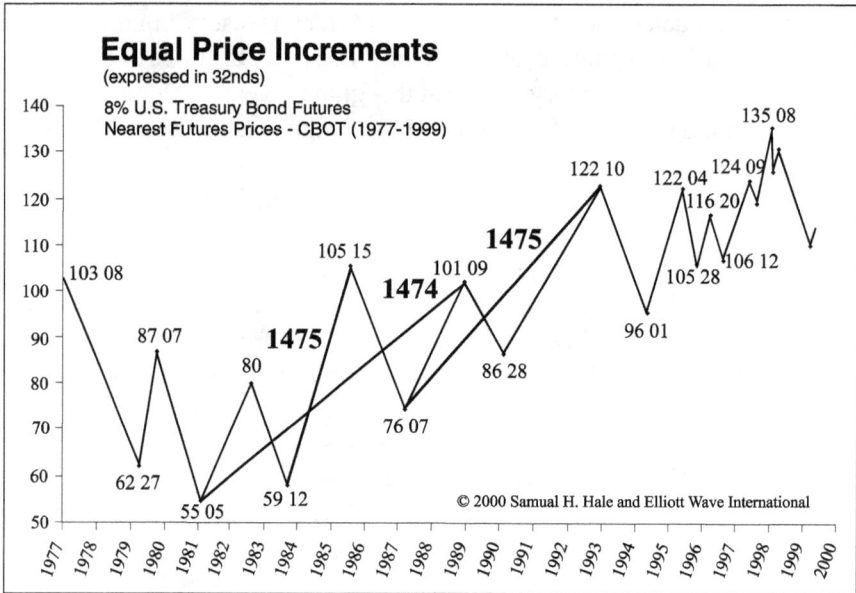

Equal Price Increments
(expressed in 32nds)

8% U.S. Treasury Bond Futures
Nearest Futures Prices - CBOT (1977-1999)

© 2000 Samual H. Hale and Elliott Wave International

Figure 3

Figure 4 shows these prices as the difference from the low to secondary low and from the high to secondary high. The 1984 low was above the 1981 low by the same amount that the 1986 high was above the 1989 high (plus one tick), and the 1987 low was above the 1984 low by the same amount that the 1993 peak was above the 1986 peak. Here is a summary of the four differentials:

$$07/02/84\ \ 59\ 12\ -\ 09/28/81\ \ 55\ 05 = \mathbf{135}\ \text{32nds}$$
$$04/17/86\ \ 105\ 15\ -\ 08/01/89\ \ 101\ 09 = \mathbf{134}\ \text{32nds}$$
$$10/19/87\ \ 76\ 07\ -\ 07/02/84\ \ 59\ 12 = \mathbf{539}\ \text{32nds}$$
$$09/07/93\ \ 122\ 10\ -\ 04/17/86\ 105\ 15 = \mathbf{539}\ \text{32nds}$$

The 1993 peak, then, marked both the duplicate of the 1475 32nds rise shown in Figure 3 and the duplicate of the 539 32nds turning-point differential shown in Figure 4. Note that from the low on 4/30/98 at 118 13 to the all-time high on 10/5/98 at 135 08 was, again, exactly 539 32nds.

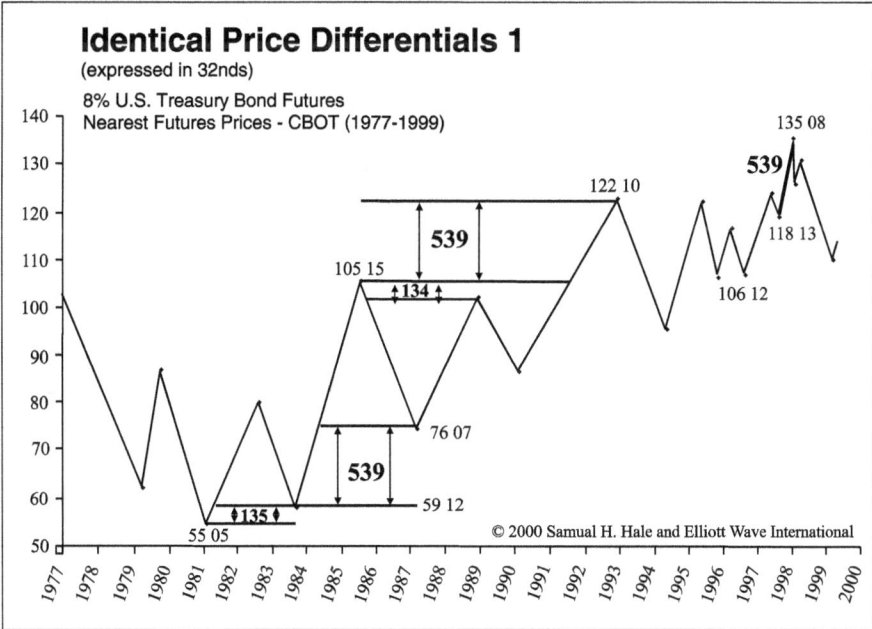

Identical Price Differentials 1
(expressed in 32nds)

8% U.S. Treasury Bond Futures
Nearest Futures Prices - CBOT (1977-1999)

© 2000 Samual H. Hale and Elliott Wave International

Figure 4

Viewed another way in Figure 5, the 1987 low was 674 32nds above the all-time low of 1981, and the 1993 peak was 673 32nds above the 1989 peak. Figure 6 also shows a smaller 128 32nds differential off the 1998 peak that was duplicated at the 1999 low.

Time Considerations

Naturalists, economists and technicians have studied cycles for decades. One often-mentioned cycle is the "four-year business cycle." The time studies in this treatise do not reveal typical trough-to-trough cycles, but *irregular rhythms* and exact *proportional balances*. Irregular rhythms are time periods that do not necessarily follow in sequence. For example, four of the major price movements marked on Figure 6 were

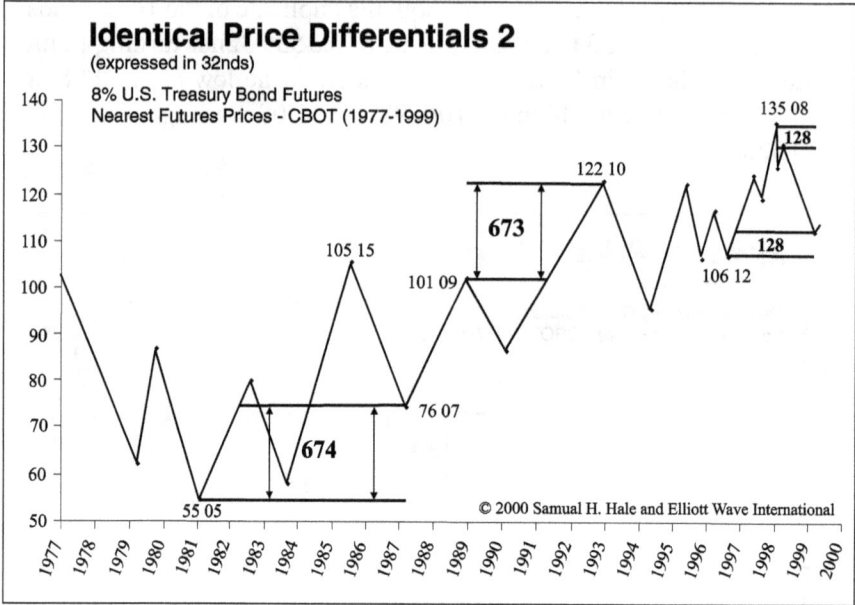

Identical Price Differentials 2
(expressed in 32nds)

8% U.S. Treasury Bond Futures
Nearest Futures Prices - CBOT (1977-1999)

135 08

128

122 10

673

105 15

101 09

128

106 12

76 07

674

55 05

© 2000 Samuel H. Hale and Elliott Wave International

Figure 5

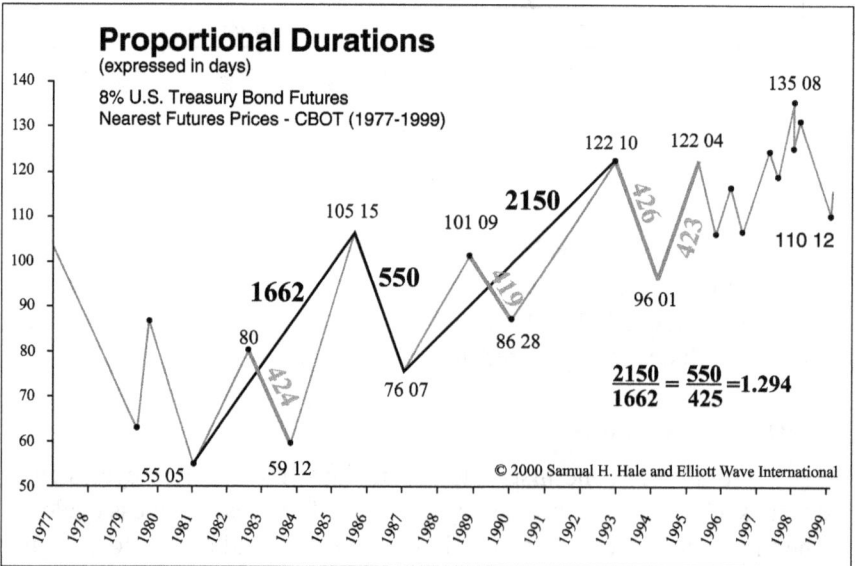

Proportional Durations
(expressed in days)

8% U.S. Treasury Bond Futures
Nearest Futures Prices - CBOT (1977-1999)

135 08

122 10   122 04

2150

426

105 15

101 09

423

110 12

1662

550

80

419

96 01

86 28

424

76 07

59 12

55 05

$$\frac{2150}{1662} = \frac{550}{425} = 1.294$$

© 2000 Samuel H. Hale and Elliott Wave International

Figure 6

within a week's time in duration – approximately 425 days each – though they were not all adjacent periods. Here is a summary:[1]

05/05/83 – 07/02/84 = **424** days
08/01/89 – 09/24/90 = **419** days
09/07/93 – 11/07/94 = **426** days
11/07/94 – 01/04/96 = **423** days.

The longest single period of reaction during the secular bull market was 550 days, from the 4/17/86 peak to the 10/19/87 low. There were 1662 days from the all time low in 1981 to the 1986 top, a level that was unsurpassed for over five years. From the 1987 low to the 1993 peak, which stood as the highest price for over four years, was 2150 days. As shown by the notes on Figure 6, these four periods are perfectly proportional. I call this type of relationship a proportional balance.

Figure 7 illustrates another proportional balance. The time period between the major peak in 1993 and the all-time high in 1998 was 1854 days. From the intervening low on 11/7/94 to that high was 1428 days.

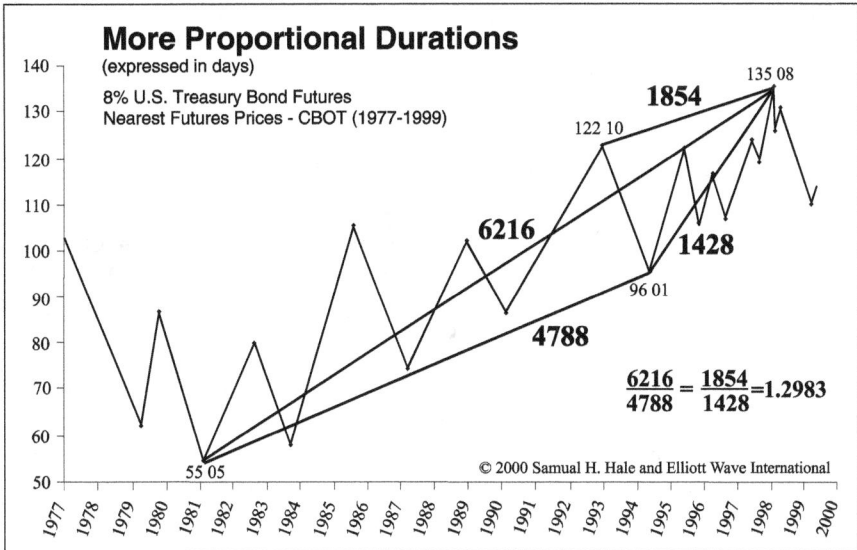

Figure 7

The ratio between these durations is 1.2983. Note that from the all-time low on 9/28/81 to that same low (11/7/94) is 4788 days. 4788 times 1.2983 equals 6216. From the all time low to the all time high was exactly 6216 days! As in Figure 6, all these time periods are proportional, and they are proportional by the same ratio.

Fibonacci-Related Observations

There are numerous golden-section phenomena observable in this market. For example, the 1474-1475 32nds increments from 9/28/81 to 8/1/89, 7/2/84 to 4/17/86 and 10/19/87 to 9/7/93 (see Figure 3) are related to the 660 32nds decline from 5/5/83 to 7/2/84 by the square root of five (2.236), an integral part of the Fibonacci formula, $(\sqrt{5}+1)/2 = 1.618$. In addition, using a monthly time frame for our graph of the nearest futures rolled on expiration,

$$09/28/81 - 07/02/84 = \mathbf{34} \text{ months,}$$
$$09/28/81 - 04/17/86 = \mathbf{55} \text{ months,}$$
$$04/17/86 - 09/07/93 = \mathbf{89} \text{ months,}$$
$$09/28/81 - 09/07/93 = \mathbf{144} \text{ months.}$$

All these monthly durations are Fibonacci numbers (see Figure 8).

Price and Time

Having considered price increments and time periods separately, we now extend the analysis to blend the two factors together. The first proportional *time* ratio displayed in Figure 6 is 1.294. The 539 32nds *price* increment highlighted in Figure 4, when divided by 1.294, equals 417. The mid-point (122 07) of the major peaks in 1993 (122 10) and 1996 (122 04) to the all time high of 135 08 reached on October 25, 1998 is 417 32nds. This same increment (417) is also obtainable by multiplying the 674 32nds move highlighted in Figure 5 by the Fibonacci ratio (.618). Thus, 539/1.294 = 674/1.618 = 417, where 417, 539 and 674 are all among our highlighted *price* increments, and 1.294 and 1.618 are some of the market's governing *time* ratios, which are now shown to be governing some of the price ratios as well.[2]

Fibonacci Durations in Months

8% U.S. Treasury Bond Futures
Nearest Futures Prices - CBOT (1977-1999)

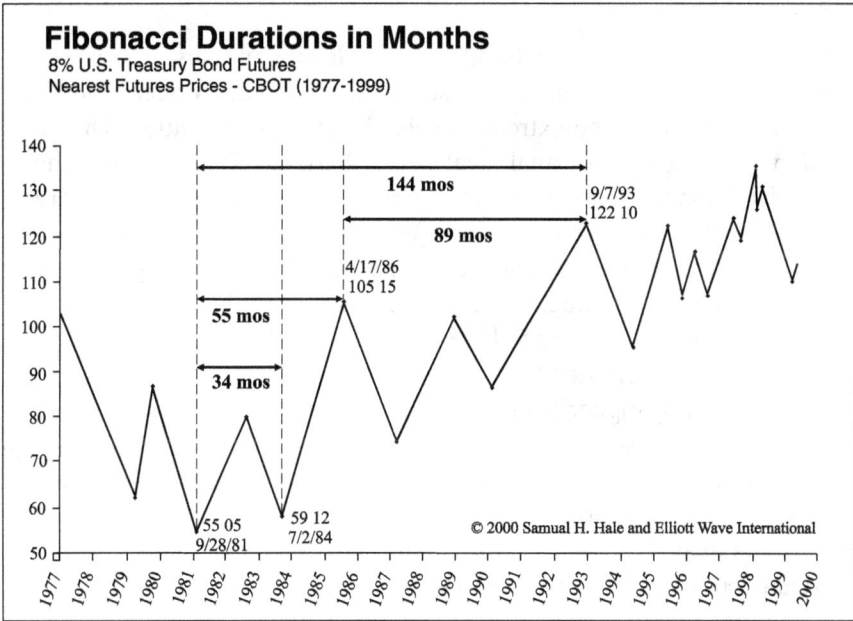

Figure 8

Time and Price Proportional Durations

(expressed in days, price in 32nds)
(Time expressed diagonally, price vertically)

8% U.S. Treasury Bond Futures
Nearest Futures Prices - CBOT (1977-1999)

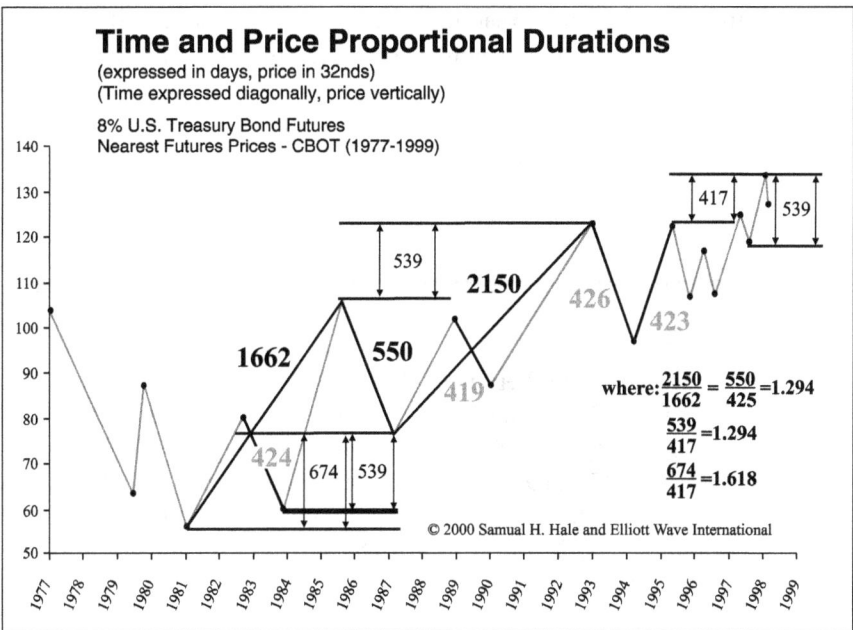

Figure 9

Practical Value

We do not yet *know* why, after trends lasting months or years, the dominance of buyers and sellers suddenly shifted and prices reversed course precisely at the extreme levels observed in this study. The developer of the field of analytical psychology, Dr. Carl Gustav Jung, theorized that we share a collective unconscious that results in our reacting to situations in similar ways. Whatever the ultimate explanation may be, it is important to know the existence of this amazing order, as it is useful in forecasting. For example, I observed these relationships in real time at the October 5, 1998 peak and concluded that the price of 135 08 would likely stand for some time. If prices were to have printed only fractionally higher or the advance lasted another few days, it would have negated the strong indications of a major turn.

These relationships were discovered without an advanced knowledge of neural networks, fuzzy logic, chaos theory or computers. Only the tools available over a half-century ago were required — a non-prejudiced and keen sense of observation. The results of this study add to the body of evidence demonstrating that old assumptions about disorder, chaos and random news causality are false. I encourage readers to step aside from the noise created by government reports, spot news, commentaries and traders' reactions thereto and review, and if necessary amend or replace, the principles on which they base their trading and investment decisions.

NOTES

[1]Not illustrated are other "irregular rhythms," including periods of 654 and 652 days (7/2/84 – 4/17/86 and 10/19/87 – 8/1/89, respectively) and **1078** and **1079** days (5/5/83 – 4/17/86 and 9/24/90 – 9/7/93). The period between 10/19/87 and 9/24/90 was just a week different, at **1071** days.

[2]Also of interest, 674 is .382 (i.e., $.618^2$) times the all-time low price of 55 05, which is 1765 32nds. Note also that the price increments of 674 and 539 from Figures 4 and 5 form a ratio of 1.250, which is not far from our time ratios of 1.294 and 1.298.

Chapter 16

CYCLIC ANALYSIS IN
THE FINANCIAL MARKETS

by Robert R. Prechter, Jr.
From a speech presented to the
Market Technicians Association Conference, May 15, 1982
originally published May 1982

Even though my main market tool is the Elliott Wave Principle, I follow a good number of other technical methods. One that is particularly useful is cyclic analysis. Many subscribers have asked me for an explanation of how to use fixed-time cycles in market interpretation, so I thought I would present an outline of my approach. This approach can be applied to cycles of any length, from days to centuries, as long as the necessary data is available.

"Cycles" refer to the occurrence of peaks and troughs in the market at regularly recurring intervals. Cycle analysts measure the time length of a cycle from *low to low*, since the dissipation of hope in the market takes longer and is less definite than a climax of fear. Thus, bottoms in the market generally occur at a single, well-defined point as most stocks converge into a "market" low on the generally prevailing fear. Tops, on the other hand, are more diffuse and less easy to pinpoint. For example, there is still argument about whether the "top" of the 1980-81 market was August 1980 (a-d line peak), November 1980 (S&P peak) or April 1981 (Dow peak). [A similar situation exists today, as the a-d line topped in April 1998, and various indexes have made highs at different times since.—Ed.] There is rarely an argument about bottoms.

It is for this reason that I find it important to illustrate market cycles with *arcs* rather than by the typical method of showing spiked peaks and troughs as shown in Figure 1. The arcs shown in Figure 2 reflect the reality of stock market cycles because of the different behavior associated with dissipating hope vs. that of climaxing fear. Commodity

One Model from The Foundation for the Study of Cycles

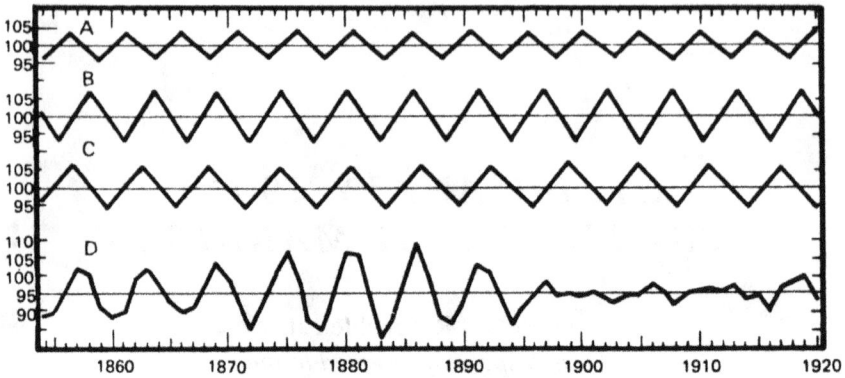

Figure 1

cycle profiles are *inverted* arcs, because price peaks in commodities are usually made not on hope, but on fear about the future. Their bottoms are often long and rounded, being generated by the prevailing complacency.

Changes in Periodicity

It is a rare market that does not exhibit clear cyclic tendencies. There is some dispute as to whether the apparent *changes* in periodicity are due to the "stretching" and "contracting" of cycles that are by nature variable in length or whether they are due to the summation of many exactly fixed periodicities occasionally canceling each other out. Figure 1, taken from *Cycles* by Edward R. Dewey, demonstrates the latter concept.

This concept does explain "cancelation," but it does not adequately explain the occasional sudden shift in a regular cycle of say, 3 weeks (or 3 years) to a new length of 4 weeks (or 4 years). This type of shift is closer to the reality of cyclic phenomena, and in fact, Dewey himself believed that cycles were inherently irregular. To apply the "fixed periodicity with fixed degree of relative force" theory, you would have to spend two years feeding all cyclic discoveries into your computer. Unfortunately, practical experience shows that you would still have an imperfect model. Massive computer programs dedicated to Fourier analysis, for example, do not produce a reliable output consistent with this hypothesis. As far as I am concerned, it is enough to understand that cycle lengths from trough to trough are not fixed forever in either periodicity or dominance. One or the other, if not both, *does* occasionally shift after a period of regularity. Thus, while dealing with an established cyclic pattern, the analyst should always be on the alert for the signs of a change, such as market action that is unexpected in terms of either direction or amplitude with respect to the presumed dominant cycle.

To stay out of trouble, I have found it practical to average the lengths of the most recent oscillations and then project only *one* cycle length into the future. As long as the next market low is in the ballpark, I repeat the process. If the market acts contrary to my expectations at the next expected cyclic low, I adjust my thinking. For instance, prior to September 1981, the basic "trading" length cycles were 3 weeks (actually 20 days) and 10 weeks (actually variable between 9 and 12 weeks). By early November, it was clear that the 3-week and 10-week cycles were being overridden by another periodicity, and by November 19, it was clear that the new dominant periodicities were 4 and 8 weeks. Despite the problem of occasional periodicity shift (or shift in dominance), it is striking how often the theory of cycles fits the action of the market.

Applying the Theory

First let me explain the lines on Figure 2. The middle line is an hourly plot of the NYSE Composite index. Currently these figures are not published regularly by any periodical [How times have changed!—Ed.], so the only way to get the figures is off the Dow Jones Newswire or directly from the NYSE tape. The arcs are a theoretical visual representation of the 4-week cycle profile. The top line is a two-day rate of change and the bottom line is a four-day rate of change. Each plot on these lines is a simple *difference* between the most current hourly price for the NYSE index and its price 12 or 24 trading hours ago. [Back then, the exchange was open only six hours a day.—Ed.] I find this method much more useful than using moving averages, which require projection into the future, concern with dropoff numbers, concern with the timing of moving average crossings, etc. The rate-of-change difference, in contrast, shows overbought and oversold readings in *real time* and lets you know visually, right at the bottom of a cycle, that you are probably there. By the way, *percentage* differences are better when dealing with long periods of time, but within the shorter time periods, the market does not move enough to invalidate arithmetic-difference

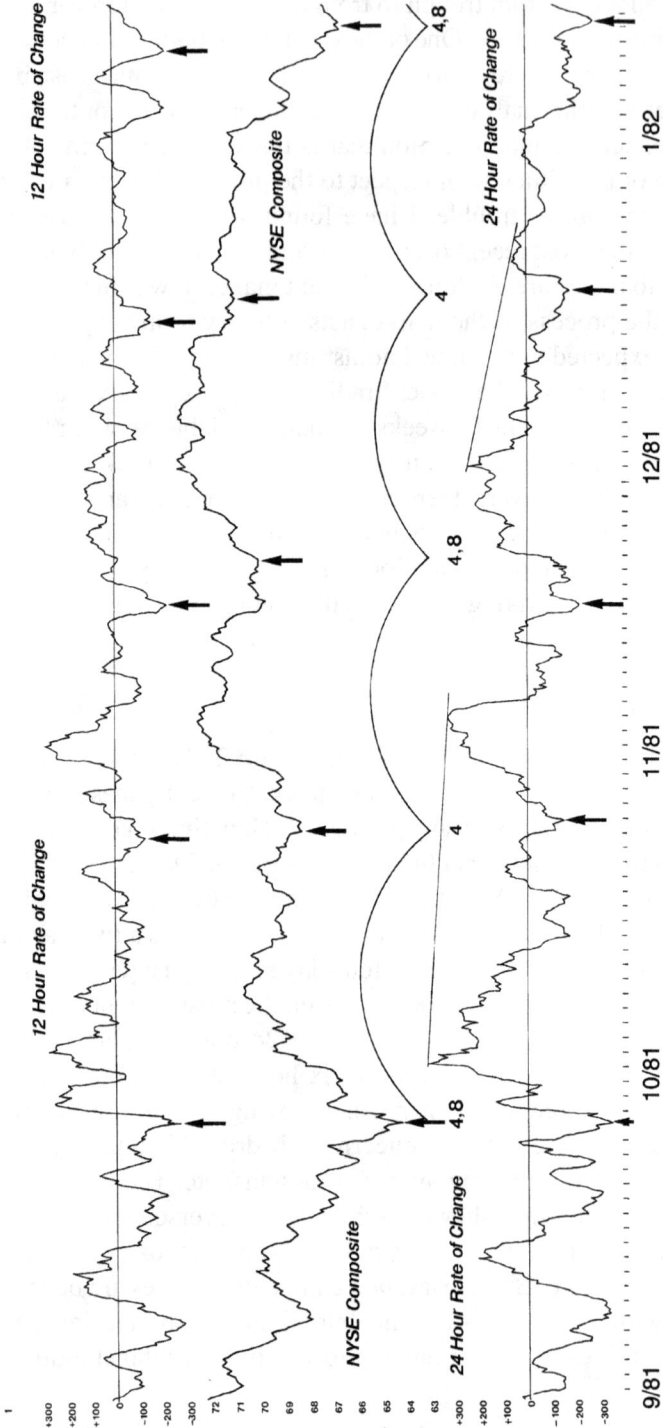

Figure 2

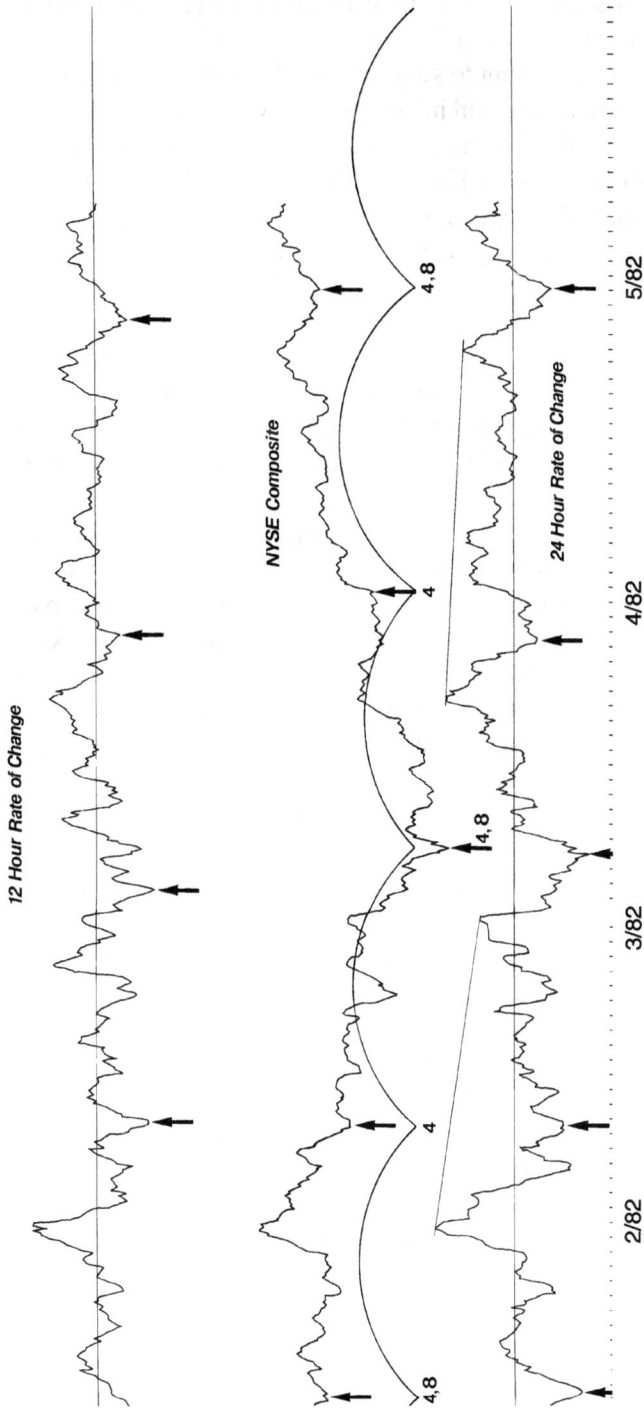

Figure 2 (cont'd)

comparisons. And since they are quicker to compute, I use them in all computations up to half a year.

It is important to keep enough different rates of change that some of them will be useful in interpreting whatever cycle lengths the market serves up. For instance, the 12-hour rate of change [Today it would be 26 half-hours.—Ed.] is compatible with the 20-day cycle, while the 24-hour rate of change is perfect for tracking the progress of the recently emerged 4-week cycle, as the chart will demonstrate. A rate of change should be from between 1/4 and 1/10 as long as the cycle it is tracking. These ratios are large enough to present a profile of the cycle yet small enough to show divergences at tops and to indicate with sharp clarity the cycle lows as they are occurring. I have also found that the ratios nearer 1/4 are more useful when the cycle further subdivides into harmonic *halves*, while those nearer 1/10 are more useful when it subdivides into harmonic *thirds*.

As a final consideration, I always make sure that my rates of change compare like to like. A 12-hour rate of change always compares the same time of day; a 10-day rate of change almost always compares the same day of the week; a 12-month rate of change (which tracks the "4-year" cycle) always compares the same month of the year. This construction elminates any "seasonal" type biases in the figures.

Isolating the two main trading-length cycles from September 1981 to May 1982, here are the key facts:

1) Every 18½ trading days, on average, a trading low has occurred in the market.

2) The *maximum* deviation from the ideal low has been only 1½ day.

3) Reckoned in calendar days, the average length is 27. Four of the eight repetitions were exactly 27 days, and one was 28. Of those remaining, the inclusion or exclusion of a weekend (Friday or Monday low) gave readings of 24, 25½, and 31 calendar days.

Currently the market is in its ninth 4-week cycle repetition since September 28, and it is still going strong. (The 3-week cycle is still present, although it has a subdued effect on the market, and I presently consider it subdominant. The smallest pullbacks in the market are due to the operation of this cycle and several even shorter ones, which are not worth following if you pay any commissions at all on your trades.)

The 4-week Cycle

What exactly does a "4-week cycle" mean? If the cycle is real, it should exhibit two traits. First, it should be clear that the market makes a low every four weeks. If you examine the charts, you will see that to be the case. Every four weeks, the NYSE Composite is positioned at the end of a sell-off phase. The rates of change show the deepest oversold readings at or very close to the cyclic lows. Second, the market action should be *worse* in the second half of the cycle than in the first half. This trait is evident in every cycle pictured. If the first half is up, the second half is flat or down. If the first half is flat or slightly down, the second half is down hard. [The power behind the stock mania of the 1990s was so strong that the first half of cycles has been up hard, the second half mildly up or sideways; this proclivity has recently changed.—Ed.]

The 8-week Cycle

Cycles show strong tendencies to occur in harmonic multiples. A cycle will often break down into either two or three cycles of a smaller periodicity. In the current market, the 8-week cycle breaks down into two 4-week cycles. Below is listed the type of evidence a cycle analyst would use to support the existence of an 8-week cycle. (Refer to Figure 2.)

1) In each case, the first 4-week cycle peak registers a higher over-bought condition in the 24-hour rate of change than the second. This consistent occurrence reflects the 8-week influence: "up" pressure in the first half, "down" pressure in the second.

2) In each case, the second 4-week cycle low registers a deeper oversold condition in the 24-hour rate of change than the first, also reflecting the 8-week cycle's influence.

3) The NYSE market action is worse during the second 4-week cycle of each pair. If the first cycle pushes the market up strongly, the second will push it up less so. If the first cycle results in a flat market, the second will accompany declining prices. Measuring from low to low, the first cycle always makes more upside or less downside progress than the second.

4) As explained at the outset, tops are extremely variable. However, it is still generally true that the market's peak within the first 4-week cycle will be later in time than it is within the second. Thus, if the first 4-week cycle's peak is 2/3 of the way through the cycle, the second cycle's peak will occur closer to the 1/3 or 1/2 mark. If the first 4-week

cycle's peak is at the 1/3 or 1/2 mark, the second cycle is often so weak that the market's highest reading within that cycle occurs on the first day or two. Of all the cycles shown in Figure 2, the only exception to the norm is the most recently completed 8-week cycle, within which the market managed a high later in time during the second 4-week cycle than during the first, despite the lesser overbought condition. The reason for this occurrence is that the subdominant 3-week cycle bottomed on April 20, providing just enough push, along with the rising 23-week cycle (see below), to get the market to edge higher near the end of that 4-week cycle.

These observations can be applied generally to harmonics of cycles of any size, since market behavior within one size of cycle always helps the analyst make assumptions with regard to the position of the next larger cycle, and in some cases, of the next smaller cycle as well. Just as the action within the 4-week cycle helps determine the status of the 8-week cycle (and the existence of the 8-week helps forecast that action), so the action within the 8-week cycle helps determine the status of the 23-week cycle, which is currently the dominant next larger harmonic.

Larger Cycles

As always, larger cycles are clearly at work. Figure 2 shows important *intermediate*-term lows on September 28 and March 9, which were 23 weeks, or exactly three 8-week cycles (and six 4-week cycles) apart. Remember, the "4-week cycle," as noted, actually averages 27 days, which is why six repetitions sums to 23 weeks. This 23-week cycle explains the general profile of the rising period from September to December, the declining period from December to March, and the rising period to the present. The next previous intermediate-term cycle low occurred in May 1981 (20 weeks prior), and the one before that in December 1980 (22 weeks prior). Until proven otherwise, we should assume that the 20- to 23-week cycle is still operative. [In fact, it was.—Ed.]

Working Assumptions

With each new data point, I take into account all the evidence and then make projections into the future. These projections serve as a backdrop for evaluating the significance of subsequent market action. To illustrate the way this input to my overall opinion would be expressed, I have put together the following projections, which now serve as working assumtions under this method. They will remain the working assumptions until the market action forces a reformulation. These projections are based strictly on cyclic analysis and based only upon the 4-, 8- and 23-week cycles. Larger cycles, which may have a *significant* impact on the overall profile of the market, are not being taken into account in this example. The purpose of these comments is to illustrate my *method* of cyclic analysis so that you can either apply it yourself or understand what I am doing in the Cycles section of *The Elliott Wave Theorist*.

As usual, I am going out only *one cycle length at a time*. A limited projection results in fewer mistakes and keeps you always on guard for the unexpected. "Scenarios" have a way of becoming embedded in one's thinking despite market action, so the best solution to that problem is to avoid unnecessary extensions of scenarios. That way, a shift in periodicity or dominance, or the sudden appearance of a longer cycle influence that you had not taken into account, can always be added to your thinking as soon as you recognize it, and you never have to scrap overly elaborate scripts of expected market behavior.

To summarize, you should generate projections *for the purpose of providing a framework of expectations to compare with the actual path of the market*. It can be taken as a forecast only if you understand it to be subject to immediate scrapping or revision upon any deviation by the market from its expected path. With these thoughts in mind, here are my current "working assumptions":

1) The next 4-week cycle low is due on May 27 (plus or minus one trading day). The market should be in an oversold condition and make a clear trading low on that date.

2) Since the current 4-week cycle is the first within an 8-week cycle, the next 4-week cycle should accompany a weaker market than the current one and generate a weaker overbought condition.

3) The next 8-week cycle low is due on or near June 23. A deeper oversold and a more significant market low should occur on or near that date.

4) Whether or not the expected timing occurs on schedule, watch for a deeply oversold reading on the appropriate rate-of-change oscillators (particularly the 10- and 30-day), probably coinciding with a 4- or 8-week cycle low, to determine when the next *intermediate*-term cyclic low is occurring. This low is most likely to occur on the third 8-week

cycle low from March 9, suggesting *mid-August* for the 23-week cyclic bottom.

[The final bear market low occurred right in the 23rd week from March 9, on the close of Friday, August 12. The date of the low may be considered August 14 (making it even closer to an exact 23 weeks), since the market was closed for the weekend and started up on Monday, August 15.—Ed.]

It should be mentioned that in severe bear phases, the actual market low often "stretches" and bottoms one cycle of the *second* smaller degree *past* the scheduled low. So given a severe selloff, an additional 4-week cycle could create a market bottom in mid-September. Either way, the condition of the rates of change should make clear exactly what is happening at the time of occurrence.

5) Perhaps most significant, the market at this moment can be assumed to have begun a general phase of decline, just as the March 9 through May 7 period has been a general phase of advance. [This is exactly what happened.—Ed.] The action during the first two weeks in May can be judged to have been very weak *against the knowledge that both the 4- and 8-week cycles were up*. In fact, the overbought condition generated in the 24-hour rate of change is lower even than that generated in the previous 4-week cycle. The selling in the past few days (May 10-14) has been described as "mild" by many market watchers, which it *would be* if trading cycles were due to bottom this week, but they're not. They are in an up phase. Therefore, *within our cyclic model*, this "mild market setback" should not be considered a buying opportunity but a harbinger of more severely declining prices. The poor showing by the market up to this point suggests that the peak of the current 8-week cycle is occurring early, and therefore that the larger 23-week cycle is past its peak and heading down. The most immediate conclusion one should draw is that the remainder of the current 4-week cycle will probably be very weak. The next most valid conclusion is that the *next* 4-week cycle will be terribly weak, since the 8-week cycle will then be in its down phase. The third most valid conclusion is that since the current 23-week cycle is topping earlier than the last, the market could be vulnerable to particularly severe downside action during the *next* 8-week cycle, which is scheduled to bottom in mid-August. These expectations will be valid *unless* any 4-week cycle between now and the expected low manages to generate an extreme overbought reading. Such a reading would *not* fit expectations and would thus cause a re-interpretation of the cycles.

These projections go out one cycle length for each category. While they now appear valid, *the analyst should stay on constant alert to see if the market is acting in any way contrary to his expectations and adjust his thoughts accordingly.* For instance, if the 10-week cycle suddenly regains dominance, the next 4-week cycle advance, due in early June, could be significantly stronger than now expected. Once you are comfortable with using the cyclic model, adjustments to thinking can be made swiftly, with a minimum of financial pain.

Why I Use Cycles

Cycles are not the final answer to markets. Even in retrospect, they often fail adequately to account for all market action. Despite their shortcomings, the theory of cycles does provide a living, working model of the market and, when used intelligently, can make you some money. The main advantages of cyclic analysis, as I see them, are listed below. It is not coincidence that they are the same ones that make the Wave Principle such a valuable discipline in interpreting and forecasting the markets.

1) Cycles give you a *frame of reference* for making decisions.

2) Cycles give you a frame of reference for *changing your opinion* on the market, and thus keep you from being "wrong too long."

3) The mere *idea* of cycles puts you in a frame of mind for *anticipating changes in market direction*, thus consistently keeping you from joining the trend-following herd in buying after rallies are well underway and selling after declines have been clearly established.

Overview

The tenors behind the affairs of men are remarkable for their recurring nature. However, a perfect machine-like repetition is conspicuously absent. The rhythms exhibited by some forms of life often occur with punch-clock regularity, but the rhythms in humanity's social life do not. The *form* of mankind's progress and regress does remain constant, however. It is for this reason that I find the Wave Principle a truer representation of the psyche of mankind than the idea of cycles. Nevertheless, what is undeniable, at the core, is that there are tides in the affairs of men.

CYCLES UPDATE

published in 1995 in Appendix B of At the Crest of the Tidal Wave

Why and When Cycles Change

As countless analysts have observed, cyclic market behavior fades in and out of reliability. Cycles enthusiasts are at a loss to explain these repeated disappointments, and some have devised methods of dealing with the shifts in length and disappearances that are quite inventive and often useful in a practical application of the approach. The reason cycles shift lengths and disappear is that *cycles are not the essence of the market's behavior*.

Cycles may be a separate overlying phenomenon, but more likely, they are a byproduct of the fractal/chaotic forces behind the Wave Principle. Times of prolonged regular periodicity may be arising out of chaotic processes upon occasion in the same way that computer-generated fractal artworks often contain, in the midst of a relatively chaotic tapestry, a perfect oval or other such geometric form. For brief times, chaotic processes show regular forms that then dissolve, like bubbles in boiling water. Because the market is a chaotic process, its regular forms, in the same way, are similarly temporary. These regular forms, such as cycles, are byproducts of the process, not its generator.

The well-documented cyclical nature of the past is likely to remain in force because the nature of collective man is impulsive and therefore not subject to change. However, counting on specific fixed periodicities to repeat is a bit like playing Russian Roulette. We *know* that any cycle that appears in market price data will disappear someday. Yet we also know that until that day comes, it can repeat many times with remarkable precision. A classic example is the three-year cycle of 1914 to 1938, a cycle that lasted for eight revolutions across nine market bottoms. The next important low was not three years later, but four years later, in 1942. From that point forward, except for a brief reprise in 1946-1949, the three-year cycle was dead. Another example is the four-year cycle, which took over and held fast from 1954 until 1982, producing seven revolutions spanning eight market bottoms. Had an observer recognized that cycle in 1962, he could have amassed a fortune over the next two decades on the basis of that one tool alone. However, in 1986, the falling portion of that cycle failed to provide a bear market, and in 1987, its *rising* portion failed to prevent the biggest two-week crash since 1929, reflecting the four-year cycle's sudden lack of dominance.

Elliott Wave Principle demonstrated the Wave Principle's fundamentality relative to the cyclic hypothesis of market behavior by forecasting, in 1978, the demise of the four-year cycle that had held sway for 24 years. In Chapter 7, Frost and I reasoned as follows:

> For those who have found success using a cyclic approach, we feel that the Wave Principle can be a useful tool in predicting changes in the lengths of cycles, which seem to fade in and out of existence at times, usually with little or no warning. Note, for instance, that the four-year cycle has been quite visible in most of the current Supercycle's subwaves II, III and IV but was muddled and distorted in wave I, the 1932-1937 bull market, and prior to that time. If we remember that the two shorter waves in a five-wave bull move tend to be quite similar, we can deduce that the current Cycle wave V should more closely resemble wave I (1932-37) than any other wave in this sequence, since wave III from 1942 to 1966 was the extended wave and will be dissimilar to the two other motive waves. The current wave V, then, should be a simpler structure with shorter cycle lengths and could provide for the sudden contraction of the popular four-year cycle to more like three and a half years. In other words, *within* waves, cycles may tend toward time constancy. When the next wave begins, however, the analyst should be on the alert for changes in periodicity.

Indeed, from that point forward, a shorter cycle of 3 to 3½ years, with lows in 1978, 1981, 1984, 1987 and January 1991, assumed dominance, while the four-year cycle became muted. [This 3.3-year cycle has continued to show up in stock prices at the lows of April 1994, October 1997 and March 2001. The 4-year cycle has also regained its power, creating lows in October 1990, November 1994 and October 1998.—Ed.]

Chapter 17

THE SUNSPOT CYCLE AND STOCKS

by Peter Kendall with Robert R. Prechter, Jr.
originally published September 2000

In the early 1930s, statisticians Felix Shaffner and Carlos Garcia-Mata set out to refute economic theories (by W. Stanley Jevons in 1867 and others) suggesting a correlation between the 10.3-year sunspot cycle[1] and changes in agricultural and business activity. They commented, "Indeed this evidence was so striking that we thought it necessary to conduct further investigations to prove the resemblance accidental. In this we were unsuccessful." Their research appeared in the November 1934 *Quarterly Journal of Economics*. Based on a study of five sunspot cycles back through 1875, Shaffner and Garcia-Mata found that industrial production repeatedly peaked before the number of sunspots did. With respect to the stock market, they also looked at the turns in 1929 and 1932 and found a high degree of correlation. Charles Collins, R.N. Elliott's original Wall Street benefactor and one of the great stock market students of his day, extended the stock market correlation with a longer-term analysis in the 1960s. Collins related 93 years of sunspot data to the trends of U.S. stocks over the same span and concurred that important stock market peaks consistently precede sunspot cycle maximums. His findings, "An Inquiry into the Effect of Sunspot Activity on the Stock Market," appeared in the November-December 1965 issue of the *Financial Analysts Journal*. By anticipating the eventual peak in the sunspot cycle, Collins asserted that investors could avoid the most serious stock market declines.

Sunspot counts range from a low of near 0 at the bottom of the cycle to 100 to 200 at their peak. One of the final contributions of Collins' long career as an investment counselor and writer was the following early warning signal: "An important stock market peak has been witnessed or directly anticipated when, in the course of each new sunspot cycle, the yearly mean of observed sunspot numbers has climbed above 50." Once the annual mean climbs above 50, Collins added, the largest per-centage decline of the stock market cycle usually follows. Based on a 1964 bottom in the sunspot cycle, Collins speculated that 1967 would bring the count above 50 and thus indicate trouble ahead for the market. The threshold was, in fact, breached in 1967, which was fair warning of the speculative peak in 1968. In 1978, Collins' sunspot indicator marked another important high that was followed by a side-ways market over the next four years (which was a decline in PPI-adjusted terms). The next signal came in May 1988. The 1987 crash had already occurred, so the warning was late. However, stocks had a second selloff in 1990 that brought the Value Line index back to its 1987 low, so the sunspot threshold did signal a period of relative weakness. Despite minor anomalies, then, Collins' observations have remained applicable. Figure 1 shows the history of the sunspot count, the stock market and those recessions most closely associated with sunspot maxima.

Charles J. Collins

1934

In November of 1934, R.N. Elliott began a correspondence with Collins that eventually resulted in *The Wave Principle*, Elliott's first treatise on his discovery, which was actually composed mostly by Collins. November 1934 was also the month Carlos Garcia-Mata and Felix Shaffner published their sunspot study. Collins was obviously impressed with the results. After three more sunspot cycles and 30 more years of market observation, he published his own "Inquiry," which has proven a useful guide to the market's direction ever since.

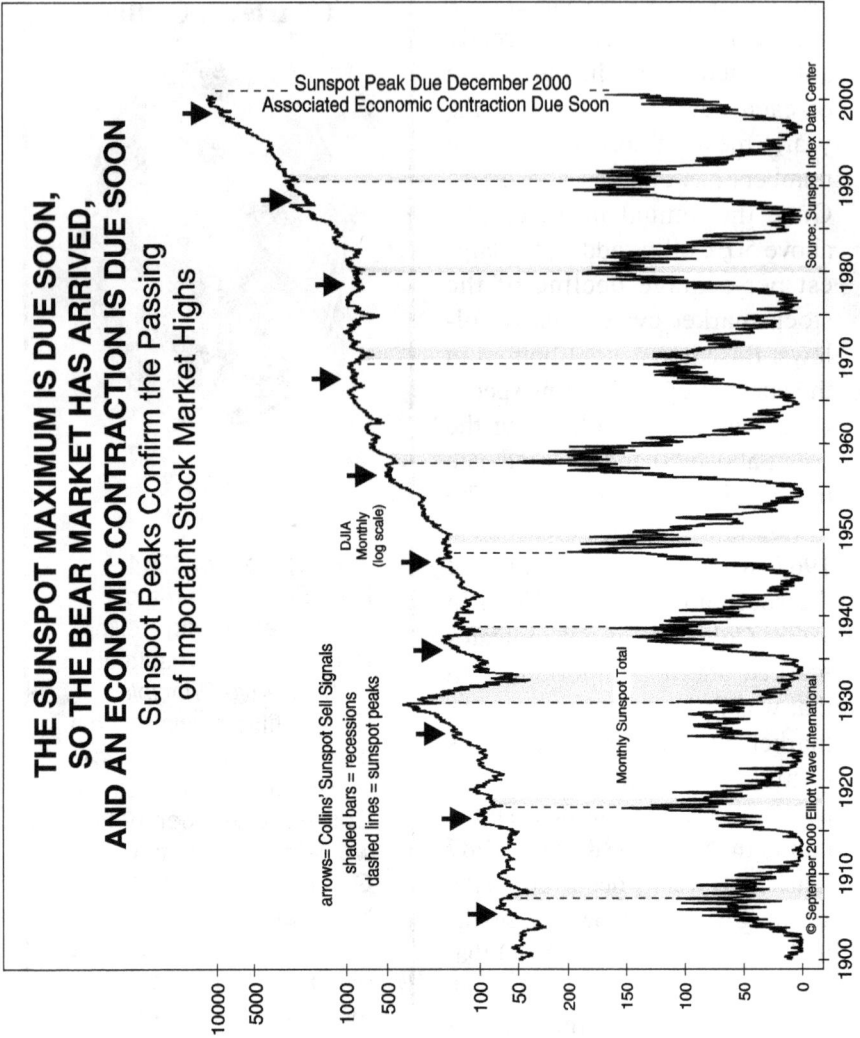

Figure 1

The current sunspot cycle began in October 1996 and appears to be adhering closely to the typical pattern. In the first two years of the cycle, the Dow Jones Industrial Average did not experience any significant stock market corrections as it gained 32%, slightly below the century-long average of 37% for this phase of the sunspot cycle. The annual sunspot mean of 50 was reached in 1998. Considering the succession of peaks in all the major market indicators and indexes, from the advance/decline line in April 1998 to the NASDAQ in March 2000, the sunspots and the market appear once again to be very much in line with historical observations. Once Collins' fair-warning sunspot signal has been given, the market may go to new highs, but it has entered a window of vulnerability that has been followed by stock market weakness in every instance over the course of the 20th century. The *end* of the time zone for a market top is just before the maximum monthly sunspot number, which is shown as a dashed line in the chart. Sunspot maxima have come 1 to 15 months after peaks in stocks. The average is **8** months. According to solar scientists, the next peak is due in December 2000, which matches the average duration over the last century. The declines that commenced in January (DJIA) and March (NDQ) 2000, then, are nicely within the window for a turn. At this point, the stock market's decline almost certainly has further to go because a two-month loss of 17% (to the early March low) would be shorter in time than any corresponding decline and shallower than all but that of 1978, when stock prices were already depressed.

Stock market weakness associated with a sunspot maximum tends to run several years, averaging 4 years and 4 months. In terms of return, the least bearish event (see table) was that of Cycle 6 in the 1950s and early 1960s, when the Dow was essentially unchanged after a period of almost six years.

How much decline should we expect this time? The largest bear markets have come off sunspot maximums that are *below the preceding maximum*. As you can see in Figure 2, the current sunspot cycle is behaving exactly that way. As with the sunspot cycles associated with the market highs in 1929 and 1968, which were followed by the two biggest bear markets of the century, the current sunspot cycle is topping out at a *lower level* than that of 1990. The recent bunching of the monthly sunspot count and the already-registered peak in the rate of change (see Figure 4) suggest a lower maximum sunspot count in this cycle.

Cycle	Duration (Peak to Peak)	Market Peak	Sunspot Peak	Lag Months	Peak to Trough Market Decline	Ultimate Duration of Market Contraction
1	8yrs, 6 mths	1/1906	2/1907	13	-48.5%	8yrs, 10 mths
2	10yrs, 6 mths	11/1916	8/1917	9	-42.0%	4yrs, 10 mths
3	12yrs, 4 mths	9/1929	12/1929	3	-89.4%	1yr, 10 mths
4	8yrs, 7 mths	4/1937	7/1938	15	-42.0%	4yrs, 1 mth
5	8yrs, 10 mths	5/1946	5/1947	12	-33.0%	3yrs, 1 mth
6	10yrs, 5 mths	7/1957	10/1957	3	+0.2%	5yrs, 10 mths
7	12yrs, 5 mths	12/1968	3/1969	4	-42.0%	6yrs
8	10yrs, 7 mths	9/1978	10/1979	12	-17.1%	3yrs, 11 mths
9	10yrs, 10 mths	7/1990	8/1990	1	-21.8%	4 mths
10	10yrs, 4 mths**	1/2000 (?)	Due 12/2000 **	11(?)		
Average	10yrs, 4 mths			8	-37.2%	4yrs, 4 mths

*As the only sunspot-related market disruption to post a gain, Cycle 6's slight rise (of 1.5 Dow points from July 1957 to June 1962) is an interesting exception. It is the period that recorded the sunspot cycle count that is easily the highest in the 250-year history of the data. From an Elliott perspective, the period is also of interest as it encompassed Primary ③ of Cycle III, one of the most powerful upward thrusts of the century-long bull market.
**Projected

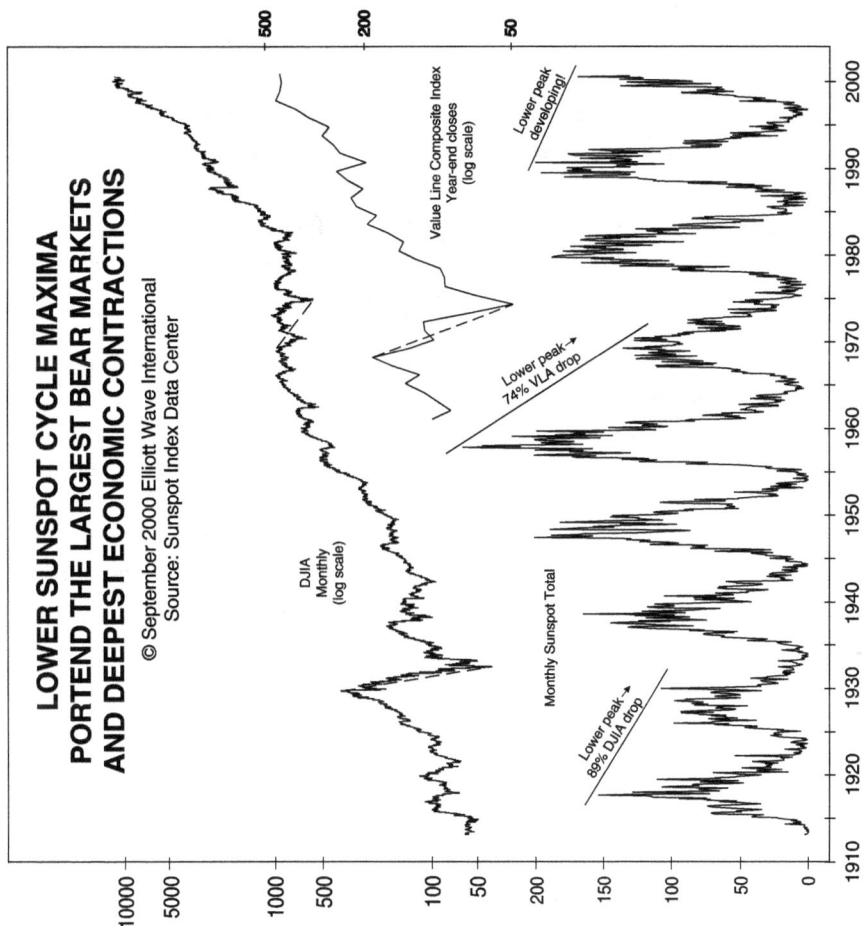

Figure 2

Outlook for the Economy

Links between sunspots and economic activity have been documented as far back as the 1720s. The shaded areas in Figure 1 show that every sunspot maximum this century has had a corresponding recession. In most cases, the recession begins when sunspots peak, which is after the top in the stock market. Only in 1938 and 1946 did the closest recession precede the sunspot maxima, but in the latter case, a second one occurred in 1948-49, roughly at the normal time. At this point in the current cycle, sunspots are approaching a peak, and a bear market in stocks is developing. The century of history shown here says unequivocally that today's economy should be heading into the early stages of a recession or depression within a matter of months.

The stock market has never bottomed in this progression until a recession occurs. Thus, another reason to expect today's new bear market to continue is that as yet, there has been no recession.

Generally speaking, *the periods from immediately before to immediately after each sunspot cycle maximum account for almost all of the major financial disruptions of the last century*. In addition to the average of 4.4 years of stock market weakness, a sunspot cycle maximum and subsequent decline is generally followed by a financial crisis and another recession. At the beginning of the century, there was also typically a third recession at sunspot lows.

Timing the Next Major Market Bottom

By the time of the sunspot cycle minimum, the most severe turmoil for stocks and the economy is almost always past. In fact, buying opportunities have presented themselves ahead of the minimum point in every cycle since 1910. The dotted lines in Figure 3 show the same relative position of the sunspot frequency at important market bottoms. Each of these bottoms, which include the starting points of Supercycle (V) in 1932, Cycle III in 1942 and Cycle V in 1974, occurred when the rate of change in the monthly sunspot count decelerated to an average of 26.5% of its prior level (using a four-month moving average to smooth sunspot volatility). Based on an average market effect of 4.4 down years, the current stock-market contraction should see a low in 2004. This date fits *The Elliott Wave Theorist*'s cycle and Fibonacci studies that have long called for a bottom in 2003-2004. Given the potential, this headline from the July 17 *USA Today* strikes us as optimistic:

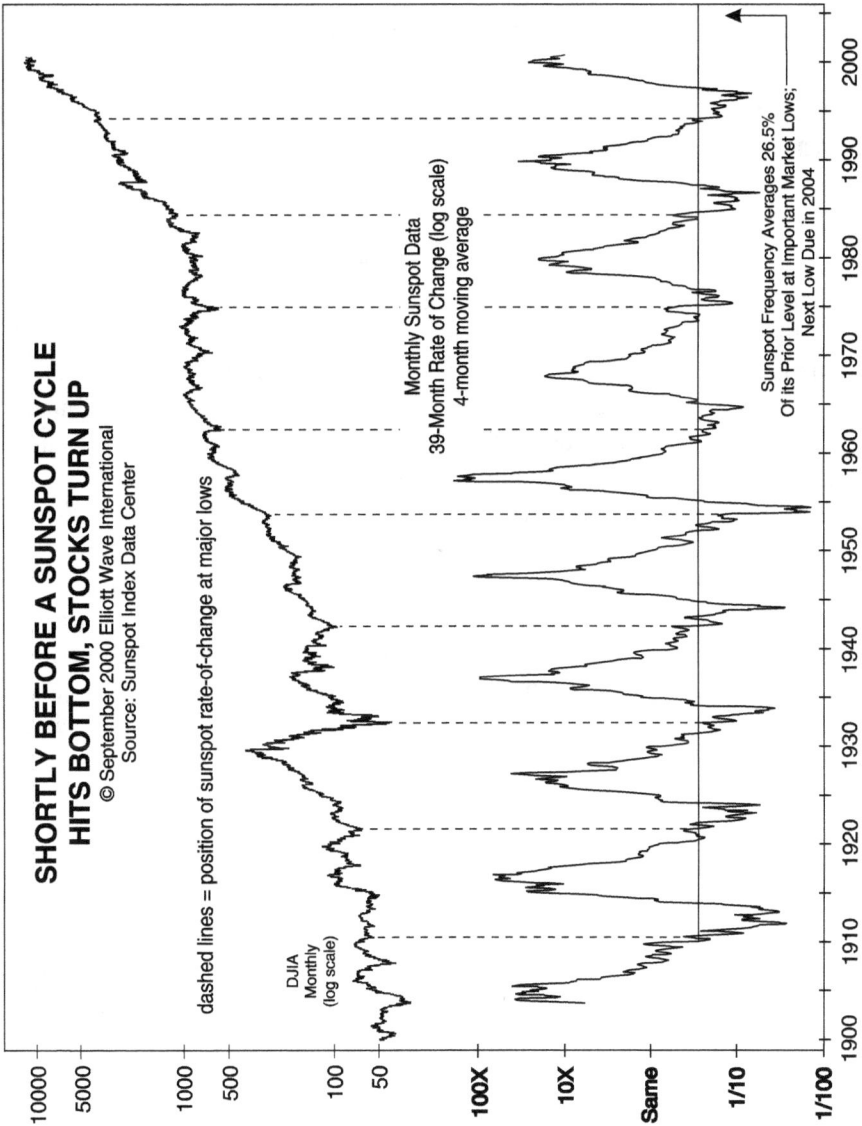

Figure 3

Solar Storm's Disruptions Mostly Over

More than likely, the disruptions have just begun, at least in the social sense.

A Broader Application?

Some effects from solar radiation are well documented. Sunspots disrupt satellite systems, radio transmissions and electric power grids. In the realm of mass human activity, the sun's role has been a source of speculation since the dawn of civilization. In 1926, Professor A.C. Tchijevsky traced sunspot activity back through 500 B.C. and found that it produced nine waves of human excitability per century. "As sunspot activity approaches maximum," Tchijevsky found, "the number of mass historical events taken as whole increases." *The Wave Principle of Human Social Behavior* describes the basis of the Wave Principle and unconscious human herding behavior as a function of the human limbic system, which is the gatekeeper of emotion within the human brain. However, the limbic system is not necessarily independent of outside forces. As the radiating center of our solar system and the wellspring of practically all the energy on the planet, the sun is certainly an intriguing contender for some degree of external mass mental influence.

Why does the stock market typically peak before sunspots do? One very plausible explanation is that the collective tendency to speculate peaks out along with the *rate of change* in sunspot activity. If sunspots affect humans' positive-mood excitability, the peak in their acceleration appears to be the point of maximum effect. When we explored this possible explanation, we found something additionally interesting. Figure 4 shows that as the solar radiation thrown off by the sun increases to a maximum rate (shown by our optimized 39-month rate of change in sunspot numbers), the human urge to speculate in general hits a fever pitch. Two months after the rate-of-change peak in 1916, the stock market established an all-time high that was not materially exceeded until the sunspot count was accelerating again in the mid-1920s. The next rate-of-change peak in October 1926 preceded the final stock market high by a full three years, but the speculative fever that accompanied the Florida land boom ended almost coincidentally, about two months earlier. The next peak was a double top that finished in February 1937,

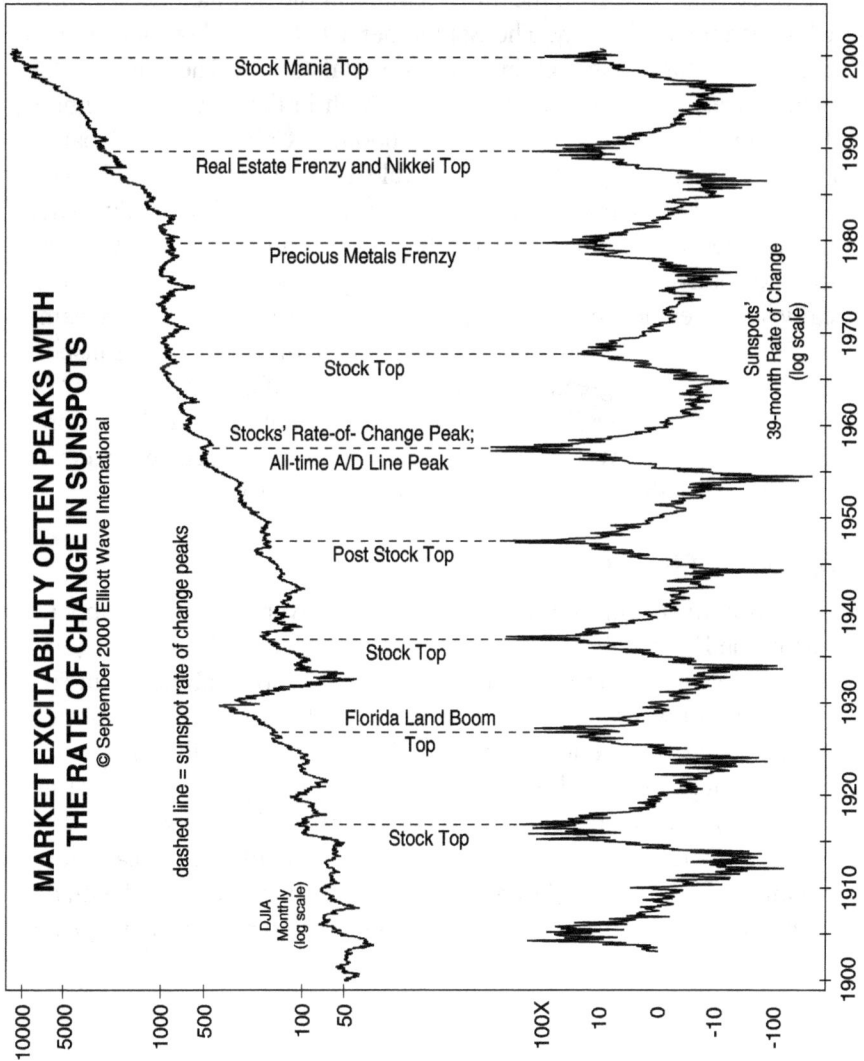

MARKET EXCITABILITY OFTEN PEAKS WITH THE RATE OF CHANGE IN SUNSPOTS

© September 2000 Elliott Wave International

dashed line = sunspot rate of change peaks

Stock Mania Top

Real Estate Frenzy and Nikkei Top

Precious Metals Frenzy

Stock Top

Stocks' Rate-of- Change Peak;
All-time A/D Line Peak

Post Stock Top

Stock Top

Florida Land Boom Top

Stock Top

DJIA
Monthly
(log scale)

Sunspots'
39-month Rate of Change
(log scale)

Figure 4

one month before a major stock market high. In 1947 and 1967, the rate of change peaked within 13 months of major stock peaks. In 1957, the peak coincided with the all-time high in the advance-decline line, which stands to this day. The September 1979 peak was four months before a century-long high in precious metals prices. The August 1989 peak closely accompanied the all-time high in the Nikkei (December 1989) and the end of a big real estate boom in California and Japan.

Scientists' grasp of the sunspot cycle is based on empirical observation rather than an understanding of what causes it. Similarly, we have not verified a causal relationship behind our observations. However, the speculative fall-off in the wake of every peak since 1916 is statistically strong evidence of an effect. The latest peak rate of change came in December 1999, and that sets up a test. Will this peak in sunspots mark the end of the greatest mania in the history of the stock market? So far, the answer is "yes," as the Dow topped a month later and the more-speculative NASDAQ peaked in March. A ninth straight correspondence will not prove the case, but it will add to the empirical evidence.

Speaking of the Sun...[2]

Speaking of sun-related phenomena, the average surface temperature of the Earth in 1997 was the *highest ever recorded* in figures going back to 1856. The higher sun radiation since 1986 combined with five El Niños in the 1990s have made the 1991-1997 period the warmest of any seven-year period on record. As climatologist Iben Browning pointed out years ago, climatic warmth and human prosperity (and thus optimism) go hand in hand. Just as the severely cold winters in the days of Valley Forge coincided with the final decade of a six-decade-long bear market, the unusually warm 1990s to date have coincided with the culmination of a prosperous mood whose roots go back over 200 years.

NOTES

[1] 10.3 years is the average duration of the sunspot cycle in the 20th Century. From the mid-18th through the 19th century, the cycle was 11.7 years (peak to peak).

[2] This paragraph was originally published in 1997.

Chapter 18

THE RESOLUTION OF A MAJOR TOP PROJECTION FOR THE CONSTANT-DOLLAR DOW USING A FIXED-TIME PERIODICITY

The Outlook in 1983

Way back in 1983 (see Appendix in *Elliott Wave Principle*), *The Elliott Wave Theorist* published a chart that forecasted a huge advance for Cycle wave V, followed by a great bear market. The bottom of the chart included a timing forecast for the *next major turn* based on a continuum of equally spaced time intervals. The interval had already marked three major turns in succession, but there was no way to project whether the next one would be a bottom or a top. At the time, I guessed it would be a bottom. Here is the commentary that went with that forecast (see Figure 1):

> Regarding time, either wave (A) or wave (C) of the Grand Super-cycle correction should bottom in **1999, + or - 1 year**, based on several observations. From a 1987 top, a decline matching the 13 years up from 1974 would point to the year **2000**. From a 1990 top, a decline matching the 8 years up from 1982 would point to **1998**. It also happens that the very regular recurrence of turning points at 16.6-16.9-year intervals (see main chart, bottom) projects **1999** for the next turning point.

As it turned out, 1987 and 1990 (as you can see in Figure 2), both proved to be turning-point years, of waves ③ and ④ (by one labeling) respectively. So the Fibonacci projections of turning points 8 and 13 years from those years remained valid.

Notice that the original projection targeted **1998** and **2000**, bracketing the year **1999**, which was targeted independently by the recurring time interval. All three of these years seem to have played crucial roles

As published by *The Elliott Wave Theorist*, April 6, 1983

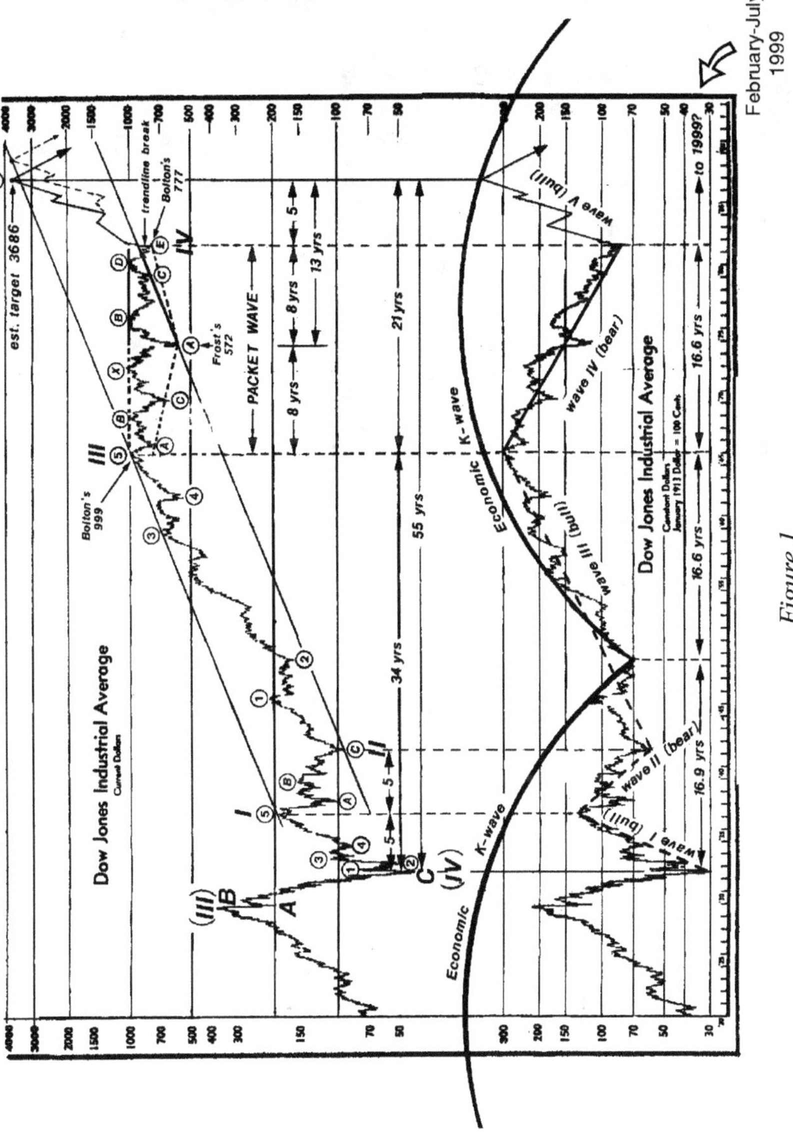

Figure 1

Figure 2

in the formation of the market's major reversal. In 1998, the Value Line geometric stock index (see Figure 2) and the daily advance-decline line peaked. In 2000, the Dow, S&P and NASDAQ all topped out in dollar terms. As we will see below, the *real* value of the Dow and the S&P topped in 1999. So all three durations were important in the cluster of years that was expected so long ago to define a major turn. The remainder of this report addresses the significance of the reversal that occurred in 1999.

The Outlook in 1999 for Constant-Dollar Stock Prices

On February 5, 1999, EWT recalled the above-quoted forecast from 1983. The idea of a major bottom was obviously wrong. Was the projection of a major turning point wrong, too? If the approaching end of the repeating time interval was still on track, it would mark not a major bottom but rather the major *top* of the great bull market. But what kind of top? Here is the commentary from that early 1999 issue:

A Mysterious Duration Signals a Major Turn

In April 1983, EWT published a special report titled "A Rising Tide" about the great bull market that lay ahead. As bullish as I was, I did not know then how high that tide would rise. Yet the main chart published in that report, reproduced as Figure 1, did indicate the time of the next major turning point. Take a look at the bottom of the graph and note that the four major turns (inflation-adjusted) of Supercycle wave (V) from 1932 were all separated by a time span of 16.6 to 16.9 years. The next major turning point was due in "**1999**." To be exact, 16.6 to 16.9 years from August 9/12, 1982 (the days of the intraday and closing lows) targets **February 6, 1999-July 18, 1999**.

Sixteen years ago, I thought that the bull market would end in 1987 or 1990 and that we would be entertaining a major low in 1999. What we have now is more satisfying academically. If wave V ends in the first half of 1999, then *every major psychological turning point of Supercycle wave (V), i.e., 1932, 1949, 1966, 1982 and 1999, will have been separated by this duration of 16.6 to 16.9 years.*

How It Turned Out

Read that section again and notice that these durations pertained specifically to the "*inflation-adjusted*" DJIA, better termed the "constant-dollar Dow." There are different ways to depict constant purchasing power for a currency. Dividing the Dow by the CPI and PPI gives the same turning date (January 14, 2000) on which the Dow topped in nominal dollar terms. However, these price benchmarks are slow to change and are subject to continual re-definition by government. When we use sensitive divisors that are consistently represented *and* freely valued in the marketplace, a different picture emerges.

Figure 3 uses real money (gold) and a basket of commodities (the CRB index) as two types of purchasing units to show U.S. stock prices in constant dollars. They demonstrate that the DJIA, adjusted to the value of physical bartering media, turned right in the incredibly narrow time

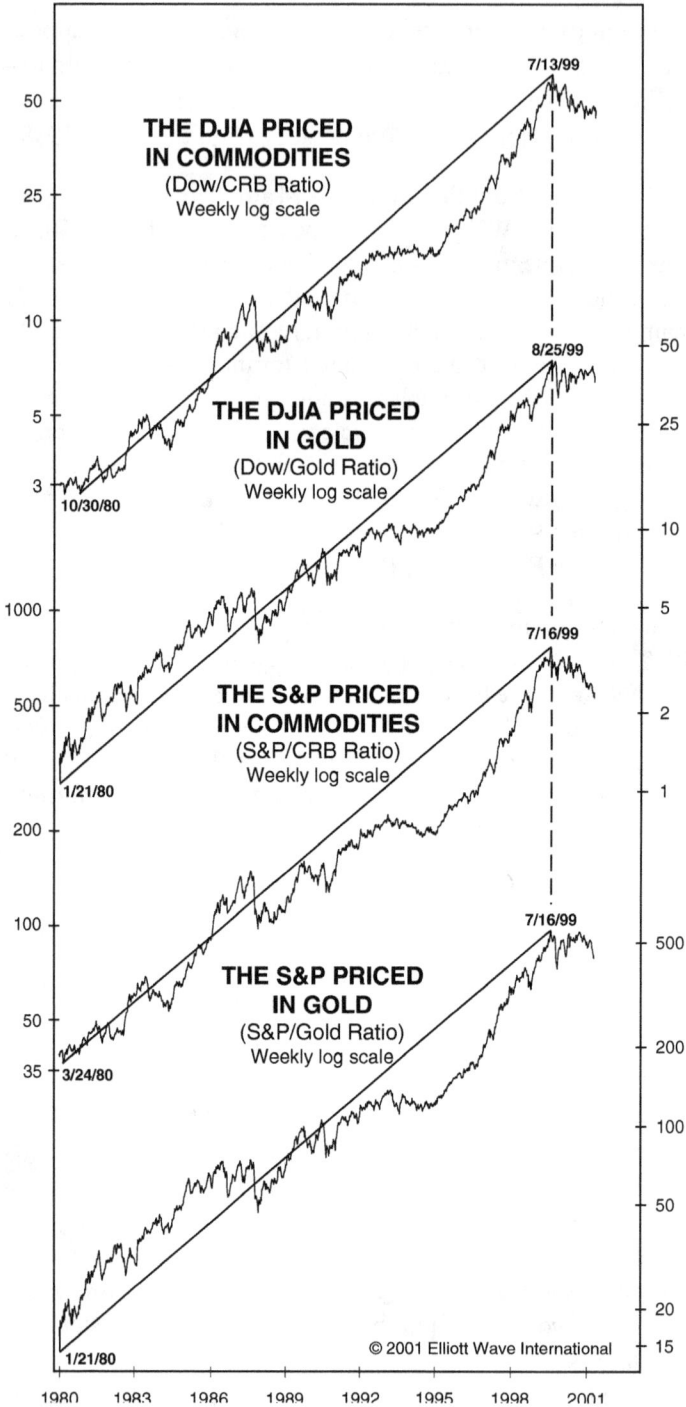

Figure 3

window set sixteen years in advance, which was **February 6, 1999-July 18, 1999**. Just look at those turns and see how they occurred right at the end of the projected range:

- DJIA top in terms of commodities: **July 13, 1999**
- DJIA top in terms of gold: **August 25, 1999**

The S&P topped on almost exactly the same dates as the Dow:

- S&P top in terms of commodities: **July 16, 1999**
- S&P top in terms of gold: **July 16, 1999**

Figure 4

The duration from the 1982 bottom to these turning dates in 1999 is within a few days of being *exactly* as long as the duration between the major turning points of 1932 and 1949. So on our chart, we now have two 16.6-year periods bracketed by two 16.9-year periods, as you can see at the bottom of Figure 4.

Other Indexes

The timing forecast pertained not only to the constant-dollar Dow Industrials and S&P but also to the Dow Jones Transports, which topped in **1999** by *all* measures as follows (see Figure 5):

- DJTA top in terms of nominal dollars (the reported index): **May 12, 1999**
- DJTA top in terms of commodities: **May 12, 1999**
- DJTA top in terms of gold: **July 19, 1999**

Two key indexes topped later than 1999 by all measures. The NASDAQ plowed upward so powerfully at the peak of the mania that it made its top in March 2000 on all measures. The Dow Jones Utilities, reflecting the last gasp of bullish psychology based on falling interest rates, topped in December 2000 in nominal terms, April 18, 2001 in terms of gold and May 31, 2001 in terms of commodities.

Caveat

There is one fly in the analytical soup. Using gold and the CRB index as deflators places the last major stock price bottom in 1980, not 1982. EWT projected the 16.6-16.9 year duration from the *1982* low, which is when stock prices bottomed in terms of the PPI. This difference may challenge our conclusion that the duration is still pertinent. On the other hand, had the components and calculation of these measures not been manipulated over the latest decade, it is possible that they also would have shown stock price highs in 1999 as well. Also, it is not necessary that these ratios mark *the* turn; marking *a* crucial long-term reversal is value enough. Regardless, one might allow that a turn in either ratio within a projected five-month period after nearly 17 years is remarkable enough to sustain the apparent validity of the observed phenomenon.

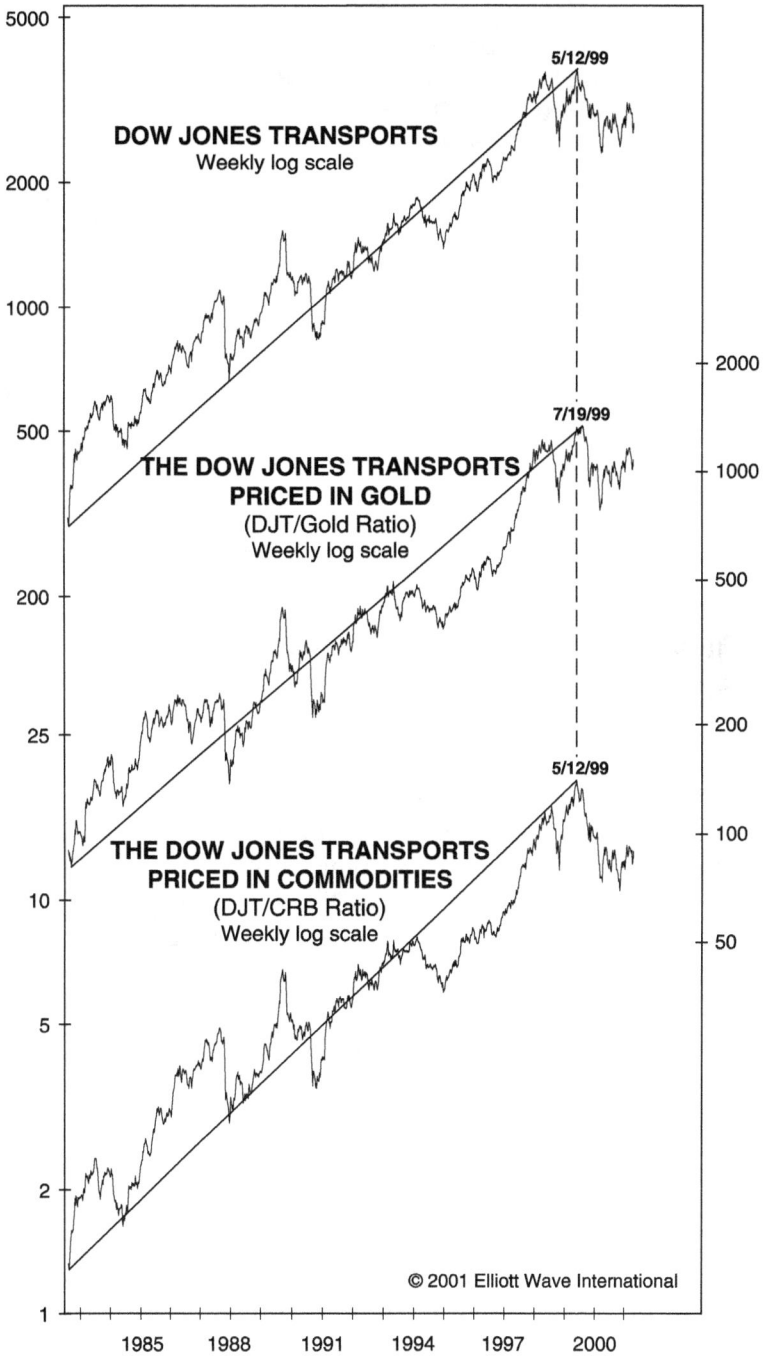

DOW JONES TRANSPORTS
Weekly log scale

5/12/99

THE DOW JONES TRANSPORTS
PRICED IN GOLD
(DJT/Gold Ratio)
Weekly log scale

7/19/99

THE DOW JONES TRANSPORTS
PRICED IN COMMODITIES
(DJT/CRB Ratio)
Weekly log scale

5/12/99

© 2001 Elliott Wave International

Figure 5

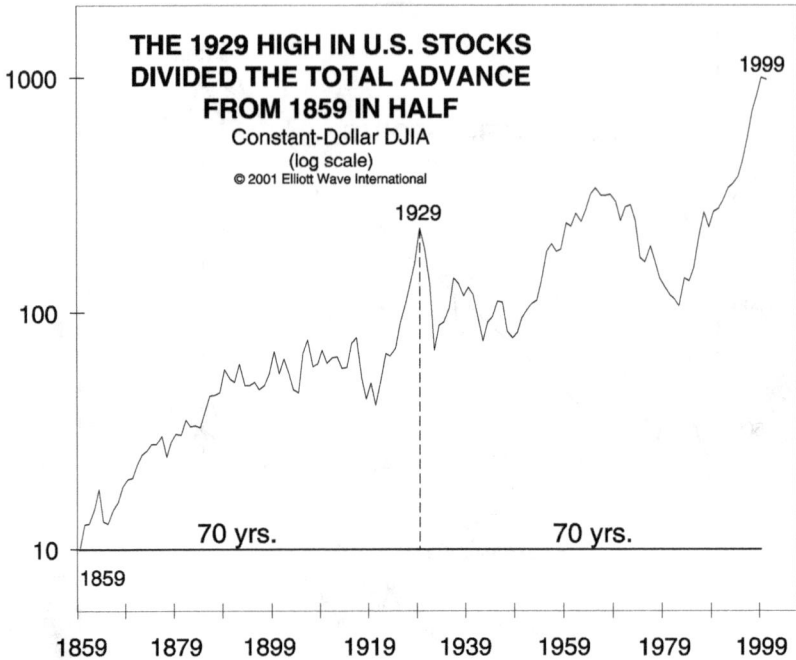

Figure 6

A Long-Term Time Symmetry with 1999

The February 2000 issue of *The Elliott Wave Theorist* (reprinted in *View from the Top of the Grand Supercycle*) shows three examples of time symmetry in long-term waves. Figure 6 illustrates another one, which pertains to the constant-dollar Dow. It is rather interesting that the famous 1929 high splits in half. The total gain from the orthodox bottom of wave (II) in 1859 to what now appears to be the top of wave (V), measured in constant dollars. This symmetry is probably more evidence that the top has passed.

The Former Dow's True Top?

The nominal (reported) Dow topped concurrently with the constant-dollar Dow, edged up to a slightly higher high five weeks later, and then fell 1400 points into October 1999. The top appeared to be in. It then staged another rally, which lasted three months into January 2000, carrying to a new high. On March 24, 2000, analyst James Rafferty in his *Market Comments* suggested one reason for that higher high:

Figure 7

Last November 1st, Dow Jones made four substitutions in the DJIA component stocks. The net effect has been to add 630 points to the average — almost all from INTC and MSFT, thus maintaining the semblance of a bull market while stock after stock continued lower.

Clearly without those extra 630 points, the Dow never would have made it to a new high, and the summer of 1999 would stand in the history books as the time of the final top. It is a testimony to the weakness in stocks of Dow Industrial companies that although Intel doubled one last time from November to August, the Dow's other components dragged it down so much that January 2000 remains the average's high-water mark (see Figure 7). Had the keepers of the Dow not made those substitutions, the nominal and constant-dollar DJIA would have topped at almost exactly the same time. They *did* make those substitutions, however, so that is the history we have.

What It Means

The array of charts in Figures 3 and 5 shows a coordinated sequence of tops, all falling right on the cusp of the 16.9-year duration projected years ago. The first conclusion we might draw, then, is that this 16.6-16.9-year periodicity marking major turning points in real (constant-dollar) stock prices is still working, in fact amazingly well. Given the market's recent plunge, we are next justified in concluding, until proven otherwise, that *the latest turn in constant-dollar stock prices was of substantial proportion*, commensurate in importance with the market turns of 1932, 1949, 1966 and 1982. This conclusion fits with our outlook for a continuing Grand Supercycle bear market. [*Editor's Note*: The DJIA in real-money terms (the Dow/gold ratio) peaked in 1999 and collapsed. It did not follow the nominal Dow to later all-time highs.]

The bottom of Supercycle wave (a) is due in 2003-2004 according to the Fibonacci array and the cluster of projected cycle bottoms detailed in Chapter 5 of *At the Crest of the Tidal Wave*. Now we have yet another bit of support for that conclusion, as 2004 is a Fibonacci **5** years from the 1999 high registered in constant-dollar terms. [The Global Stock Index registered a bottom in March 2003.—*Ed.*]

The Next Turn for the 16.6-16.9-Year Periodicity

Whether this periodicity will extend into the next Grand Supercycle is unknown and perhaps unlikely, since I have seen — and even predicted — changes in cyclic durations at major changes in Elliott waves. For now, we can simply observe that this repeating duration between turning points next calls for a major turn in the inflation-adjusted prices of stocks to occur in the first half of the year 2017. The projected year of 2017 is also a Fibonacci **13** years from 2004, the last year likely to mark the bottom of Supercycle wave (a). Just as with 1999, the two *encompassing* years are also indicated by Fibonacci durations, since 2016 is **34** years from the 1982 bottom, and 2018 is **89** years from the 1929 high. I surely wish we could have known back in 1983 that the turn due sixteen years later would be a high, but the *direction* of reversal for this periodicity does not seem to be indicated in advance. Thus, there is no way to know that detail until we get close. In the meantime, we may rest assured that the latest turn is definitely a *top*.

PART V

Requirements for Successful Forecasting and Speculation

Chapter 19

ACHIEVING SUCCESS IN MARKET ANALYSIS

by Robert R. Prechter, Jr.
*excerpted from material originally published December 1983,
September 1984 and from a speech to the
International Elliott Wave Conference, September 1991*

Art or Science? (1983)

The study of the Wave Principle must be, and is, a science, albeit one in its early stages of development, as most social sciences are. Therefore, as Charles Collins often said, application of the Wave Principle is an objective discipline. For this reason, only rigorously honest interpretations can be accepted as valid. If you want your hopes or whims fulfilled regardless of the evidence, the market will punish you for that weakness. Take it from someone who had to figure that out the hard way. The worst interpreters of the theory are those who view it as art, to be "painted" with their own impulsive or imprecise "interpretations." However, until the probabilities of the various patterns and ratios can be quantified, *applying* the Wave Principle will retain many of the characteristics of a craft (Webster's: "skill acquired by experience or study; systematic use of knowledge in doing things"), to be mastered not only by thinking but by doing.

The Importance of Thinking Technically (1984)

Technical data is that which is generated by the action of the market under study. Supposedly "fundamental" data is that which is outside the market but assumed to impact the market. Conventional analysts use the latter almost exclusively and to miserable result. A conventional analyst was quoted in the August 24 *Wall Street Journal* as saying, "As long as the budget deficit problem remains unresolved, and you have a restrictive monetary policy combined with an expansionary fiscal policy, you're going to have a worried stock market. The market will continue to vacillate as long as there are such inconsistencies in government economic policy." Now, I'm only 35, but I will bet that my 80-year-old subscribers cannot recall a time when half the country wasn't screaming about the government's economic policies. The stock market has gone every direction but backwards with that situation in the fundamental background. Yet without any kind of study, this point is being offered as a reason for a market opinion.

The main problem with this ubiquitous style of analysis is that its indicators are removed from the market itself. The analyst assumes causality between external events and market movements, an idea that is almost certainly false. But just as important, and less recognized, is that such analysis almost always requires a *forecast of the supposedly causal data itself* before one can draw conclusions about the market. As one analyst recently claimed, "interest rates are too high *and rising.*" Rates certainly *had* been rising, but whether or not they were still rising involved a forecast. In actuality, on Wednesday of that week, long term rates had already begun *falling.* Another example is contained in a WSJ article mentioned in the July letter. The argument was made on May 29, after a full year of rising interest rates, that interest rates could not decline because (1) the economy is too healthy and (2) the Fed will fail to clamp down on inflation in an election year. Whether or not these things come to pass, what is important to recognize is that this "fundamental" analysis begins with a *forecast* of its own indicators, beginning with what the economy, the Fed, inflation and politicians will do. The analyst is then forced to take a *second* step in coming to a conclusion about how those forecasted events will affect the markets! Technicians only have one step to take, which gives them an edge right off the bat. Their main advantage is that they don't have to forecast their indicators.

As stated above, even the fundamentalists' second step is probably a process built on quicksand. Assuming causality between outside and the market action is a highly questionable approach. For instance, suppose you had supplied the analyst who turned bearish in June with the information that by late August, short term interest rates would be a full percentage point *higher* than they were at the time of his pronouncement. He would have stuck to his opinion even more strongly and would have been as wrong as one could possibly be.

The most common application of fundamental analysis is estimating companies' earnings for both the current year and next year and recommending stocks on that basis. As you can see, this method *first requires a forecast of the fundamental data.* The record on that basis alone is very poor, as *Barron's* pointed out in a June 4 article, which showed that earnings estimates for the 30 DJIA stocks averaged 18% error for any year ahead. The weakest link in the chain, however, is the assumption that earnings estimates are a basis for choosing stock market winners. According to a table in the same *Barron's* article, a purchase of the ten DJIA stocks with the most favorable earnings estimates would have produced a ten-year cumulative gain of 40.5%, while choosing the ten DJIA stocks with the least favorable earnings estimates would have produced a whopping 142.5% gain.

Successful Forecasting is Probabilistic

Forecasting necessarily involves probabilities. Sometimes, the probabilities are close to 50-50 for two outcomes, and while reasonable analysts should agree *on that fact*, they might disagree as to which side the advantage belongs. Sometimes probabilities are 80% for a particular outcome, and competent analysts using the same method should agree on the probable outcome. However, even when the odds of a particular outcome are 80%, that does not mean that the outcome *will occur*. It means that *even given that favorable circumstance*, one out of five times your investment decision will still be wrong.

You cannot deviate from an objective application of your rules and guidelines just because your last market call was a bad one. If you do, you'll ruin your long-term ability to anticipate market direction correctly much of the time, which is all that good analysis promises. In other words, *some percentage of error is a requirement for overall success*, and trying to avoid it or achieve perfection by overriding your proven methodology will ruin your *chances* for success.

Independence and Objectivity

At minimum, successful analysis and speculation require that you be independent in your thinking. Thinking independently of the crowd, however, does not mean always *fighting* the crowd. For example, "contrary opinion" is a term often bandied about as the correct orientation to markets because it reflects fierce independence. However, the tendency to want to fight every trend with contrary thinking is just as destructive to success as the lemming-like desire to jump on trends after they are well aged. Although it is difficult to be truly independent, you must avoid both a lazy willingness to conform to the group and the curmudgeonly desire always to fight it. You must also be know-ledgeable, which is one point of this presentation. Finally, you must be as objective as possible at all times.

What are the factors that allow you to be objective? First is the knowledge that the essential dynamics of crowd psychology are immutable because human beings have a fundamental nature with respect to emotionally charged social situations, and that fundamental nature is precisely what is primarily at work in the speculative marketplace. Next, it is necessary to understand that this truth also applies to you. From that solid foundation, success in markets then demands a tremendous effort, the goal of which is nothing less than *using your rational cerebral cortex to tame the emotions and motivations produced by your primitive brain stem*. One must understand, contrary to the erroneous assumptions of your unconscious, that buying in a high and rising market is not the same as putting food on the table. The "food" in this case is a mental image, not a reality. Similarly, selling in panic as the market falls is not equivalent to running from a wild animal on the attack; indeed, the wilder the "animal" appears, the greater the panic, and the closer to a bottom the market is. At such times, reason argues that you should contemplate buying, not selling. The "wild animal" is an ephemeral image, a mirage, and only by resisting the urge to flee can one maintain his advantageous position in the berry field, picking the best of the crop after others have fled. Developing such paradoxical knowledge about the investment marketplace provides a survival *advantage* over those who instinctively chase rallies and flee declines. This knowledge is difficult to obtain because it is the opposite of the more natural assumption upon which the unreasoning "primitive" brain has issued its commands.

Thus, in order to think and act objectively in the marketplace, you must pit your reason and knowledge against your deeply inbred emotional tendencies. It takes a tremendous effort first to understand how it feels when the primitive part of your brain tries to compel you to take specific action in certain circumstances — such as the "fight or flight" reaction when you see a tiger ten feet away or the herding instinct when the group gets up to leave for another location — and then to learn to override these tendencies with calm and independent reason when the fear is created *not* by the presence of a tiger but by a rapidly decreasing value for your investment or a powerful consensus opinion of your peers. Difficult as it is to attain, this ability is *required* for success in the fields of analysis and speculation. It is clear why so few people excel at the task. Intelligence is not enough. Knowledge is not enough. Independent thinking is not enough. You also need the ability to *recognize*, and then to *control*, your deepest and most powerfully overwhelming emotions.

The Inescapability of Having an Opinion

While investors have some leeway in their choice of methods for forming an opinion on the prospects for their investment, one thing is for certain. *Every investment posture requires a market opinion.* People try to avoid the responsibility of an opinion by "diversifying" for its own sake (usually just prior to a deflation that brings down all assets) or by claiming that their market "always goes up long term," whether it is stocks, gold or real estate (usually just prior to a major and/or long lasting decline in that market), or by claiming they are not making an investment when they put their money in Treasury bills, the bank or the mattress (usually just before markets are ready for highly profitable moves, governments are about to go bankrupt, banks are ready to fail or the currency is about to be devalued). No investment approach is guaranteed, and therefore none is safe, and therefore *each requires an opinion*. Since, if you are an investor, you cannot escape having an opinion, you might as well obtain a *good* one, and the best way to do that is by objective thought and knowledgeable analysis. In acting on an opinion, you should pay attention to that old adage, first uttered, as far as we know, by the Roman orator, Cicero, who counseled, "There is grief in indecision." On the other hand, there is also that time honored observation made by an acquaintance of mine, who said, "It's never too late to panic."

Always Right? (1984)

While this chapter and Chapter 20 address the soundness of the *essence* of technical analysis, they do not mean to imply that all specific conclusions or methodologies based thereon are therefore valid. Indeed, that is hardly the case. Are there incompetent technicians? Of course. Are there non-objective technicians? Yes. In fact, some people who call themselves technicians rely on techniques that are little more

than numerology. Are there technicians who are closet fundamentalists? Everywhere. This type of erroneous thinking permeates the world
of financial analysis. For example, someone who bills himself as a
technician was the one on television on June 1, explaining that he just
turned bearish on stocks because now "interest rates were too high and
still rising." Such practitioners are subject to the widespread errors of
conventional thought. Are there unknowledgeable technicians? Yes.
Are there dependent technicians, who conform to group opinion? Yes.
That's why polls of technicians' opinions differ only slightly in result
from polls of other market observers and make good technical indicators themselves. Will competent technicians using the same method
always agree? Not necessarily. The science of market forecasting is
young and undeveloped.

If you are a pure technician and still come to a wrong conclusion
about the market, does that necessarily mean your method is flawed?
Read this article from the Associated Press about an occurrence in New
Orleans.

100 Lifeguards There - He Drowns

New Orleans (AP)—Although 100
lifeguards were present, a fully clothed
man drowned at a party to celebrate
the first summer in memory without a
drowning at a city pool, officials said
yesterday.

Jerome Moody, 31, was found on the
bottom at the deep end of a Recreation
Department pool at the end of the party
Tuesday, said Madlyn Richard, department director.

Moody, a guest who was not a life-
guard, was fully dressed, she said.

Four lifeguards were on duty and
more than half the 200 people there were
certified lifeguards, she said.

The body was found as the pool
was being cleared. It was not known
when Moody got in the water or how
he drowned.

> Lifeguards attempted to revive Moody until emergency attendants arrived. An autopsy confirmed Moody had drowned, said Coroner Frank Minyard.
>
> —August 2, 1985[1]

How many of you would have assumed that pool to be relatively safe? Would your conclusion have been proved invalid? No. Sometimes intelligent people, trained in a valid craft, just commit errors. The only way to achieve a successful record over the long term is to accept the fact that you will be wrong sometimes.

Nevertheless, the fact remains that technical analysis (particulary wave analysis) is vastly superior to "fundamental" analysis in forecasting general market trends. As Martin Pring (*Pring Market Review*, Washington Depot, CT) recently said in an article for *Futures* magazine, "[few] market letters are completely devoted to technical analysis. They usually include comments about fundamental factors such as the money supply. You have to let the indicators speak for themselves. Other stuff clouds your judgment."

Pure technicians are very rare. But from what I've seen over the past ten years, their market calling and forecasting records are vastly superior to those of conventional fundamentalists and significantly better than those of the hybrids.

NOTES

[1] "100 Lifeguards There — He Drowns." AP News Service, August 2, 1985

Chapter 20

A CALL TO ARMS

by Robert R. Prechter, Jr., CMT
Past President of the MTA, 1990-1991
From a speech presented to the
Market Technicians Association Conference
Wesley Chapel, Florida, May 1994
and published in the MTA Journal *of Summer/Fall 1994*

I have designed this talk so as not to disappoint anyone who came to hear Bob Prechter say something radical. I haven't made a speech outside our own conferences for five years and probably won't for another five years, so I hope you'll indulge me while I push the envelope a bit with something I feel passionate about.

Despite the evidence of this well attended conference, today the term "technical analysis" is in lower repute than many of us realize. I'm not speaking only of its status in the eyes of money managers, TV commentators and the public. Of course, it has always been ignored in mature bull markets, when paper profits appear to have validated all kinds of incorrect decision making processes. No, I'm speaking of the fact that the term "technical analysis" is in low repute with technicians.

Some of you may not know that a former president of the MTA who for years had the word "technical" on the masthead of his institutional publication recently took it off. Why did he do that? Part of the reason is that we ourselves have not defended the term to the extent that it deserves. We compromise like Neville Chamberlain and say that "technical analysis is useful *in conjunction with fundamentals*," "it can help the money manager decide when to buy the stocks he has *already chosen* using fundamentals," and all sorts of other mealy mouthed non-defenses of our craft.

In January, I read in a newspaper that (quote) "stocks *have* been interest rate driven, and now they will be earnings driven." Of course, we have all heard that statement a hundred times over the past six months. However, this time, the statement was made not by a fundamentalist money manager but by a technician. In fact, it was an MTA member.

Four days ago, I heard on television a long discussion about the stock market that focused on interest rates, the economy, corporate earnings and the Fed. This is, of course, quite common on financial television. However, the discussion was provided by a technician. In fact, it was an MTA member.

When I encounter such presentations, I become disturbed beyond measure. This kind of talk undermines our profession, our case, our cause and our principles.

In case there is any question about it in this room, let's examine the question, "Are stocks *driven* by earnings?" "Are they *driven* by the latest economic statistics?" Well, since 1932, corporate profits have been down in 19 years. The Dow *rose* in 14 of those years. In 1973-74, the Dow *fell* 46% while earnings *rose* 47%. 12-month earnings peaked at the bear market low. Earnings do *not* drive stocks. As Arthur Merrill showed years ago, earnings *lag* stocks. As many observers have pointed out, the *economy* lags stocks. It is therefore *impossible* for earnings or the economy to drive stocks. Even most economists know this, since they use the stock market as a leading indicator. Yet technicians, who are supposed to be looking at charts, which means studying history to see if their statements are valid, have been making these statements to the media.

Why do such false ideas continue to hold sway even, apparently, among many technicians? The fault lies in failing to grasp the profound depth and validity of our basic premise, particularly in contrast to that of our competition.

Necessity of Utilizing Technical Analysis

To understand the value of our craft, it is first necessary to understand that in fact, *all* effective forecasting *requires* technical analysis. While technical analysis can be utilized perfectly well on its own, there is *no such thing* as valid analysis *apart* from technical analysis. How can I make such an outrageous statement?

First, let's define our terms. Technical analysis is the study of *intramarket* data, that is, data generated by the action of a market and by the behavior and psychology of that market's participants and observers, in other words, a study of events, conditions and processes in the marketplace.

Conventional analysis is the study of *extramarket* data, that is, events, conditions and processes outside the marketplace, which are deemed to be the factors, or "fundamentals," that drive the market.

Events outside the marketplace cannot provide a sufficient basis for anticipating the trend of a market. Let me explain by example. If someone is bearish on stocks because interest rates are rising, you are justified in asking, "How do you know that interest rates didn't stop rising today, in which case stocks are a buy?" He might respond, "well, the latest economic report shows strength," in which case you are justified in asking, "How do you know that the economy didn't peak last month?" At some point he must respond that he will wait for a change of some kind, a report of a slower economy or a lowering of rates by the Fed. Then you can ask, "How do you know that that economic report won't reflect the *only* economic downtick or that the Fed won't lower rates *once* and then start raising them again?" If he answers that he doesn't know, then he remains stuck with no basis for a decision. On the other hand, he might say, quite thoughtfully, "Well, the Fed has usually moved in multiple steps in the past." Now, by forecasting the behavior of his supposed cause, he is engaging in technical analysis of his "fundamental" data. He is forecasting the behavior of an agency based on *the history of its own behavior*, in this case using the technical idea of trending. This agency is then considered to affect a market (i.e., interest rates) that will affect the one he actually wants to predict, i.e., stocks. *He cannot avoid employing technical analysis at some point.* Since he *must* employ it, we should ask him, "isn't it far easier merely to perform technical analysis directly on the market in question?" Instead of saying, "the trend of Fed action is toward higher rates until that trend changes," he simply could have said, "the trend of stocks is down until *that* trend changes." He would have saved all that effort and avoided the pitfall of requiring his whole chain of causality to maintain itself, for which history shows numerous exceptions. My point is *not* that markets are unrelated to events. It is rather that even if one can show that certain financial actions or events are related to whatever market is under analysis, it is useless information without employing technical analysis, and each step removed weakens any market conclusion.

We have now uncovered another secret, which is that conventional analysts must *predict their own indicators*. What's more, the chain of predictions concerning each supposedly causal indicator will be endless until the conventional analyst finally provides a prediction based on technical analysis. More often than not, he simply says that he sees no evidence of a change in trend for his supposed cause, which is a technical statement. Trend following, of course, is the crudest form of technical analysis, and nearly all conventional analysts and economists employ it. Unfortunately for them, they make it far *less* useful by extrapolating the trends of *lagging events*. Some such indicators, such as earnings, can time themselves exquisitely to produce maximum error in forecasting the stock market. These analysts would do far better to trash all of their supposed indicators and just trend-follow the market with a single moving average, like Dick Fabian does.

A technician is not reduced to predicting his own indicators. This is not to say that such indicators are always right, but at least the chain of argument is direct and finite. The indicator speaks to the future, and that's that.

Furthermore, a conventional analyst cannot adjust for error. If interest rates fall and stocks fall with them, or if earnings fall and stocks are going up, he has no basis upon which to modify his stance. Many technical approaches to market analysis provide a built-in method for changing one's mind.

The indicators that conventional analysts use are truly not indicators at all. They are typically presented on the basis of a simple *presumption* that they are valid, not because of any rigorous back testing. Conventional analysts do not bother to study history. They merely assert, for instance, that the passage of a trade agreement will affect stock prices because it *seems* as if it should. Wouldn't it be a delightful shock if some reporter suddenly asked, "Pardon me, but have you by any chance *checked the historical record* to see if trade agreements in fact are typically followed by what you assume will happen?" But don't hold your breath. The reason conventional analysts get away with their suppositions is that they sound utterly reasonable to the average man on the street, who, as we all know, is sophisticated in the ways of Wall Street. Technicians, on the other hand, *do* study history. That's what a chart *is*. When a correlation recurs often, it at least has a *chance* of indicating causality.

There is a hybrid form of analysis called "fundamental analysis" that involves both technical and conventional ideas. This is the Graham and Dodd approach of searching for stock value by comparing stock price to company performance. Clearly this is a measure of investor psychology and thus crosses into the domain of the technical, so I have no quarrel with this approach as an *adjunct* to technical analysis. I do, however, have a quarrel with those practitioners who say it is the *only* valid approach, as many of them do. Those who hold that opinion are philosophically conventional analysts as per the definition I gave earlier, despite their closet use of technical principles. Actually, the reliance on corporate performance statistics, which is the "fundamental" factor, weakens the reliability of the message, because profits, earnings and dividends can all change after an investment decision has been made. An apparently cheap stock by such formulas can fall 50%, after which the company reports poor performance and dividend cuts and so on, so that it is no longer cheap by the *same* measures.

Like conventional analysts, fundamental analysts rarely appreciate the fact that they must incorporate technical thinking at some point for their analysis to have any validity. One occasionally hears of fundamentalists who realize what they're doing and become technicians. In fact, several of our past presidents began their careers as fundamental analysts. Rarely does a conversion take place the other way around. In fact, I've never heard of one.

Sadly, even many technicians don't understand the true value of their craft. To be successful, you must always, always think technically. Let me give you some examples of what I mean.

Thinking Technically About Events and Conditions

Suppose you make a good call on the market, a sector, a group or a stock, and your clients tell you they are too afraid to follow it. The market goes your way, and seven or eight weeks later you get a call congratulating you on your work. You might just say thanks and hang up the phone and feel very satisfied. Or, you might understand that the phone call has a technical meaning. If you get three more calls that day, you may want to take a good look at your indicators. Similarly, if you are ever so fortunate and simultaneously unfortunate as to be granted a certain measure of fame — or infame — you will find that overstated praise for your abilities reflects prevailing market psychology, and the stronger it is, the more mature is the trend. Likewise, publicly voiced attacks against you for all sorts of real and imagined sins are excellent market indicators, and the more vicious and inaccurate they are, the better they are as indicators. In other words, instead of taking such things at face value, see if they are a comment on the prevailing psychology. Let's try a less obvious example: in the 1950s, people built bomb shelters. They were responding to events that had already happened, preparing for the past, in essence, fearing the last bear market. This year, the Smithsonian Institution placed a bomb shelter in its collection as a relic. Observers, conventional analysts all, hailed it as signaling the beginning of a new era of peace for mankind. What is the *technical* importance of that occurrence?

R.N. Elliott said quite properly in 1946, "In the matter of investment, timing is the most essential element. *What* to buy *is* important, but *when* to buy is more important." Regardless of today's rhetoric, that is still true. *Once you are satisfied that the trend is safe*, you can then concentrate on stock selection. In fact, just to demonstrate an application of this idea, I will read a quote from *The Elliott Wave Theorist* of April 1983: "Large institutions will probably do best by *avoiding a market timing strategy and concentrating on stock selection*, remaining heavily invested until a full five Primary degree waves can be counted." That statement of the value of stock selection was possible only because of having a perspective on the market from a timing standpoint. However, the past twelve years have brought back into fashion the recurring belief that market timing is passé and useless, if not counterproductive. "*All* one needs is good stock selection. Just stay in good stocks, and you will make money *and* be safe." Many of you might agree substantially with that assessment. Indeed, I have heard many technicians say it.

But think about the *technical* meaning of that belief. Few people made this case in June 1984. Few said it in December 1974. Few said it in 1942, 1932, 1859 or 1842. What technical conclusion can you draw from the pervasiveness of this opinion today? *It is a symptom of complacency about the trend of the overall market.* In fact, it is *philosophically* impossible for today's most successful money managers to sell stocks or bonds and take a cash position. After all, it was that kind of thinking that brought them to their current state of success. This is not only the kind of thinking necessary to create a major overvaluation; it is the kind that will force money managers to hold their increasingly less valuable paper all the way down in the next bear market until a new philosophy assumes dominance. Now contemplate the kind of irony that one continually notices when thinking technically. *It is precisely the position of the market in its overall trend that induces people to say that the position of the market in its overall trend is irrelevant.* At the bottom of a bear market, *timing* becomes the new philosophy, which assumes its place on the pedestal just when it is actually time to concentrate on holding and selecting stocks. Technicians can observe and profit from such irony in the marketplace every day; conventional analysts produce irony every day without knowing it.

All right, we have explored a few of the shortcomings of the conventional approach. But that is not enough to make us understand the value of our own approach. Let's tackle that task next.

The Proper Direction of Causation

Almost everyone believes, in regard to the market, that *events determine psychology*. If that is true, then events must be so perfectly determinist that they create the patterns that we technicians observe in prices, value and market opinion. However, if *mass psychology guides the tenor of events*, then it is only mass psychology that is patterned. Human actions then express that psychology in countless diverse ways that give rise to the myriad events of human history. If I have anything to contribute to technical analysis, it is this idea, that the behavioral patterns inherent in human interaction shape social events. In my opinion, all of history flows from the technical truth that men have a nature, that this nature produces patterns of interaction, and that these patterns of interaction produce results. Thus, the true fundamentals of the financial markets are the patterns of shared human emotions.

In my opening discussion about the claim that stocks will be "earnings driven," some of you were probably thinking, "I know better than that. Earnings lag stock prices because smart investors anticipate, or discount, the future," in other words, guess the future correctly. While this position is a time-honored and valiant attempt to explain why events lag stock prices, I believe it is false. In fact, because markets are patterned, it *must* be false. The truth is that the actions of human beings spurred on by an increasingly ebullient social mood *create* rising earnings, and a bull market in stocks reflects the presence of such a mood. *This* direction of causality explains why the movement of aggregate stock prices can almost always predict aggregate earnings. Rising earnings are the fruits of a bull market. When the fruit is ripe, the tree is already in its declining season. If you wait for the fruit to ripen in order to turn bullish on the trend of the tree, it is too late.

This is a radical idea of causality and the only one that makes sense. With this background, we can begin to discuss the wider applications of technical analysis on the way to elevating it in our minds to the status it deserves.

The Wide Applicability of Technical Analysis

Why are feature length Disney cartoons popular again at the theaters? From 1966 to 1982, most people thought such films were outmoded, silly and sentimental. Indeed, the studio hardly made any. In the past decade, they are back, and they have been blockbusters. Let's take the long route to answering this seemingly trivial question.

If one knows the species of a tree, he can predict what kind of fruit it will bear. Events are the fruits of a bull or bear market. Since stock prices are a direct reflection of social mood, we can use stock price trends to predict to some degree the forms of social behavior that mood affects, such as entertainment trends, the tone of the media, cultural themes and symbols, the styling of consumption items such as clothing and automobiles, social harmony vs. conflict, politics, peace, war and even such deeply emotional tendencies as the social preference for relying on reason vs. relying on emotion to solve both individual and social problems.

Almost everyone believes that behaviors such as those I have just listed are "fundamentals," i.e., *determinants* of the value of stocks and investments, and come *before* such valuation. This false premise leads to a fog of uncertainty in every conceivable area of anticipating the social future, from market forecasting to anticipating cultural trends to predicting elections to planning for the comfort and well being of one's family or the safety of one's nation. However, they are *results*, and when you know what they result *from*, i.e., social mood trends, you can often predict the general tenor of such behaviors. I was happy to hear Bob Farrell say that he finds he can often make a number of forecasts about upcoming "fundamental" changes using technical analysis. That is exactly my point, except that I am arguing further that such is the *only* logically sensible direction of forecasting between the two sets of data.

I find that the *guidelines* of the Wave Principle are often useful in forecasting certain specifics of social behavior. For example, one guideline is that a fifth wave attempts to re-live the technical glory of the third, but falls somewhat short of doing so. This observation has a specific technical meaning in wave formation, but is also applicable to social trends. It explains, for example, why Disney movies became popular again in wave V; they were popular during wave III from 1942 to 1966. That's why we have oldies radio, playing the music of the 1950s and 1960s. That's why in the early 1980s we elected a president, Ronald Reagan, who called for a return to the values of Calvin Coolidge and Dwight Eisenhower, presidents during previous bull markets. Notice that in most of these cases, the extent of innovation in the fifth wave is very low; innovation occurs in the third wave, copying in the fifth.

Some people "explain" such trends with demographics, but of course, they do not explain the forces behind the demographics. The Wave Principle explains population trends quite well. People fall in love more, have more stable marriages and have more babies in bull markets. Bear markets feature more fractured homes, illegitimacy, divorce and a glorification of sex over love. These results are the reflection of polarization in the realm of the family.

Bull markets result in increased harmony in every aspect of society, including the moral, religious, racial, national, regional, social, financial, political and otherwise. Bear markets bring polarization. With that realization, you can predict relative harmony in all those areas in bull markets and relative conflict in those areas in bear markets. For example, apartheid was made official South African policy in the 1940s at the end of the last Supercycle bear market and the peak of society's negative mood. It has been eliminated in the approach to the peak of this bull market and its positive mood. Wednesday's paper showed black and white leaders, enemies for decades, clasping hands over their heads in the spirit of brotherhood. Religious wars were big in the Dark Ages and for a while afterward but have been a minor concern in the past eight centuries of rising long-term trend. Indeed, Catholic, Jewish and Arab leaders are all shaking hands today at the top of a centuries-long bull market for civilization. Nationalism was the political theme in the 1940s during a bear market; as this bull market has been peaking out, we have seen plans for a European Community, a New World Order, and for the former Communist countries of Eastern Europe to join NATO. Several months ago, the leaders of the U.S. and Russia, enemies for decades, clasped hands over their heads in the spirit of cooperation. These trends reflect classic bull market sentiments of human social harmony. The bear market will bring back nationalism, racial exclusion and perhaps even religious conflict. The bull markets of 1949 to 1966, and 1974 to today, were nearly free of war. War will also return by the end of the bear market, just as it did on the heels of the Supercycle bear market of the 1850s and that of the 1930s. Each time one of these grand events occurs, whether viewed as good or evil, the world sees it as a turning point for mankind. Such observations are true, but because people think conventionally in terms of the direction of causality, it is a turning point in precisely the *opposite* direction that they assume it to be. They are therefore entirely unprepared for the next chain of events. Thinking *technically* about events, that is, observing what they reveal about social psychology, prepares you for those changes.

If you're still not convinced, I beg you to consider this question. Who is more sensible, a technician who says, "War is the *result* of a negative social psychology, which is why it occurs near the end of bear markets," and therefore counsels you to beware of the impending risk of war in such environments, or an economist who says, "I can see that stocks and the economy tend to pick up during or after wars, so war must create economic expansion and is therefore *a good thing*"? Who would you rather have advising the President? Or another country's leader? Was Hitler's coming to power in 1933 *bullish* for stocks worldwide, as a conventional analyst is *forced* to conclude, or was he put in power at a market low as a result of the most negative social psychology since 1859, as I would postulate? Which explanation makes more sense?

All right. Technical analysis can be used to forecast social trends and events. What else?

I find wave analysis useful in anticipating turning points in my personal and professional life. My business ebbs and flows in waves that have been entirely predictable at major junctures. Let's bring it close to home and see if technical analysis might be useful in predicting trends within our own Market Technicians Association. One of my observations with respect to bull vs. bear markets is that bull-market psychology is *in*clusionary of other people, and bear market psychology *ex*clusionary. In a bull market, the social mythology increasingly sees mankind as a brotherhood. At a bear market low, in contrast, everyone is a potential enemy, for whatever silly reason: his color, his religion, his nation, his social status, his planet. How might this theme apply to the MTA?

Old timers will recall that the MTA was a small club of professionals from its commencement in 1970 to the end of the inflation- adjusted bear market in 1982. During the bull market, it suddenly became highly inclusionist and expansionary. In the process, the advocates of exclusion were overridden. The association changed its by-laws in 1985 to accommodate more people. We dropped the requirement of being a full time professional *practitioner* of technical analysis so that we could include people who extensively *use* technical analysis, substantially widening the universe of potential members. *This is classic bull market behavior.*

So what can we expect next? In the bear market, the MTA will become more *ex*clusionist and polarized. Like the nation, which will finally take action against illegal aliens, like regions, which will in a few years begin demanding secession from larger political entities, and like races, who will begin to support separatist leaders, the MTA will become more desirous of identifying an "us" and a "them." This "us vs. them" dynamic could show up ultimately in a tightening of the MTA's membership requirement. Or perhaps in secession by a regional affiliate. Or perhaps in an east/west split of the entire organization. The bear market low is years away, so specifics cannot be surmised yet. But as time passes, the specific divisionary forces will become clear. Such oscillation between division and cohesion will continue in our organization as long as there is an MTA, just as it does in politics. And the styles of the changes are predictable based upon the principles of technical analysis. By the way, I didn't know until this morning that the reason this conference has only 160 attendees despite an impressive roster is that the membership overwhelmingly voted for the first time in years *not to advertise it to the public* because it wanted to have a more intimate professional gathering. This is an exclusionist policy, one that wasn't on my list!

I believe that technical analysis is also applicable to the study and understanding of history. If man's actions are patterned over five days, five weeks, five years and fifty years, they might be patterned over 500 years and 5000 years. Indeed, it is my contention that all of history can be understood from a technical standpoint and in fact *only* from a technical standpoint. The Wave Principle appears to govern the ebb and flow of social progress all the way back to the start of the Bronze Age. It is the pattern of a progressive life form, and mankind has been following it relentlessly. This kind of analysis can give you a panoramic view not only of the past but also of the future.

Scientific Forecasting

With knowledge of how the patterns unfold, to the extent of your ability and effort, you will be able to *anticipate the tenor of the future* in all kinds of fields. That is an ability that has deftly eluded man throughout his existence and indeed has been considered impossible. Nevertheless, we finally have a way to anticipate much about our social future, not with magic or revelation or sorcery, but with science.

Not only is our profession roaring toward the realm of science, but science itself is roaring toward technical analysis. In fact, it will change our profession over the next decade in a most shocking way. The latest scientific frontier, that of chaos science, will eventually make conventional analysis, involving the idea of causality from events to markets, *obsolete*, just as those same studies have quite swiftly made obsolete the idea of Random Walk, which held academia captive for decades. The modern field of complexity theory addresses nature's processes of *self-organization*. Now that this principle is understood, it is only a short step to realize, as some have already done, that *society operates the same way*. That's why free societies are more successful and productive than controlled ones. They self organize far more efficiently than any human directors could make them do. Nature's processes of self-organization, furthermore, are patterned. This applies to human self-organization as well, which is exactly what R.N. Elliott said and *exactly the phenomenon that technical analysis studies*. Just like the Communists who could never figure out who was directing the industrial success of the United States, conventional analysts keep trying to find the unidentified "directors" (the Fed, the gnomes, the shorts, the specialists, bankers, politicians, etc.) that make everything in the market happen, and guess what, *there aren't any*. The only director is the behavioral dynamic that human interaction produces. Complexity theorists are beginning to understand this fact, albeit in a foggy way to date. Academics are years behind, presenting studies that admit to a *slight* psychological component to stock price activity by investigating whether the stock market occasionally "overreacts," when in fact it does not "react" in the first place. I have always maintained that analytical study should be focused upon the patterns of human self-organization, and at least increasingly, if haltingly, that is exactly where it is being focused. We as technicians will benefit immensely from this trend *if we have the sense to know* that it is providing a ringing validation of our approaches.

Championing Our First Principles

In general, advocates of technical analysis have been content to defend it meekly as having an ancillary value, as providing a little extra input that might help some investors make some decisions. However, the truth is *far* more profound than that. Technical analysis is not just one approach to determine value or a trend. It is based upon a fundamental overriding *fact*, that collective human behavior is patterned. Conventional analysis is not a hallowed sensible approach; it is nonsense. It is founded upon a false premise, which is that there are no patterns, only unpredictable, random causes of behavior to which society responds like puppets. Conventional analysts can't see their own contradiction, that it is society that causes the causes. It is society that determines interest rates, creates earnings, steers politics and all the rest. But to the conventional analyst, each of these realms is as detached from social cause as a meteorite striking the earth. Because many of us have not made this distinction and contemplated and validated its meaning, we have been afraid to defend technical analysis as one would defend any dearly held fundamental truth of human existence. We are afraid to say that the *real fundamentals* of market analysis are human beings and their patterns of behavior. The result is that today, university professors, who have recently validated the spread between futures and cash prices, relative IPO volume and even trend following as being predictive of stock prices, are getting credit for work we did decades ago. Why? Because today too many of us are talking about the economy, the Fed, interest rates and the health-care bill instead of breadth, volume, rates of change, non-confirmation, divergence, trendlines, relative strength, institutional cash levels, allocation percentages, derivative premiums, short-selling ratios, public participation ratios, fear, hope, greed, and the cycles and patterns of human behavior.

So how do we deal with the low repute of the term "technical analysis" among our own practitioners? My recommendation years ago was that we drop the term "technical," which is used as if it is some subspecies in a universe of various acceptable types of market analysis. Our craft *is* market analysis. At a larger scale, it is sociology. And the approaches we take are the *only* valid approaches to performing it. Conventional analysis and "fundamental" analysis are something else entirely, and we can leave it up to their practitioners to define and defend them. When someone asks whether you use corporate earnings in your stock market analysis, tell him no, you analyze markets, not their lagging results. In the end, however, the label doesn't matter. You can call yourself a technical analyst. You can call yourself a market analyst. You can call yourself an analyst of the behavior patterns of human beings. Whichever label you choose, do not be ashamed of it; do not excuse it; do not compromise it. Announce it with firmness, finality and authority, but above all, *with a deep and justified pride, letting the world see in you the respect that our field deserves, and the respect that* **you** *deserve by practicing it.* Thank you.

Chapter 21

WHAT A TRADER REALLY NEEDS
TO BE SUCCESSFUL

by Robert R. Prechter, Jr.
originally printed November 1986

*In 1984, Bob Prechter won the United States Trading Cham-
pionship, setting a new all-time profit record of 444.4% in a
monitored real money options account in four months. That
February through May period presented a difficult and choppy
market to the effect that the second highest reported gain in
the options division was just 84%, and 83% of the contestants
lost money. According to contest sponsors, many market letter
writers have entered the contest over the years, but almost all
have lost money. In the average 4-month contest, over 75%
of contestants, most of whom are professionals paying $200
to prove their abilities, fail to report profits.*

Ever since winning the United States Trading Championship in
1984, subscribers have asked for a list of "tips" on trading or even a
play-by-play of the approximately 200 short-term trades I made while
following hourly market data over that four-month period. Neither of
these would do anyone any good. What successful trading requires is
both more and less than most people think. In watching the reports of
each new Championship over the past three years, it has been a joy to
see what a large percentage of the top winners have been *Elliott Wave
Theorist* subscribers and consultation clients. (In fact, in the latest
"standings" report from the USTC, of the *top three profit producers*
in each of four categories, *half* are EWT subscribers!) However, while
good traders may want the input from EWT, not all EWT subscribers are

good traders. Obviously the winners know something the losers don't. What is it? What are the guidelines you *really* need to meet in order to trade the markets successfully?

When I first began trading, I did what many others who start out in the markets do: I developed a list of trading rules. The list was created piecemeal, with each new rule added, usually, following the conclusion of an unsuccessful trade. I continually asked myself, what would I do differently the next time to make sure that this mistake would not recur? The resulting list of "do's" and "don'ts" ultimately comprised about 16 statements. Approximately six months following the completion of my carved-in-stone list of trading rules, I balled up the paper and threw it in the trash.

What was the problem with my list, a list typical of so many novices who think they are learning something? After several months of attempting to apply the "rules," it became clear that I made not merely a mistake here and there in the list, but a fundamental error in compiling the list in the first place. The error was in taking aim at the *last* trade each time, as if the next trading situation would present a similar problem. By the time 16 rules are created, all situations are covered and the trader is back to square one.

Let me give you an example of the ironies that result from the typical method of generating a list of trading rules. One of the most popular trading maxims is, "You can't go broke taking a profit." (The brokers invented that one, of course, which is one reason that new traders always hear of it!) This trading maxim appears to make wonderful sense but only when viewed in the context of a recent trade with a specific outcome. When you have entered a trade at a good price, watched it go your way for a while, then watched it go against you and turn into a loss, the maxim sounds like a prounouncement of divine wisdom. What you are really saying, however, is that in the context of the last trade, "*I should have sold when I had a small profit.*"

Now let's see what happens on the next trade. You enter a trade, and after just a few days of watching it go your way, you sell out, only to stare in amazement as it continues to go in the direction you had expected, racking up paper gains of several hundred percent. You ask a more experienced trader what your error was, and he advises you sagely while peering over his glasses, "Remember this forever: Cut losses short; let profits run." So you reach for your list of trading rules and write this maxim, which means only, of course, "*I should NOT have sold when I had a small profit.*"

So trading rules #2 and #14 are in direct conflict. Is this an isolated incident? What about rule #3, which reads, "Stay cool; never let emotions rule your trading," and #8, which reads, "If a trade is obviously going against you, get out of the way before it turns into a disaster." Stripped of their fancy attire, #3 says, "*Don't panic during trading,*" and #8 says, "*Go ahead and panic!*" Such formulations are, in the final analysis, utterly useless.

What I finally desired to create was a description not of each of the trees, but of the forest. After several years of trading, I came up with —guess what— another list! But this is *not* a list of "trading rules"; it is a list of requirements for successful trading. Most worthwhile truths are simple, and this list contains only five items. (In fact, the last two are actually subsets of the first two.) Whether this list is true or complete is arguable, but in forcing myself to express my conclusions, it has helped me understand the true dimensions of the problem and thus provided a better way of solving it. Like most rewards life offers, market profits are not as easy to come by as the novice believes. Making money in the market requires a good deal of education, like any craft or business. If you've got the time, the drive, and the right psychological makeup, you can enter that elite realm of the truly professional, or at least the successful, trader or investor. Here's what you need:

1. A Method.

I mean an *objectively definable* method for making trading or investment decisions. It must be thought out in its entirety to the extent that if someone asks you how you make your decisions, you can explain it to him, and if he asks you again in six months, he will receive the same answer. This is not to say that a method cannot be altered or improved; it must, however, be developed as a totality before it is implemented. A prerequisite for obtaining a method is acceptance of the fact that perfection is not achievable. People who demand it are wasting their time searching for the Holy Grail, and they will never get beyond this first step of obtaining a method. I chose to use, for my decision making, an approach that was explained in our book, *Elliott Wave Principle.* I think the Wave Principle is the best way to understand the framework of a market and where prices are within that framework. There are a hundred other methods which will work if successful trading is your only goal. As I have often said, a simple 10-day moving average of the net figure of daily advances minus declines, probably the first indicator a stock market technician learns, can be used as a trading tool, if objectively defined rules are created for its use. The bad news is that as difficult and time consuming as this first major requirement can be, it is the easiest one to fulfill.

2. The Discipline to Follow Your Method

This requirement is so widely understood by the true professionals that among them, it almost sounds like a cliché. Nevertheless, it is so crucial to your success that it cannot be sidestepped, ignored or excepted. Without discipline, you really have no method in the first place. It struck me one day that among a handful of consistently successful professional options and futures traders of my acquaintance, three of them are former Marines. In fact, the only advisor, as ranked by *Commodity Traders Consumer Report*, consistently to beat my Telephone Hotline record from 1983 to 1985 was a former Marine as well (he has since retired from the advisory business). Now, this is a ratio *way* out of proportion to former Marines as a percentage of the general population. Why should this anomaly exist? Think about it. At some point in their lives, these people *volunteered* to serve in an organization that requires, above all, *discipline.* These are people who *asked* for the opportunity to go charging through a jungle pointing a bayonet and pitching grenades, surviving on roots and bugs when necessary. That's an overdramatization perhaps, but you get the point. These people knew they were "tough" and wanted the chance to prove it. Being "tough" in this context means having the ability to supress a host of emotions in order to act in a manner that would strike fear in the hearts of most people. I was never a Marine, but years ago while attending summer school with Georgia's "Governor's Honors Program," I was given a psychological test and told that one of my skewed traits was "tough-mindedness" (as opposed to "tender-mindedness"). I didn't exactly know what that meant, but after trading and forecasting the markets for fourteen years, it is clear that without that trait, I would have been forced long ago to elect another profession. The pressures of trading are enormous, and they get to everyone, including me. If you are not disciplined, forget the markets.

3. Experience

Some people advocate "paper trading" as a learning tool. Paper trading is useful for the testing of methodology, but it is of no value in learning about trading or investing. In fact, it can be detrimental, by imbuing the novice with a false sense of security. A novice may have successfully paper-traded over the past six months and thus believes that the next six months with real money will be no different. In fact, nothing could be further from the truth. Why? Because the markets are not merely an intellectual exercise. They are an emotional (and in extreme cases, even physical) challenge as well. If you buy a computer baseball game and become a hitting expert with the joystick while sitting quietly alone on the floor of your living room, you may conclude that you are one talented baseball player. Now let the Mean Green Giant reach in, pick you up, and place you in the batter's box at the bottom of the ninth inning in the final game of the World Series with your team behind by one run, the third base coach flashing signals one after another, a fastball heading toward your face at 90 miles an hour, and sixty beer-soaked fans in the front row screaming, "Yer a bum! Yer a bum!" Guess what? *You feel different!* To put it mildly, you will find it impossible to approach your task with the same cool detachment you displayed in your living room. This new situation is real, it matters, it is *physical,* it is *dangerous, other people are watching,* and you are being *bombarded with stimuli.* This is what your life is like when you are actually speculating in the market. You know it is real, you know it matters, you must physically pick up the phone and speak to place orders, you perform under the scrutiny of your broker, your spouse, your business acquaintances or your clients, and you must operate while thousands of conflicting messages are thrown at you from the financial media, the brokerage industry, analysts, and the market itself. In short, you must conquer a *host* of problems, most of them related to your own inner ability to battle powerful human emotions, in order to trade real money successfully. The School of Hard Knocks is the *only* school that will teach it to you, and the tuition is expensive.

There is only one shortcut to obtaining experience, and that is to find a *mentor.* Locate someone who has proved himself over the years to be a successful trader or investor, and go visit him. You will undoubtedly find that he is very friendly, since his runaway ego of yesteryear, which undoubtedly got him involved in the markets in the first place, has long since been humbled, matured by the experience of trading. Watch this person operate. Observe not only what he does, but far more important, what he *does not allow himself to do.* This person does exist, but it is hard to find him. He will usually welcome the opportunity to tell you what he knows.

4. The Mental Fortitude to Accept the Fact That Losses Are Part of the Game

There are many denials of reality that automatically disqualify millions of people from the joining the ranks of successful speculators. For instance, to moan that "pools," "manipulators," "insiders," "they," "the big boys," "program trading" or anything else is to blame for one's losses is a common fault. Anyone who utters such a conviction is doomed before he starts. My observation, after eleven years "in the business," is that the biggest obstacle to successful speculation is the failure merely even to recognize and accept the simple fact that *losses are part of the game,* and that they must be accommodated. The perfect trading system does not exist. Expecting, or even hoping for, perfection is a guarantee of failure. Speculation is akin to batting in baseball. A player hitting .300 is good. A player hitting .400 is great. But even the great player *fails to hit* 60% of the time! He even *strikes out* often. But he still earns six figures a year, because although imperfect, he has approached the best that can be achieved. You don't have to be perfect to win in the markets, either; you "merely" have to be better than almost everybody else, and that's hard enough. Practically speaking, you must include an objective "money management" system when formulating your trading method in the first place. There are many ways to do it. Some methods use stops. If stops are impractical (such as with options), you may decide to risk only small amounts of total capital at a time. Personally, I prefer letting my analytical method dictate my action. After all is said and done, learning to handle losses will be your greatest triumph.

The last on my list is one I have never heard mentioned before.

5. The Mental Fortitude To Accept Huge Gains

This comment usually gets a hearty laugh, which merely goes to show how little most people have determined it actually to be a problem. But consider. How many times have you had an experience like this:

For a full year, you trade futures contracts, making $1000 here, losing $1500 there, making $3000 here and losing $2000 there. Once again, you enter a trade because your method told you to do so. Within a week, you're up $4000. Your friend/partner/acquaintance/broker/advisor calls you and, looking out only for your welfare, tells you to take your profit. You have guts, though, and you wait. The following week, your position is up $8000, the best gain you have ever experienced. "Get out!" says your friend. You sweat, still hoping for further gains. The next Monday, your contract opens limit against you. Your friend calls and says, "I *told* you so. You got greedy. But hey, you're still way up on the trade. Get out tomorrow." The next day, on the opening, you exit the trade, taking a $5000 profit. It's your biggest profit of the year, and you click your heels, smiling gratefully, proud of yourself. Then, day after day for the next six months, you watch the market continue to go in the direction of your original trade. You try to find another entry point and continue to miss. At the end of six months, your method finally, quietly, calmly says, "Get out." You check the figures and realize that your initial entry, if held, would have netted $450,000.

So what was your problem? Simply that you had allowed yourself unconsciously to define "your" "normal" range of profit and loss. When the big trade finally came along, you lacked the self esteem, or the esteem for your method, required in order to take all that it promised. You looked at a job requiring the services of Paul Bunyan and decided that you were just Pee Wee Herman. Who were *you* to shoot for such huge gains? Why should *you* deserve more than your best trade of the year? You then abandoned both *method* and *discipline.*

To win the game, make sure that you understand why you're in it. The big moves in markets only come once or twice a year. Those are the ones that will pay you for all the work, fear, sweat and frustration of the previous eleven months or even eleven years. Don't miss them for reasons *other than* those required by your objectively defined method.

The I.R.S. categorizes capital gains as "unearned income." That's baloney. It's *hard* to make money in the market. Every dime you make, you *richly deserve.* Don't ever forget that. I wish you success.

Appendix

A CAPSULE SUMMARY OF
THE WAVE PRINCIPLE

The Wave Principle is Ralph Nelson Elliott's discovery that social, or crowd, behavior trends and reverses in recognizable patterns. Using stock market data as his main research tool, Elliott isolated five specific patterns of movement, or "waves," that recur in market price data. He named, defined and illustrated those patterns and described their variations. He then described how these structures link together to form larger versions of those same patterns, how those in turn link to form identical patterns of the next larger size, and so on. In a nutshell, then, the Wave Principle is a catalog of price patterns and an explanation of where these forms are likely to occur in the overall path of market development.

Pattern Analysis

Until a few years ago, the idea that market movements are patterned was highly controversial, but recent scientific discoveries have established that pattern formation is a fundamental characteristic of complex systems, which include financial markets. Some such systems undergo "punctuated growth," that is, periods of growth alternating with phases of non-growth or decline, building fractally into similar patterns of increasing size. This is precisely the type of pattern identified in market movements by R.N. Elliott some sixty years ago.

The basic pattern Elliott described consists of *motive waves* (denoted by numbers) and *corrective waves* (denoted by letters). A motive wave is composed of five subwaves and moves in the same direction as the trend of the next larger size. A corrective wave is composed of three subwaves and moves *against* the trend of the next larger size. As Figure 1 shows, these basic patterns *link* to form five- and three-wave structures of increasingly larger size (larger "degree" in Elliott terminology).

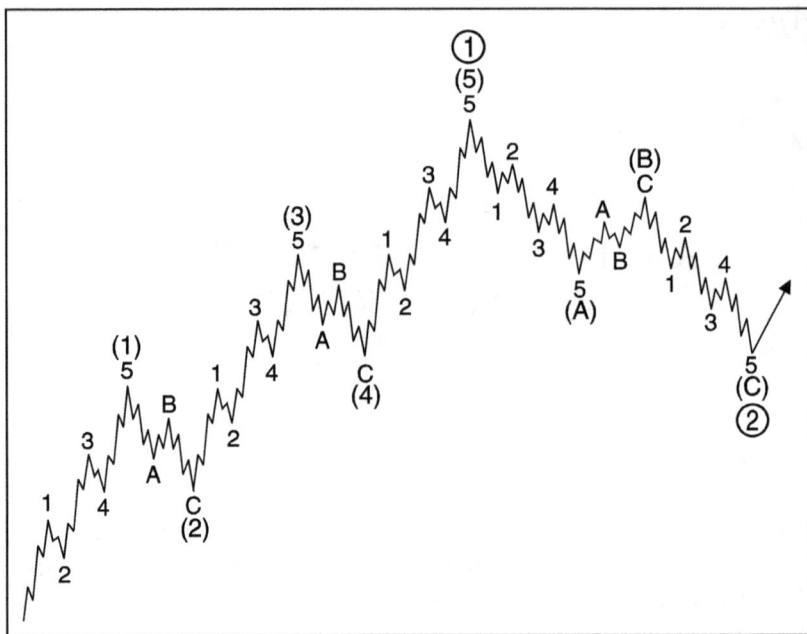

Figure 1

    In Figure 1, the first small sequence is a motive wave (called an
"impulse") ending at the peak labeled 1. This pattern signals that the
movement of one larger degree is also upward. It also signals the start
of a three-wave corrective sequence, labeled wave 2.

    Waves 3, 4 and 5 complete a larger motive sequence, labeled wave
(1). Exactly as with wave 1, the five-wave structure of wave (1) tells us
that the movement at the *next* larger degree is upward and signals the
start of a three-wave corrective downtrend of the same degree as wave
(1). This correction, wave (2), is followed by waves (3), (4) and (5) to
complete a motive sequence of the next larger degree, labeled wave 1.
Once again, a three-wave correction of the same degree occurs, labeled
wave 2. Note that at each "wave one" peak, the implications are the same
regardless of the size of the wave. Waves come in degrees, the smaller
being the building blocks of the larger.

Wave Degree	5s With the Trend					3s Against the Trend		
Grand Supercycle	Ⓘ	ⒾⒾ	ⒾⒾⒾ	ⒾⓋ	Ⓥ	ⓐ	ⓑ	ⓒ
Supercycle	(I)	(II)	(III)	(IV)	(V)	(a)	(b)	(c)
Cycle	I	II	III	IV	V	a	b	c
Primary	①	②	③	④	⑤	Ⓐ	Ⓑ	Ⓒ
Intermediate	(1)	(2)	(3)	(4)	(5)	(A)	(B)	(C)
Minor	1	2	3	4	5	A	B	C
Minute	ⓘ	ⓘⓘ	ⓘⓘⓘ	ⓘⓥ	ⓥ	ⓐ	ⓑ	ⓒ
Minuette	(i)	(ii)	(iii)	(iv)	(v)	(a)	(b)	(c)
Subminuette	i	ii	iii	iv	v	a	b	c

Within a corrective wave, waves A and C may be smaller-degree motive waves, consisting of five subwaves. This is because they move in the same direction as the next larger trend, i.e., waves (2) and (4) in the illustration. Wave B, however, is always a corrective wave, consisting of three subwaves, because it moves *against* the larger downtrend. Within motive waves, one of the odd-numbered waves (usually wave three) is typically longer than the other two. Most motive waves unfold between parallel lines except for fifth waves, which occasionally unfold between converging lines in a form called a "diagonal triangle." Variations in corrective patterns involve repetitions of the three-wave theme, creating more complex structures that are named with such terms as "zigzag," "flat," "triangle" and "double three." Waves two and four typically "alternate" in that they take different forms.

Each type of market pattern has a name and a geometry that is specific and exclusive under certain rules and guidelines, yet variable enough in other aspects to allow for a limited diversity within patterns of the same type. If indeed markets are patterned, and if those patterns have a recognizable geometry, then regardless of the variations allowed, certain relationships in extent and duration are likely to recur. In fact, real world experience shows that they do. The most common and therefore reliable wave relationships are discussed in *Elliott Wave Principle*.

Applying the Wave Principle

The practical goal of any analytical method is to identify market lows suitable for buying (or covering shorts) and market highs suitable for selling (or selling short). The Elliott Wave Principle is especially well suited to these functions. Nevertheless, the Wave Principle does not provide *certainty* about any one market outcome; rather, it provides an objective means of assessing the relative *probabilities* of possible future paths for the market. At any time, two or more valid wave interpretations are usually acceptable by the *rules* of the Wave Principle. The rules are highly specific and keep the number of valid alternatives to a minimum. Among the valid alternatives, the analyst will generally regard as preferred the interpretation that satisfies the largest number of *guidelines* and will accord top alternate status to the interpretation satisfying the next largest number of guidelines, and so on.

Alternate interpretations are extremely important. They are not "bad" or rejected wave interpretations. Rather, they are valid interpretations that are accorded a lower probability than the preferred count. They are an essential aspect of investing with the Wave Principle, because in the event that the market fails to follow the preferred scenario, the top alternate count becomes the investor's backup plan.

Fibonacci Relationships

One of Elliott's most significant discoveries is that because markets unfold in sequences of five and three waves, the number of waves that exist in the stock market's patterns reflects the Fibonacci sequence of numbers (1, 1, 2, 3, 5, 8, 13, 21, 34, etc.), an additive sequence that nature employs in many processes of growth and decay, expansion and contraction, progress and regress. Because this sequence is governed by the Fibonacci ratio (.618), it appears throughout the price and time structure of the stock market, apparently governing its progress.

What the Wave Principle says, then, is that mankind's progress (of which the stock market is a popularly determined valuation) does not occur in a straight line, does not occur randomly, and does not occur cyclically. Rather, progress takes place in a "three steps forward, two steps back" fashion, a form that nature prefers. As a corollary, the Wave Principle reveals that periods of setback in fact are a requisite for social (and perhaps even individual) progress.

Implications

A long-term forecast for the stock market provides insight into the potential changes in social psychology and even the occurrence of resulting events. Since the Wave Principle reflects social mood change, it has not been surprising to discover, with preliminary data, that the trends of popular culture that also reflect mood change move in concert with the ebb and flow of aggregate stock prices. Popular tastes in entertainment, self-expression and political representation all reflect changing social moods and appear to be in harmony with the trends revealed more precisely by stock-market data. At one-sided extremes of mood expression, changes in cultural trends can be anticipated.

On a philosophical level, the Wave Principle suggests that the nature of mankind has within it the seeds of social change. As an example simply stated, prosperity ultimately breeds reactionism, while adversity eventually breeds a desire to achieve and succeed. The social mood is always in flux at all degrees of trend, moving toward one of two polar opposites in every conceivable area, from a preference for heroic symbols to a preference for anti-heroes, from joy and love of life to cynicism, from a desire to build and produce to a desire to destroy. Most important to individuals, portfolio managers and investment corporations is that the Wave Principle indicates in advance the relative *magnitude* of the next period of social progress or regress.

Living in harmony with those trends can make the difference between success and failure in financial affairs. As the Easterners say, "Follow the Way." As the Westerners say, "Don't fight the tape." In order to heed these nuggets of advice, however, it is necessary to know what is the Way, and which way the tape. There is no better method for answering that question than the Wave Principle.

To obtain a full understanding of the Wave Principle, including the terms and patterns, please read *Elliott Wave Principle* by A.J. Frost and Robert Prechter, or take the *Comprehensive Course on the Wave Principle* on Elliott Wave International's website at www.elliottwave.com.

ABOUT THE AUTHORS

Michael Buettner has covered business and finance for more than 20 years for a number of news and research organizations, including Dow Jones, EuropeanInvestor.com, American City Business Journals, Media General and Elliott Wave International. His work has received awards from the Society of American Business Editors and Writers, the Florida Press Association and the Florida Press Club as well as an honorable mention from the Market Technicians Association in the Charles Dow Award competition.

John Casti is a resident member of the Santa Fe Institute and a professor at the Technical University of Vienna. He received his Ph.D. in mathematics from the University of Southern California and then worked at the Rand Corporation, the University of Arizona, New York University, Princeton University and IIASA (Vienna, Austria). A prolific author, his books include *Reality Rules*, *Paradigms Lost*, *Searching for Certainty*, *Five Golden Rules*, *Would-Be Worlds*, *Paradigms Regained*, *The Cambridge Quintet* and *Complexification*. Mr. Casti's recent interests center on the use of large-scale microsimulation to study properties of complex, adaptive systems, such as stock markets, the business world and road-traffic networks.

Anne Crittenden holds a B.A. with Honours in Government from the University of Sydney and an M.A. in English from the University of Toronto. An Australian, she and her husband lived in North America for several years. When Anne came upon the Elliott Wave Principle, she found that it alone helped explain the fluctuations of political history and literary fashions. Then she turned to financial matters and realized that Jungian thought supplied the key psychological concepts about how these pivotal changes arise.

Dr. Sally J. Goerner is the director of the Triangle Center for the Study of Complex Systems, past-president of the Society of Chaos Theory in Psychology and the Life Sciences and on the scientific advisory council of the European Academy of Evolution Research. With advanced degrees in computer science, psychology and nonlinear dynamics she is one of the leaders of the international movement to integrate complexity research with evolution and to apply the resulting findings to human systems and social change. Dr. Goerner has lectured extensively throughout Europe and North America on dynamic evolution and deep ecology. Her specialty is showing how major social, scientific, economic and spiritual changes of our time are all part of one common evolutionary transformation.

Dr. Michael K. Green received his PhD in philosophy from the University of Chicago and is currently Professor of Philosophy at State University College of New York at Oneonta. His publications include articles in the *Journal of Business Ethics, History of European Ideas, Social Theory and Practice, Kant-Studien, Political Theory, International Studies in Philosophy* and *The Elliott Wave Theorist*. He works closely with the Hartwick Humanities in Management Institute, which is developing a series of leadership case studies combining business theory with works from history, the humanities and the social sciences. He also contributes to EWI's new Socionomics Institute.

Benjamin Graham and **David Dodd** are the authors of the Wall Street classic, *Securities Analysis*, originally published in 1934 and still in print. A money manager, author, and adjunct professor at Columbia University, Graham became a millionaire by buying beaten-up stocks following the 1929 crash.

Sam H. Hale, CMT began his financial career 35 years ago with a predecessor firm of Morgan Stanley, Dean Witter. After seven years, he formed his own NASD research boutique, where he served as president. Three years later, he became a member of the CBOE and a registered market maker in IBM, EK and GM. While on the floor, he remained a market timing consultant to other market makers as well as to a member firm. He was recruited by A.G. Edwards & Sons, Inc. in 1984 where, as the senior technical analyst for the Futures and Options Department, he has since provided daily comments and forecasts on stock index futures and options as well as U.S. Treasury bond and soybean futures. Sam was awarded the Chartered Market Technician designation by the Board of Governors of the Market Technicians Association in 1995. He is a past MTA Board Member and was Chairman of the Association's 25th Anniversary Seminar Committee, past president of the Atlanta chapter and is an affiliate member of the New York Society of Security Analysts.

Peter M. Kendall was a financial reporter and columnist from 1983 to 1992. He wrote the "On the Money," a column for *The Business Journal* from 1991 to 1997. Pete joined Elliott Wave International as a researcher in 1992 and has been contributing to its publications since 1995. Pete is Director of EWI's Center for Cultural Studies, where he focuses on popular cultural trends and the new science of socionomics. Pete graduated from Miami University in Oxford, Ohio with a degree in Business Administration.

Jordan Kotick is Vice President, Technical Market Strategist at JPMorgan Chase in New York. Previously, he worked at Elliott Wave International as Senior Interest Rate analyst and at CIBC World Markets in Toronto as technical analyst on the Research, Strategy and Trading Desk and as a Government bond trader. He is a contributing author to the textbook for the technical analysis course offered by the Canadian Securities Institute, is the Past President of the Canadian Society of Technical Analysts and is currently the international (IFTA) liaison for the MTA in New York. Mr. Kotick holds an Honours Bachelor of Arts degree with a double major in Philosophy and Economics, a Master of Arts degree in Philosophy and is a Chartered Market Technician.

Paul M. Montgomery received his MBA from the University of Virginia. Professionally active for thirty years, Montgomery is a market analyst, financial writer, money manager and stock broker with Legg Mason Wood Walker, Newport News, VA. Forecasts in his *Universal Economics* periodical, published since 1971, are widely acclaimed for independence and accuracy. He has created numerous original market indicators, and his work is often covered in *Barron's* and quoted by other analysts.

Robert R. Prechter, Jr. is the founder and president of Elliott Wave International. He has been publishing Elliott Wave commentary since 1976. During the 1980s, Prechter won numerous awards for market timing as well as the United States Trading Championship, culminating in Financial News Network (now CNBC) granting him the title, "Guru of the Decade." Bob served for ten years on the Board of Directors of the national Market Technicians Association and in 1990 was elected its president. He also served on the Board of Directors of the Foundation for the Study of Cycles and is a member of Mensa and Intertel. Today, Elliott Wave International is the largest technical analytical firm in the world, covering all major markets globally, 24 hours a day. Before starting out independently, Bob worked with the Merrill Lynch Market Analysis Department in New York as a Technical Market Specialist. He obtained his degree in psychology from Yale University in 1971.

Walter E. White graduated with degrees in Mathematics and Economics from the University of Oxford. In the 1960s, he was associated with the Atomic Energy Commission of Canada, and in the 1970s and 1980s he held a research position at the University of Toronto.

www.ingramcontent.com/pod-product-compliance
Lightning Source LLC
Chambersburg PA
CBHW061136220326
41599CB00025B/4252